Human Rights and Global Diversity

"Think for yourself."
prentice hall
philosophy—2002

Prentice Hall's *Basic Ethics in Action* series in normative and applied ethics is a major new undertaking edited by Michael Boylan, Professor of Philosophy at Marymount University. The series includes both wide-ranging anthologies as well as brief texts that focus on a particular theme or topic within one of four areas of applied ethics. These areas include: Business Ethics, Environmental Ethics, Medical Ethics, and Social and Political Philosophy.

Anchor volume
Michael Boylan, *Basic Ethics*, 2000

Business Ethics

Michael Boylan, ed., *Business Ethics*, 2001

James Donahue, *Ethics for the Professionals*, forthcoming

Dale Jacquette, *Journalistic Ethics*, forthcoming

Murphy, Laczniak, Bowie and Klein, *Ethical Marketing*, 2005

Joseph Des Jardin, *Environmental Business*, forthcoming

Edward Spence, *Advertising Ethics*, 2005

Environmental Ethics

Michael Boylan, ed., *Environmental Ethics*, 2001

J. Baird Callicott and Michael Nelson, *American Indian Environmental Ethics: An Ojibwa Case Study*, 2004

Lisa H. Newton, *Ethics and Sustainability*, 2003

Mary Anne Warren, *Obligations to Animals*, forthcoming

Medical Ethics

Michael Boylan, ed., *Medical Ethics*, 2000

Michael Boylan and Kevin Brown, *Genetic Engineering*, 2002

Rosemarie Tong, *New Perspectives in Healthcare Ethics*, forthcoming

Social and Political Philosophy

R. Paul Churchill, *Human Rights and Global Diversity*, 2006

Seumas Miller, Peter Roberts, and Edward Spence, *Corruption and Anti-Corruption: An Applied Philosophical Approach*, 2005

Deryck Beyleveld, *Informed Consent*, forthcoming

Kia Nielsen, *Social Justice*, forthcoming

Please contact Michael Boylan (mboylan@phoenix.marymount.edu) or Prentice Hall's Philosophy & Religion Editor to propose authoring a title for this series!

Human Rights and Global Diversity

Robert Paul Churchill

George Washington University

Upper Saddle River, New Jersey 07458

Library of Congress Cataloging-in-Publication Data

Churchill, Robert Paul.
   Human rights and global diversity / Robert Paul Churchill.
     p. cm.
   Includes bibliographical references and index.
   ISBN 0-13-040885-9
   1. Human rights—Moral and ethical aspects. 2. Ethical relativism. 3. Cultural relativism.
   4.   Intercultural communication. I. Title.

JC571.C565 2005
323—dc22

2004022492

VP, Editorial Director: Charlyce Jones Owen
Assistant Editor: Wendy Yurash
Editorial Assistant: Carla Worner
Marketing Manager: Kara Kindstrom
Marketing Assistant: Jennifer Lang
Production Liaison:
   Marianne Peters-Riordan
Manufacturing Buyer: Christina Helder

Cover Art Director: Jayne Conte
Cover Design: Bruce Kenselaar
Composition/Full-Service Project
   Management: Linda Duarte/Pine
   Tree Composition
Printer/Binder: Courier Companies
Inc.
Cover Printer: Lehigh Press

Pearson Education LTD.
Pearson Education Singapore, Pte. Ltd.
Pearson Education Canada Ltd
Pearson Education—Japan
Pearson Education Australia Pty. Limited

Pearson Education North Asia Ltd.
Pearson Educación de Mexico, S.A. de C.V.
Pearson Education Malaysia, Pte. Ltd.
Pearson Education, Upper Saddle River,
  New Jersey

10 9 8 7 6 5 4 3 2 1
ISBN 0-13-040885-9

For Eileen,
My Guiding Light

Contents

PREFACE   xi

chapter one
REASONING ABOUT HUMAN RIGHTS   1
1. The Concept of Rights   2
    Social context   3
    Entitlements   4
    Correlative duties   6
    Objects of rights   8
    Individual discretion   10
    Universalizability   10
    Moral rights   12
2. The Justification of Human Rights   13
    Natural law and natural rights   15
    Difficulties with natural rights   17
    From natural rights to human rights   20
    Good reasons approach   22
    Problems with the good reasons approach   25
    Dialectical justifications   28
3. Applications: The Anikwata Case   33
    Do the Anikwatas Have a Right to Asylum?   34
    Considering justifications   38

chapter two

DEBATING THE UNIVERSALITY OF HUMAN RIGHTS   **42**
1. Universalism Versus Exceptionalism   43
2. Is It Possible for Human Rights Norms to Apply
   Universally?   48
3. Should Human Rights Norms Apply Universally?   66
4. Diversity, Human Rights, and Cross-Cultural
   Negotiation   87

chapter three

HUMAN RIGHTS AND CROSS-CULTURAL NEGOTIATIONS   **89**
1. A Transformational Strategy   92
2. A Strategy of Accommodation   97
3. Internal Validation as a Strategy   108
4. The Strategy of Worldview Integration   118
5. Summing Up and Looking Forward   125

appendix a

THE INTERNATIONAL HUMAN RIGHTS REGIME   **128**
1. Conceptualization of the Program   128
   a. Charter of the United Nations   128
   b. Universal Declaration of Human Rights   129
2. Definitions of Human Rights and Creation   130
   a. International Bill of Human Rights   130
   *b. Convention of the Prevention and Punishment
      of the Crime of Genocide   130*
   c. International Covenant on Civil and Political Rights (ICCPR)   131
   *d. International Covenant on Economic, Social, and Cultural
      Rights (ICESCR)   132*
   *e. Convention Against Torture and Other Cruel, Inhuman,
      or Degrading Treatment or Punishment (CAT)   133*
   f. Convention on the Rights of the Child (CRC)   134
3. Monitoring and Implementation   134
   a. Implementation Provisions of Treaties and Covenants   135
   b. Influences on National Law   135
   c. Role of the UN Commission on Human Rights   136
   d. Office of the High Commissioner for Human Rights   136
   e. Peacekeeping and Humanitarian Intervention   137
   f. Tribunals   137
4. Instruments and Organizations Regional in Scope   138
5. International Citizens' Advocacy Groups   139
Concluding Comment   140

appendix b

SELECTED RESEARCH AND/OR ACTIVIST NONGOVERNMENTAL
ORGANIZATIONS (NGOs), SELECTED INTERGOVERNMENTAL
ORGANIZATIONS (IGOs), WITH OTHER SELECTED RESOURCES **142**
Selected NGOs and Web Sites   142
Selected IGOs and Web Sites   144
Other Selected Resources   144

INDEX   **145**

Preface

As is customary, an introduction or a preface of a book should give readers a clear indication of the author's objectives. Consequently, I have divided this preface into three brief parts. First, I explain what the book attempts to accomplish. Second, I offer an overview of the importance of human rights for our future as global citizens. Third, there is much in discussions and arguments over human rights that falls outside the scope of this book; consequently, in order to avoid confusion, I comment on what this book does *not* cover.

THE ARGUMENT OF THE BOOK

This book is intended as an unabashed argument for the *universality* of human rights. As such, the book is guided by three main theses. First, all human beings everywhere have the same human rights. To speak of rights as "human rights" means that, simply in virtue of a person's status as a human agent, every human being has moral entitlements that outweigh contrary considerations except in rare and unusual circumstances. An argument for human rights as a special category of rights and for their reality as prescriptive and preemptory moral entitlements is made in Chapter One, Reasoning about Human Rights.

It follows from the logic of Chapter One that human rights are necessarily universal. Thus, all human beings everywhere can make the same legitimate claims to the enjoyment and protection of basic goods and liberties, and are therefore universally the same in the possession of human dignity as agents. The absence of protection of a human right or of people's enjoyment of it within a particular state or society is *not* evidence of its nonexistence in that place or time. And persons not able to enjoy the goods or objects of their human rights are victims of serious moral wrongs.

The argument of Chapter One thus entails that all versions of *exceptionalism*, or *particularism*, are false. Contrary to particularism, and despite cultural and social diversity—much of which is to be valued and preserved—human rights are *not* created by, or exist as a consequence of, or are otherwise dependent on, relative and particular cultural or social arrangements. Neither are human rights (in contrast to legal rights) created by states or societies (they are not enacted or legislated), nor can they be modified in essential respects by conditions arising within a particular society, nor overridden except in extreme emergencies. Indeed, in the rare instances when a human right must be derogated—for example, a suspected terrorist is deprived of freedom to protect the right to life of others—we recognize that the circumstances would justify the derogation universally. That is, derogation of the suspected terrorist's right to liberty would be justified in the same relevant circumstances in any social group or country experiencing the same threat.

Chapter Two, Debating the Universality of Human Rights, is an extension of the argument for the universality of human rights. Because, as previously noted, the argument of Chapter One already implies logically that human rights are universal (a claim that I characterize as *universalism*), Chapter Two is presented as a rebuttal of arguments advanced by those who are not yet persuaded. The chapter is intended to show that no plausible particularist, or exceptionalist, argument can succeed, including the following contenders: the view that universalism is false because ethical relativism is true; the view that human rights cannot be universal because they have their origins in particular (North Atlantic) cultures; the view that human rights are incommensurable with key values in some societies and therefore cannot be "translated" into meaningful norms for those societies; the view that human rights are a (sometimes disguised) form of cultural imperialism; the view that human rights are destructive of values that are native, or indigenous, to local social groups; and the view that human rights, or some of them, may be set aside or "traded off" to attain other social values deemed important by opponents of the universality thesis.

The argument from ethical relativism receives the greatest amount of attention for two reasons; first, historically the argument has had greatest currency (at least within intellectual circles in the North Atlantic) and has misled more people than the others. Of more importance, however, is the logical status of this objection to universalism. It serves as grounding for particularist arguments in the sense that, were it to be true, not only would universalism be false, but also the particularist arguments would obtain philosophical justification. It is critical, therefore, to appreciate why ethical relativism is false, and indeed, as I show, is even self-refuting.[1]

This book is in the *Ethics in Action Series*, which is edited by Michael Boylan, and for this reason, Chapter Three, Human Rights and Cross-Cultural Negotiations, is very much about applied ethics. This chapter considers the impact of the universalist human rights position in cultures and geopolitical regions of the globe in which there is still strong resistance to the growing international consensus on human rights. In some cases rejection centers on women's rights, as in some Muslim societies; in other cases, as in China, it involves serious infringement of civil and political liberties; or in still other cases, as in the United States, unacceptable infringements of welfare, or subsistence, rights prevail, as in inadequate provision of food, housing, and health care.

My approach in Chapter Three is to emphasize ways of finding consensual and cooperative approaches to the debate. Given that particularist arguments fail (Chapter Two), the objective is to show that there is no inherent contradiction between human rights norms (defensible interpretations of what respect for human rights requires) and social and cultural values, practices, and forms of life *worthy* of preservation. My hope is to show that human rights can be incorporated into every social or cultural order without threat to fundamental and morally defensible values and practices defended by members of the social order, and often in a way that strengthens plurality (for example, by protecting minorities and expression of diversity) or that protects traditional values (for example, the authority of tribal order against the destructive effects of modernization).

The four methods discussed in Chapter Three successively reflect efforts to bring to bear resources of communicative theory; efforts to employ cultural, spiritual, and ethical resources already embedded within a particular

---

[1]Some readers might be tempted to view the logical structure of Chapter Two as what logicians call an *argumentum ad ignorantiam,* or "negative proof." In other words, they might aver that it does not follow from my showing that the particularist arguments presented fail, that every possible particularist argument will fail. I believe that such objectors misplace the burden of proof, however. I regard the argument of Chapter 1 as *sufficient* to establish the universality of human rights. Thus, I do not attempt to prove this thesis by refuting contenders in Chapter Two. My objective, instead, is to overcome bias against the argument of Chapter One by demonstrating the untenability of particularist positions.

society or culture to embrace human rights or to embrace them more completely; efforts of accommodation that recognize permissible differences in cultural or social "interpretations" or "forms" of human rights; and, in addition, efforts to bring the benefits of worldview perspective to bear on the debate.

WHY EMPHASIZE THE UNIVERSALITY OF HUMAN RIGHTS?

The argument of Chapter Three is underscored by the conviction that we should respect human rights because we accept and admire one another's basic humanity. But for political, social, and other practical reasons, human rights norms will be of critical importance for the twenty-first century. This last claim has both an empirical and a normative dimension. On the empirical, or factual, plane, human rights are emerging as the most dominant ordering principles in international affairs and global society. Among the causes of the increasing prominence of human rights is each of the following:

1. The vast expansion of international activity in protecting refugees and providing humanitarian assistance in countries devastated by ethnic conflict and civil war;

2. The expansion of United Nations peacekeeping efforts to protect civilian populations, to secure the distribution of relief supplies, and to supervise elections, among other things;

3. The extensive "internationalization" of human rights in certain regions, especially the European Union where the European Court of Human Rights hears cases on appeal and makes decisions binding on participating member states;

4. The evolution of the international human rights "regime" as a formidable body consisting of conventions, or treaties, customary law, and techniques for implementation and compliance;[2]

5. The requirement that newly independent states seeking membership in the United Nations accept the aspirations of the Universal Declaration of Human Rights, and more significantly, the incorporation of provisions of human rights covenants into the constitutions of many new states, as well as the expression of the aspirations of the peoples of many "third world states" in terms of human rights, such as in the Declaration of the Right to Self-Determination and the Declaration of the Right to Development;

6. The increasing recognition among states leaders and peoples generally that sovereignty cannot be unlimited, in fact, that the sovereignty of a state or the authority of a social group (for example, a tribal council) is limited by the rights of citizens, members, or any persons under its power.

[2]Gene M. Lyons and James Mayall, eds., *International Human Rights in the 21st Century* (Lanham, MD: Rowman & Littlefield, 2003), pp. 10–2.

In saying that human rights have a normative dimension, I mean, in addition, that it is *good* that state relations and that our lives as global citizens are ordered by these principles rather than others less conducive to the development of our full potential as agents. But I also assert that there are additional reasons why we should want to organize our interactions on the basis of human rights. These reasons refer to a future characterized by increasingly scarce resources needed to sustain life and increasingly severe competition for these resources; environmental degradation that, unless addressed, will threaten the opportunities of increasing millions to live lives of dignity; and globalization that drives states to adopt open markets and to remove restrictions on the free movement of capital. This new international economic orthodoxy makes it increasingly difficult for states to redistribute income or to implement welfare policies. Additionally, globalization leads to the increased privatization of the necessities of life, such as potable water.

As anthropologist Barbara Rose Johnston notes, "The past few generations have seen a rapid expansion of technology and industries, intensified use of environmental resources, exponential population growth, and unprecedented destruction of our global habitat. Accompanying these changes in human action are changes in the culture and structure of power: fewer and fewer people control more and more of the world's resources, and most people are far removed from the consequences of their actions."[3] Because the severest problems of the twenty-first century are intrastate and transnational—often truly global in reach—as are economic globalization, information technology, infectious disease, terrorism, and despoliation of the environment—the traditional, nation-state international system is incompetent to deal with them.

Yet, insofar as there are human causes (or human links in the causal chain) of our problems, they all involve *power*. We all know that those who suffer the most from economic globalization or environmental despoliation are typically those with the least power in society, either the power to insulate themselves from threats or the power to rebuild their lives after catastrophe. And it is precisely because human rights developed their prominence as the way persons assert their moral entitlements to limit forms of power exercised against them (first in relation to states, now increasingly in relation to nonstate "actors" such as industrial conglomerates), that human rights will be of increasing importance in the years to come. The focus of human rights is always on the protection of humanity, as meaningfully embodied and individuated in persons, against whatever forces might seek to stifle or crush human beings. Thus, because human rights are more directly related to and more easily fashioned to deal with power relations as they affect persons, it *ought* to be the normative system, selected first among

---

[3]Barbara Rose Johnston, ed., *Life and Death Matters: Human Rights and the Environment at the End of the Millennium*, "Introduction" (Walnut Creek, CA: AtaMira Press, 1997), p. 15.

---

others, to be developed further and expanded to meet the challenges of the future.

SUBJECTS OUTSIDE THE SCOPE OF THIS BOOK

This book represents an exercise in applied philosophy and applied ethics, most particularly. Consequently, no attempt has been made to cover subjects thoroughly discussed elsewhere. In particular, there is no effort here to present the historical development of the Universal Declaration of Human Rights or of the subsequent "International Bill of Rights."[4] In addition, I have not attempted to replicate or to advance the work on human rights of empirical political sciences or of other social and behavioral scientists.

Margaret Keck and Kathryn Sikkink examine a type of pressure group that had largely been ignored by political analysts: networks of activists that coalesce and operate across national boundaries. Keck and Sikkink argue that, in the last two decades, transnational activism has had a significantly positive impact on human rights.[5] Likewise, Sikkink and others have examined the impact of human rights norms on the behavior of national governments in many regions of the world, demonstrating how and why human rights norms influence the actions of states and are internalized in domestic policies.[6] Equally outside the scope of the book, but also important for the promotion and implementation of human rights, are the numerous intergovernmental organizations (IGOs), such as the United Nations Commission on Human Rights, and numerous nongovernmental organizations (NGOs), such as Amnesty International, Human Rights Watch, and the World Labor Organization.

The central focus in this book is on the universality of moral principles, or norms, in what is known as the International Bill of Rights (IBR). The IBR comprises the Universal Declaration of Human Rights and the two subsequent conventions of 1966, the International Covenant on Economic, Social, and Cultural Rights (ICESCR) and the International Covenant on Civil and Political Rights (ICCPR). The IBR is, however, only one part of what might be called the "international human rights regime" that includes additional important covenants, monitoring instruments, regional human

---

[4]An excellent account of the former is Mary Ann Glendon, *A World Made New: Eleanor Roosevelt and the Universal Declaration of Human Rights* (New York: Random House, 2001). A collection of materials relevant to the development of the International Bill of Rights is to be found in Henry J. Steiner and Philip Alston, eds., *International Human Rights in Context*, 2nd ed. (Boulder, CO: Westview Press, 1988). See also their extensive bibliography.

[5]Margaret E. Keck and Kathryn Sikkink, *Activists Beyond Borders: Advocacy Networks in International Politics* (Ithaca and London: Cornell University Press, 1998).

[6]Thomas Risse, Stephen C. Ropp, and Kathryn Sikkink, eds., *The Power of Human Rights: International Norms and Domestic Change* (Cambridge: Cambridge University Press, 2001).

rights organizations, and enforcement mechanisms such as the European Court of Human Rights. Although mention is made of the international human rights regime in certain places in the main text and the international human rights regime is briefly desribed in Appendix A, readers will need to go to other sources for a fuller account of its various parts and operation.[7]

In recent years, considerable attention has been given to group rights, or collective minority rights. Their prominence in discourse arises when rights of individuals cannot be achieved or protected except by members of groups acting in concert or by granting to all members of a group what, in Chapter One, I characterize as the "object" of the right. Some authors believe that protection of group rights is a necessary part of any attempt to democratize a deeply divided society, especially where constitutional guarantees and the rule of law may not be sufficient to overcome ethnic or racial animosity and rivalry.[8] Group, or collective, rights thus make sense in the context of institutional arrangements to protect a minority against an oppressive majority, such as the apportioning of seats in a national assembly, or to protect the customary practices of indigenous persons against the inroads of a majority culture, by allowing an indigenous group to follow tribal practices by making special provisions or exemptions. Thus, although I cannot make the argument here, I regard group rights as derivative and not primary. As group rights exist to facilitate the realization of the individual rights of persons, they are legal or social rights, but not human rights.

Finally, there are abundant philosophical issues that are not considered in this introductory work. Some, such as the long-standing controversy over the relative priority of "negative" (liberty) rights versus "positive" (social and economic) rights, I pass over because I am persuaded that this division is artificial and unhelpful, at least for my purposes here.[9] There are other philosophical justifications of human rights worthy of consideration, but I must leave the discovery and savoring of these to interested and industrious readers.

ACKNOWLEDGMENTS

Many hands, minds, and hearts are involved in the making of a book. In this case, I would especially like to acknowledge the continual loving support of my wife Eileen; my students in my graduate course "Normative Issues in

[7]For a general overview see Jack Donnelly, *Universal Human Rights in Theory and Practice* (Ithaca and London: Cornell University Press, 1989), pp. 205–27. Donnelly distinguishes between global and regional human rights regimes and analyzes regimes in terms of three variables: promotion, implementation, and enforcement.
[8]*International Human Rights in the 21st Century*, p. 4.
[9]The classical argument against the distinction is Henry Shue, *Basic Rights: Subsistence, Affluence and U.S. Foreign Policy* (Princeton: Princeton University Press, 1980).

U.S. Foreign Policy," who read and offered helpful comments on earlier
drafts of two chapters; Katherine Hamilton who, as recipient of a Pre-
Doctoral Scholars Summer Internship from the State of California, was able
to serve as my research assistant in the summer of 2001 and who brought a
number of significant issues to my attention and offered many important insights, especially on the status of women in Islam; the helpful and cheerful
assistance of my editors Ross Miller, Wendy Yurash, and Linda Duarte; the
anonymous reviewers for Prentice Hall whose comments were challenging
and most helpful; and especially, the Series Editor, Michael Boylan, without
whose consistent and generous assistance and friendship this book would
not have been possible. Finally, I am grateful to scores of friends and ac-
quaintances around the globe, especially in the Middle East and Southeast
Asia who did their best to help me appreciate their cultural values and
worldviews and with whom I spent many, many fruitful hours discussing
human rights.

Robert Paul Churchill

Human Rights and Global Diversity

chapter one

Reasoning about Human Rights

"What are human rights?" This general question may be a request for a number of different answers. One might be asking about the existence of human rights, for example, "What evidence is there that anyone has human rights?" or about specific rights that persons claim, for example, "Is privacy a human right?" By contrast, one might be asking how human rights differ from other kinds of rights such as legal or moral rights. In the latter case, one asks for the reasons for regarding human rights as a special category of rights. Some people might be disposed to think that human rights must first exist as some kind of "entity" before they can be justified as good. Others share the view (endorsed here) that, in saying a right is a human right, we mean that it can be given a specially compelling justification. In this view, the concept of human rights as a distinct category arises when we consider the justification of rights.

First things first. To fully understand the issues involved in controversies over the *existence* of human rights and the *justification* of human rights, we need to perform a *conceptual analysis*. In this connection the opening question can be interpreted as asking about the *concept* of human rights, as, for instance, in "What ideas or notions are involved in our talk, or discourse, about human rights?" For someone just beginning to participate in the discourse, this last question could be rephrased as "How should we think about human rights?"

In addition, because the concept of rights is more basic (or logically prior) to the concept of human rights, we first need a conceptual analysis of the more general concept. This conceptual analysis is presented in the first section of this chapter. It is followed in the second section by a discussion of justifications for human rights. In the third section, we consider how the analysis and reasoning about rights introduced in Sections 1 and 2 might be applied to a contemporary cross-cultural problem.

1. THE CONCEPT OF RIGHTS

Philosophers turn to conceptual analysis when the ideas designated by an indefinite term such as *rights* (or *democracy, justice, equality,*) are too complex or too controversial to be defined in simple and nonambiguous terms.[1] In a conceptual analysis, we examine the ideas and notions that commonly arise when frequent users of the term think and write about rights. We look for a network of ideas that are logically connected, or "packed" together. These ideas are first separated so that each can be illuminated or explained, and then their connections are clarified. And—unlike the case with a definition that we look up or stipulate—reasons are offered and weighed for certain interpretations and uses of the term. The process of analysis usually is complete when users of the term would accept it as a more or less adequate and neutral account of what they mean in speaking and writing about rights (or at least as a very reasonable account).[2]

As you work through the conceptual analysis in this section, it is important to bear two things in mind. First, the analysis concerns the concept of rights; *a theory* of rights (such as natural rights theory) is intended to supply *justifications* for the rights we claim or defend, although a formal theory is not necessary for a justification. Likewise, whether an *application* of the concept is correct or incorrect depends on the facts of particular cases as well as on reasons supplied for applying the concept in a certain way.

Second, obviously a concept of rights presupposes possible consensus over the meaning of certain terms and beliefs. Every concept must be situated within a group that shares an understanding of its significance. As many commentators have noted, historically ideas about rights were first articulated and debated in Western Europe and North America by thinkers

---

[1] As used here, a *concept* may be understood to include those ideas that necessarily form parts of it. For instance, the concept of a square necessarily includes the ideas of a straight line, a plane figure, a rectangle, a right (90°) angle, and equal sides.

[2] "Analysis," in *Cambridge Dictionary of Philosophy*, Robert Audi, ed. (Cambridge: Cambridge University Press, 1995), p. 22. See also Robert Paul Churchill, *Logic: An Introduction* (New York: St. Martin's Press, 1990), pp. 135–7 for some limitations on this kind of analysis.

such as Thomas Jefferson, John Locke, and Thomas Paine.[3] The concept analyzed here has the same historical origins although it has achieved universal
scope in discourse as indicated, for example, by the "International Bill of
Human Rights."[4] Nevertheless, it may be controversial whether this conceptual analysis applies cross-culturally around the globe or whether there can
be anything like a "universal" conception of rights.[5] Detractors claim that
the concept analyzed here is meaningful only within cultures and linguistic
communities of Western Europe and the North Atlantic. Although this is an
issue to be taken up in Chapter 2, it can be said here that the following
analysis might at least promote reasonable disagreement. Following the
analysis, those who are still unwilling to accept the concept at least should
find it easier to specify why they object to it.

Social context

Reflection shows that rights are social in character. Philosopher Martin
Golding helps us see this by calling to mind the story of Robinson Crusoe.[6]
Although shipwrecked on a desert island, Crusoe was presumably as rational and as normal as most other persons. He could and did consciously
engage in purposive activity on his own, he continued to have hopes and
desires, and his capacities to suffer pain and feel loneliness remained unim-
paired. Nevertheless, it is extremely odd to speak of rights while Crusoe remained alone on his island, when no other person knew or cared about him.
Although he can speak, he lacks another human being to speak and interact
with. Notice how strange it seems to ask, "Does Crusoe have a right to eat
whatever he likes?" or "Has Crusoe a right to go wherever he wants on his
island?" while he is alone on his island.

The point is not that Crusoe *lacks* rights, for if he were rescued and re-
turned to English society, then questions about Crusoe's rights would be relevant and meaningful. The point is rather that on his island Crusoe lacks a
social environment, and outside such an environment, discourse about
rights has no relevant point. But as soon as Friday arrives, similar questions,
for example, "Does Crusoe have a right to keep for himself all the food he
has grown or gathered?" make a great deal of sense. Of course, we can also

---

[3]Thomas Jefferson, "Declaration of Independence," in *The Life and Selected Writings of
Thomas Jefferson,* eds. Adrienne Koch and William Peden, (New York: Modern Library, 1972);
John Locke, *Second Treatise of Government* [1690] C. B. Macpherson, ed. (Indianapolis, IN: Hack-
ett Publishing, 1980); Thomas Paine, *Rights of Man* [1791] (Buffalo, NY: Prometheus, 1989).

[4]This consists of three documents, the United Nations Universal Declaration of Human
Rights (1948), the International Covenant on Civil and Political Rights (1976), and the International Covenant on Economic, Social and Cultural Rights (1976).

[5]See, for example, Jay Drydyk, "Globalization and Human Rights," in *Moral Issues in
Global Perspective,* Christine Koggel, ed. (Peterborough, Canada: Broadview, 1999), pp. 3–42.

[6]Martin Golding, "Towards a Theory of Human Rights," *The Monist* 52 (1968), pp. 521–49.

ask about Friday's rights, such as, "Does Friday have a right to be on Crusoe's island?" Or, "Does Friday have a right to Robinson Crusoe's help in hiding him from the cannibals?"

The Crusoe example underscores the fact that only in social contexts are rights claimed, defended and protected, or violated. Whether or not rights can exist anterior to or outside of a community of some sort (as Natural Rights theorists claim), they come into play and are applicable only in social contexts. All claims of rights are directed to and made in relation to audiences that, *in principle,* are capable of responding by satisfying (at least in part) or frustrating those demands. Furthermore, the existence of rights is dependent upon persons who, *in principle,* are willing to take a stand, make demands on one another, and accept the possible outcomes of these demands as pertinent to their sense of self and self-respect in their relevant communities. To claim a right is to assert a warrant for doing or having something despite the possibility that doing or having it may adversely affect the interests of others.

Entitlements

To illuminate an important aspect of rights, contrast the way that we think about rights, on the one hand, and about privileges and gifts, or gratuities, on the other. What distinguishes a privilege or a gratuity from a right? Consider these characteristics of privileges and gratuities. First, one must often apply for a privilege (e.g., a driver's license) or must assume the burden of demonstrating that one is competent or worthy of it (e.g., by passing a test or by giving good service as in the case of a tip). Second, a privilege or gift is granted or given at the discretion of the institution or person that grants or gives it. Third, privileges and especially gifts are given out of benevolence or charity; the grantor or giver is under no duty to confer the privilege or gift, and either may be withheld when giving is inconvenient to the giver. Certainly a privilege or gift is not something an individual can claim as one's due.

By contrast, we think of rights as involving demands that require others to respond that are not dependent on feelings of goodwill or assessments of convenience. We say of a right that it is some person's due—that he or she is *entitled* to it and that he or she is wronged if the right is violated.[7] In addition, to regard oneself as a rights-holder is to view oneself as having personal dignity and moral worth as an individual.

To consider the idea of rights as entitlements, consider the following example. All college students know that professors sometimes grade stu-

---

[7]Joel Feinberg, "The Nature and Value of Rights," *Journal of Value Inquiry,* 4 (1970), 243; and *Social Philosophy* (Englewood Cliffs, NJ: Prentice Hall, 1973).

dents' papers unfairly.[8] The reasons for this outcome vary from case to case, and the incidence of unfair grading is probably no greater at one institution than it is at another. It is also fairly common for students who believe that they have been unfairly graded to want to inquire about the grading. Moreover, it seems correct to say that students have a right to a respectful response to their concerns.

For those involved in academia, it is natural to believe that a student is entitled to impartial review upon request. It should not be left up to the professor whose fairness is being challenged to decide whether to consider a student's request. For these reasons many colleges and universities have established student-faculty commissions or other formal bodies that respond to student complaints of unfairness through established procedures designed to be effective and impartial.

Now imagine a university—Lower State University—at which the situation is entirely different. If a student at Lower State wishes to question grading, he must petition the professor who graded the paper for an appointment. The professor herself decides whether or not to accept such a petition. And, even if the petition is granted, it is entirely up to the professor whose fairness is being questioned whether or not to review the paper. Of course, many faculty members at Lower State are conscientious and kind men and women. They generally would not dream of turning down a student's petition or refuse a review. Also, they would attempt to be as objective as possible, and they may even call in colleagues to review a student's complaint.

However, whether or not a professor at Lower State chooses to respect a student's request and to respond impartially is solely subject to his or her sense of justice or benevolence, or to factors such as the inconvenience that the review would cause. If some professors choose to review grade complaints and if others do not, then unfortunate students have no grounds for asserting that they have been wronged. At Lower State, then, students are privileged to receive faculty review of a complaint; faculty indulgence is a gratuity that is dispensed only with goodwill. Students have no *claim* on the faculty, nor are they *entitled* to impartial review.

What does the difference between these two cases illustrate? It shows that rights are *entitlements.* To be entitled to something is to have a case meriting serious consideration; it is to be in a position to demand or insist upon something that one wants or has, as one's *due.* The claim of students for review ought not to depend on faculty goodwill or permission. Likewise, a claim of right is not defeated or deflected because the response called for causes inconvenience for others.

---

[8]This example is adapted from Norman E. Bowie and Robert L. Simon, *The Individual and the Political Order* (Englewood Cliffs, NJ: Prentice Hall, 1977), pp. 56–7.

In addition, a rights-holder is someone who is also *wronged* by the violation of the right itself and apart from deprivation of a benefit. Faculty at Lower State who turn down petitions deny students of a benefit (the opportunity for impartial review), and faculty may be acting unkindly and ungenerously, but—given the imaginary scenario—they do not wrong the students by violating rights. But the imaginary scenario of Lower State is counterintuitive. College students who have serious concerns about grading but whose cases are not reviewed suffer the wrong of a rights violation as well as deprivation of a benefit. The violation is an assault on their dignity and integrity as persons. If they are subject to discrimination (e.g., their cases are not taken seriously although other students' cases are), then they are treated as having less inherent worth as persons. If their concerns are ignored or dismissed out of hand, or belittled, then these students are treated as less than fully competent and responsible moral agents. Thus, we see that in asserting one's rights, a person asserts oneself as a moral agent and demands respect as an autonomous agent. Rights-holders have a recognized moral authority in their dealings with one another.

To be sure, people may make claims to things to which they are not entitled. This might be the case, for example, if students claimed that they had a right to receive grades of *A* even if they did not pass exams or turn in assignments. In the latter case, unlike the one involving appeals of unfair grading, it is much more likely that the asserted justification is inadequate, and the warrant empty. In deciding whether or not people are entitled to what they claim as a right, we must therefore attend to the persuasiveness of the reasons that can be given for the rights-claim. The justification of rights-claims is considered in Section 2. Here we have been concerned only to examine connections between ideas of entitlement and the concept of rights.

Correlative duties

If rights involve an entitlement to do or to have or to be free from something, then they also involve claims against others to act or to refrain from acting in certain ways. Thus, if a student has a right to have his or her case heard, then there must be other persons who have a duty to provide that opportunity. This concept is often described as the *correlation between rights and duties.*[9]

To clarify the correlation between rights and duties, consider what rights add to freedom, or liberty. Let us define freedom for the present simply as the absence of restraint, interference, or hindrance. Thus, for example, when we say that Joel is free to speak his mind, we ordinarily mean that Joel's attempts to voice his opinions will not be restrained or obstructed by

---

[9]S. I. Benn and R. S. Peters, *Social Principles and the Democratic State* (London: George Allen and Unwin, 1959), p. 89.

others. What the right adds to the freedom is the obligation of others not to interfere, as well as a further duty—usually a public duty—to provide social protection for the freedom. Thus, more fully, to say that Joel has a right to speak his mind is to say that Joel is free to do so *and* that there is a reasonable expectation that his freedom to do so is protected in some significant way. Thus, if Ahmed tries to deny Joel his right to speak, we expect that Ahmed will be subjected to social or moral criticism, or censure, and possibly to arrest and a fine or punishment.

As the discussion of entitlement showed, rights are claimed as one's due whether or not they inconvenience the interests of others. For these reasons, rights are properly understood as providing individuals with social protections from standard threats against persons, whether these threats originate in state power or in the power of private individuals or of other corporate bodies.[10] For instance, rights guaranteed by the United States Constitution protect individuals against imprisonment without trial by jury, from the silencing of antigovernment views, and against unreasonable search and seizure, among others.

In thinking about correlative duties, it is helpful to distinguish general, or in rem, rights from special, or in personam, rights.[11] A right is said to be special (in personam) if it imposes a correlative duty on some distinct and "assignable" individual. Most often, special rights arise from particular roles and the responsibilities attached to them, such as the roles between parents and children, or the arrangements made voluntarily between prospective rights-holders and duty-bearers. For instance, if you loaned me one hundred dollars and I promised to repay you tomorrow, then you have a special right to receive my money tomorrow. I have a correlative duty to repay you, but no one else has this duty.

By contrast, a right is said to be general (in rem) if it imposes a correlative duty generally on others. For instance, an individual's right to be free from physical assault imposes an obligation of restraint on anyone who might be inclined to or in a position to harm the person. Likewise, a person's right to speak freely means that anyone's interfering with his or her speech is violating a correlative duty.

Although rights imply duties, two important qualifications must be noted. First, it may be difficult to determine who is charged with duties correlative to general rights and what exactly is required to discharge them. Indeed, this is a notoriously difficult aspect of applying rights,[12] and a

---

[10]See, for example, Jack Donnelly, *Universal Human Rights in Theory and Practice* (Ithaca, NY: Cornell University Press, 1989), Ch. 13; Henry Shue, *Basic Rights: Subsistence, Affluence, and U.S. Foreign Policy* (Princeton, NJ: Princeton University Press, 1996), pp. 32–3.

[11]Wesley N. Hohfeld, *Fundamental Legal Conceptions* (New Haven, CT: Yale University Press, 1919, repr. 1964); John T. Salmond, *Jurisprudence*, Glanville Williams, ed. (London: Sweer & Maxwell, 1957), p. 286.

[12]*Basic Rights*, pp. 52–69.

conceptual analysis cannot supply answers. To illustrate, even if we are persuaded that Sudanese who are stricken by famine have a general right to food, it may be difficult to decide who must respond. (For instance, must the government act for us collectively or must each of us respond through individual contributions, and must you or I respond whether or not others do?) It may also be difficult to determine how much must be done to fulfill duties. (For instance, must we do the best we can to end starvation, or must we provide a level of nutrition beyond requirement for survival?) A theory of rights is often needed to justify the assignment, or distribution, of correlative duties and to justify claims that certain responses, among alternatives, are required.

Second, the relationship between rights and duties is not symmetrical. Not all duties imply correlative rights. In Western societies especially, duties are thought to form a broader category. For example, a physician may have a moral duty to put his or her knowledge and skill to the best possible use. But it may not be clear who has a right to benefit from the exercise of those abilities. But there are also contexts in which it is common to speak of rights consequent on duties—for example, a child's right to subsistence from parents' income. In addition, it is claimed that in some societies or groups in which duties are owed in recognition of membership, these duties do give rise to rights. This is claimed to be the case in some traditional African cultures, for example. As Kwasi Wireda points out with reference to the Akan peoples of West Africa, despite the absence of talk about rights, "obligations are matched by a whole series of rights that accrue to the individual simply because he lives in a society in which everyone has those obligations."[13]

Objects of rights

In discussing the correlation between rights and duties, we spoke of a *right* to do or to have *something*. This represents a distinction between a right (X) and the *object*, or *substance*, of the right (Y). For example, I have a right to eat the food I have purchased with money I earned. But the object of this right is the salmon and broccoli on my plate. Likewise, I have the right to speak freely, but the object of the right is—on the present occasion—my part in the conversation that I enjoy over lunch. Do these examples seem trivial? Well, what if I am systematically deprived of food and faced with the threat of starvation? What if I am arrested, imprisoned every time I attempt publicly to express my political views, even to voluntary audiences?

---

[13]Kwasi Wirendu, "An Akan Perspective on Human Rights," in *Human Rights in Africa: Cross-Cultural Perspectives*, Abdullahi Ahmed An-Na'im and Francis M. Deng, eds. (Washington, DC: Brookings Institute, 1990), p. 247.

In such cases, I am likely to assert a basic right to sustenance and a right to free speech.

Philosophers and rights theorists have increasingly come to recognize as most basic, or fundamental, those rights that have as their objects the goods that individuals require in order to function as moral agents. Henry Shue regards rights as basic if the enjoyment of them is essential to the enjoyment of all other rights.[14] Diana Meyers refers to basic rights as "inalienable" and identifies four: life, personal liberty, freedom from gratuitous acute pain, and satisfaction of basic needs (adequate food, water, clothing, shelter, and medical treatment for survival).[15] Alan Gewirth also recognizes as most basic those goods minimally necessary for agency.[16] Gewirth maintains that whether or not some good can be claimed as a right is its centrality to agency within society. He divides goods into three categories: basic, nonsubtractive, and additive (see Section 2). Whereas basic goods are necessary for any effective action within society, nonsubtractive goods are the goods a person already possesses. Additive goods are nonbasic goods that a person seeks to possess.[17]

The distinction between rights and their objects helps us understand why a right is not negated or erased when it goes unfulfilled, that is, when the rights-holder is deprived of or not provided with the object. Thus, someone who snatches my food violates my right to eat it, but the right is not negated although it is violated. Likewise, although a dictator may prevent me from speaking—from attaining the object of my right—he or she cannot erase the right itself.

Generally, as these examples indicate, we *claim* rights in large part because we seek the object of the right. Now, attaining this object may be subject to the interference of others. Usually, I will not claim a right to eat my food, if I care nothing for it—go ahead and snatch the plate. Likewise, I am not very likely to claim my rights if I do not perceive them under threat. I need not claim a right to speak freely, for example, when there is no threat to such action. So, claiming a right comes into play when, because of the actions or likely actions of other agents, there are conditions that put the attainment of the object of the right at risk. But we also claim rights because we seek others' recognition and respect for our decision to seek the object in question as a result of autonomous choice. In other words, rights claims are also made when the behavior of others manifests a tendency to disregard—that is, disrespect—rights in general. In cases of this latter type, by claiming our rights we reaffirm the moral importance *in principle* of having rights.

---

[14]*Basic Rights.*

[15]Diana T. Meyers, *Inalienable Rights: A Defense* (New York: Columbia University Press, 1985), p. 53.

[16]Alan Gewirth, *Community of Rights* (Chicago: University of Chicago Press, 1996).

[17]Michael Boylan, *Basic Ethics* (Upper Saddle River, NJ: Prentice Hall, 2000), p. 108.

Individual discretion

Whereas gifts and privileges are given or allowed at the discretion of the grantor, rights-holders often have the discretion to exercise or to waive their rights. There is a "self-administrative" aspect about rights. That is, it is ordinarily left up to the individual rights-holder to decide whether or not to claim a right, how to assess violations of it, and whether or not to seek assistance in enforcing a correlative duty. Thus, in claiming or waiving his or her rights, the rights-holder either binds others to prearranged duty relationships or releases others from them. As suggested by the phrase "exercising rights," rights empower rights-holders in addition to benefiting them.[18]

In many cases an individual may *waive* a right at his or her discretion. One can choose not to claim a right and can agree that others need not regard a request for action or redress as something to which the requester is entitled. The more basic an object or service is for the benefit or agency of an individual, however, the more difficult it is to conceive of a right to that object or service as "waivable." It is not consistent with the concept of rights that an individual would voluntarily abandon the right to life (the right not to be killed) or the right to food and water necessary for life. Basic rights protecting what is minimally necessary for individuals to function as agents can be understood to be *inalienable* in the sense that they cannot be meaningfully waived.[19]

Thus, discretion over the claiming and waiving of rights usually relates to exercises of rights that are special, or in personam, because the effects of waiving the right at one time and on one occasion do not impair the enjoyment of other rights at present or in the future. There is no parallel self-administrative aspect to most general rights, however. For instance, when violation of a right is punishable under a criminal code, then it generally is not up to the person whose right was violated to decide whether or not to press charges or to invoke the aide of the community or the state.

Universalizability

To be sure, some persons may be protected in their ability to have or to enjoy rights, whereas others are not. Nevertheless, the concept of rights is very closely connected with the notion of *equal* rights, or what we may call the "universalizability" of rights. It is a logical feature of the way we think and talk about rights that, given a specific right, we generalize, or "universalize," it. Now, appeals to the principle of equal rights invariably arise when attempts are made to justify access to an object or a service on the basis of a human right. But it is important to understand that this principle

---

[18]Jack Donnelly, *International Human Rights* (Boulder, CO: Westview Press, 1998), p. 19.
[19]*Inalienable Rights*, pp. 51–2.

of equality can be used—justifications can be made in a certain way—because of the logic of universalizability.

Consider any person, say Rashid, who is said to have some right X. Suppose that Rashid or others claim that Rashid's right to X is justified. What is the basis for this claim? It must be because of the necessity of the object of X for Rashid's agency, for instance, in the way that it fulfills his basic physical needs, prevents his suffering, preserves his personal liberty, and so forth. But then, anyone else who has the same relevant basic physical needs, liability to suffering, threats to personal liberty, and so forth, ought, logically, to have the same right as Rashid. The right ought to be an equal right for all claimants with the same relevant qualifying characteristics— whatever those may be, in fact—because it would be irrational to distinguish between persons when there is no relevant difference between them.

Note also that rights of the same kind do not differ in degree; no one has a greater degree of a particular right than another does. It is not possible for rights-holders to possess the same rights but to differ in their degree of possession. Napoleon the pig attempts to obscure this point in George Orwell's *Animal Farm* when he declares that all animals are created equal but that some are more equal than others.[20]

Universalizability demands rationality in reasoning and coherence in one's outlook. Differences that some might want to regard as important, for example, differences in skin color, national origin, and language, are wholly irrelevant to basic needs or capacities to benefit, and hence to rights. Arguments are needed to support claims that any differences are relevant. The actual presentation and evaluation of these arguments is a matter of the justification of the claimed right, not an aspect of its conceptualization. It needs to be emphasized, however, that claiming rights entitle one to certain goods, calls into play a logical requirement for consistency. One must concede that, by the same reasoning, others must have the same rights unless their situations are materially different.[21]

Universalizability, as a logical property, should not be confused with a claim made by advocates of "natural rights," or "human rights." These advocates maintain that some rights are universal in the sense that persons possess them for no other reason than that they are humans, or persons. People possess natural, or human, rights independently of the particular political and legal relationships in which they find themselves. This

---

[20]George Orwell, *Animal Farm* (New York: Harcourt, Brace and Company, 1946).

[21]Moreover, the person arguing for unequal or differential treatment must bear the burden of proof. And it is important not to forget who must bear this burden. For instance, critics of equality have maintained that there is no proof that persons have the same rationality or capacities and therefore could equally benefit from the same goods; the factual evidence is insufficient to support the claim. But the factual information also does not show that people are fundamentally unalike in the ways claimed and, since the burden falls on the critics, there is no justification for discriminating among people on the grounds that some have rights but that others, like them in relevant respects, do not.

position involves two sorts of views. One view, to be discussed in the next section on natural rights, maintains that universal rights are based on the common possession among humans of common attributes or characteristics. A second view is that at least some rights are not contingent, or dependent, upon there being legal protection or enforcement for them. Since the second view involves a conceptual issue, it is considered as the next subtopic in this section.

Moral rights

As indicated before, people may have rights even though they are denied the objects of those rights. Likewise, they may have rights even though their rights claims are disrespected. As we have seen, a person may possess a right even if the right is not, or cannot be, protected by or enforced by law. So, although it is part of the concept of rights that they entail correlative duties, a failure to perform or to enforce these duties does not negate the rights involved.

It is important to distinguish between legal and moral rights. Thus, for example, each of us has the moral right to be told the truth about political events that may affect us in a serious and possibly adverse manner, although we may not enjoy the right through its legal enforcement. On the other hand, although power can create benefits and privileges, often power alone is not sufficient to create rights. Often, a legal enactment said to "confer" a right actually formalizes relationships of cooperation and reciprocity already recognized as legitimate in a society.

To be sure, the categories of "moral" and "legal," including political and civil, are broad and often overlap. So, some moral rights are politically recognized and reasonably well protected by law, whereas others are not. In the United States, for example, freedom of conscience is very well protected, whereas protections against homelessness or medical calamity are quite inadequate. Basically, the primary difference between moral rights and other rights has to do with the *kinds of reasons* to which one appeals in claiming entitlement and the *kinds of reasons* to be considered in assessing justifications for the rights claim. A secondary difference has to do with the way the right came to be publicly recognized—for example, as a legislative enactment—or receives protection. Even when a right is moral, often rights-holders turn first to public guarantors of rights, if such are available, for a redress of grievances. But when the reasons are moral, then the right is a moral right whether or not it is also a legal (including civil or political) right, and whether or not it is general or special.

It was noted at the beginning of this section that rights find applicability within social contexts. It is now important to clarify that point by adding that although rights necessarily require social interactions among persons, they do not require legal order or political states. References to "society" are ambiguous because they fail to convey the distinction between a moral community and a legal or political order. To avoid this confusion, I shall follow the lead of philosopher John Locke and distinguish between the moral community on the one hand and the legal system and political state on the other.[22] There seems to be no difficulty in conceiving of persons possessing moral rights independently of their membership in a given *legal* or *political union*. We can accept that these rights are "natural" when the word "natural" has as its opposites the words "artificial" and "conventional," even if we suspend judgment on Locke's further claims that these rights are also universal and absolute in some important way.

2. THE JUSTIFICATION OF HUMAN RIGHTS

When the reasons supporting a rights-claim and a correlative duty are *moral* and these reasons are *persuasive*, then we regard the rights claim to be *morally justified*. It should become clear, if not so already, that we do not first identify a right as a moral right, and then consider its justification. To constitute a right as a moral right, it is sufficient to present persuasive *moral* reasons for the right. So, in considering the justification of moral rights, we want to consider whether the supporting reasons are *moral* reasons, in contrast to strictly special, legal, or political reasons. For instance, we might consider whether a defendant's case is morally compelling although, because of precedent and the strictures of legal interpretation, a court may decide that a plaintiff wins the lawsuit.

In addition, in considering whether reasons are *compelling*, we want to consider both their relevance and their strength. We want to consider the strength of reasons for an individual's claim to an object of a right, and the relevance and strength of that individual's or others' reasons for believing that what is at issue is an entitlement. That is, we evaluate reasons for maintaining that the individual's claim should be respected, and—in connection with the correlation between rights and duties—that others should respond in appropriate ways, such as by restraining themselves or by providing help or relief.

The analysis of the concept of rights, as undertaken before, shows that rights involve cooperative and reciprocal forms of behavior. When the concept of rights is recognized and widely accepted within a group, then we may characterize the group as having a *practice of rights*.[23] Now it will be

---

[22]Locke distinguishes between the "state of nature," which is regulated by moral duties, and "civil government," which is formed by social contract. See *Second Treatise*, Chs. 2 and 7–8.

[23]Richard E. Flathman, *The Practice of Rights* (Cambridge: Cambridge University Press, 1976).

noted that, within a practice of rights, references to what is recognized and accepted about the practice are often enough for a justification. When practices are well developed, the assertion of a right is partly, as we saw before, the claim for a warrant. So, if a question such as "Why did she get to vote for the prime minister?" is asked in Canada, a response such as "Because she's a citizen and citizens have this right" may be taken as sufficient justification.

The problem is that appeals to the practice often are not particularly persuasive, let alone compelling. This is especially the case when the practice itself is incomplete or defective, or when it is challenged. One can always demand a justification for the practice itself. It is very important, therefore, to be able to provide and to evaluate arguments for the right itself.

We are familiar with the rights called "natural rights" by John Locke in the *Second Treatise of Government* and identified as the "rights to life, liberty, and property."[24] Likewise, the Declaration of Independence speaks of the "rights to life, liberty, and the pursuit of happiness" as natural rights. Today, the "International Bill of Human Rights," which consists of the United Nations *Declaration of Human Rights* first adopted in 1948 and subsequent Covenants, is regarded by most nation-states as the authoritative document on "human rights."[25] Since the eighteenth century, natural rights, and then human rights, have been regarded in the West as the most fundamental of moral rights.[26] And to say that they are the most fundamental of moral rights is to say that the strongest possible reasons can be given for them.[27] For instance, among other things, to claim that a right is a natural, or a human, right, is to say that especially strong reasons can be provided for respecting it. For example, unless a person has access, when he or she needs it, to adequate physical shelter, then he or she cannot attend to one's most basic physical functions—eating, sleeping, bathing, and excreting—in private. Those who are not homeless are shocked by the suggestion that they could fulfill these needs only through luck, the kindness of strangers, or under the supervision of others. Such a life, they admit, would be subhuman—continually demeaning and lacking in dignity as well as (often) physically distressing. Thus, there is a strong reason for claiming that regular access to and private use of adequate shelter is an inalienable human right.

---

[24]*Second Treatise,* p. 66.

[25]There are two major covenants in addition to the UN Declaration: the International Covenant on Civil and Political Rights (1976) and the International Covenant on Economic, Social and Cultural Rights (1976).

[26]In terms of the distinction between general and special rights, human rights are always general (in rem), and sometimes, depending on circumstances, special (in personam) rights. For instance, although a prisoner's right not to be tortured is a general right, it is also a special right against any "interrogator" who threatens to use implements of torture against the prisoner.

[27]Note that this point can be also be made the other way around. Rights defended by the strongest moral arguments are "elevated" to the "category" of natural and human rights.

And as we noted in an earlier section, to say that a right is *inalienable* means that persons possess the right in virtue of their humanity and that therefore the right cannot be separated from, or "alienated" from, one's status as a person.

It is crucial to consider justifications for natural and human rights because it is widely thought that the best moral arguments have been made for them. Yet, some advocates of global diversity criticize these rights as artifacts of Western culture and argue that Eurocentric conceptions of rights do not apply to their own societies. By contrast, advocates of human rights must maintain, however, that all human beings equally possess these rights. Consequently, this debate will be the focus of our attention in the very next chapter.

Natural law and natural rights

In general, it was with the advent of the American and French revolutions that the theory of natural rights became influential in Western politics. Natural rights developed out of the theory of natural law, and the natural rights advocates of the Enlightenment (Hooker, Grotius, Locke, Kant, Paine, Jefferson, Montesquieu) regarded natural law as a necessary prerequisite of natural rights.[28] According to John Locke, men in the state of nature before they are united into a government are in "a state of perfect freedom to order their actions and dispose of their possessions and persons as they think fit *within the bounds of the law of Nature,* without asking leave or depending on the will of any other man."[29]

Note that freedom within the "bounds of the law of Nature" is not unlimited freedom to do as one likes, or "license" as Locke calls it. Rather, "the state of nature has a law of nature to govern it," and this law teaches "all mankind who will but consult it, that being all equal and independent, no one ought to harm another in his life, health, liberty, or possessions."[30] The law of nature is the supreme moral law. It can be known by reason and intuition by all "who will but consult it." Every person is free to live as he or she chooses, so long as the person does not harm another's life, health, liberty, or property. Saying that the natural law entitles me equally to these things is tantamount to saying that they are natural rights. We all can claim them as entitlements sanctioned by a natural law that also imposes correlative duties upon us all.

Thus, by converting natural law theory into the doctrine of natural rights, Locke was able to advance four important points. First, because

---

[28]See A. P. d'Entreves, *Natural Law: An Historical Survey* (New York: Harper & Row, 1965).
[29]*Second Treatise*, p. 8.
[30]*Ibid.*, p. 9.

natural rights are moral rights possessed by *individuals* in a "state of nature" governed by a law of nature, they are "inalienable." Governments do not create or confer these rights, nor are they consequent on group membership. We possess them simply in virtue of our existence as persons. As Locke says, "Every man has a property in his own person: this nobody has a right to but himself."[31] In other words, natural rights are a part of the "personhood" of each individual and could not be "taken away" without a violation of personhood.

Second, through natural reason and intuition we can all know that we have natural rights and what rights we have. There is no need for Scripture, or esoteric knowledge, or any parochial tradition or custom, to interpret them. Third, natural rights are universal; all persons possess them equally and not only as members of some society, or because of such things as status, wealth, or nationality.[32] Fourth, by asserting the supremacy of universal God-made law, Locke could justify civil disobedience of man-made laws that were unjust because they conflicted with natural law.

Moreover, for Locke and the liberal tradition he influenced, the justification of government was based on natural rights. On the basis of Locke's social contract theory, government was created by consent so that individuals, as citizens together, could enjoy the greater protection and fulfillment of their individual rights. Force could not be justly used against any individual unless it was necessary to vindicate a right that he or she had infringed. In addition, should government itself violate citizens' natural rights, then that government, in undermining trust, had destroyed or "dissolved" its own legitimacy. The people were then free, Locke asserted, to establish a new government.[33] Similarly, an individual forfeited his or her right not to be interfered with, if the individual violated the natural right of another citizen.[34]

Despite early associations with a Christian God and higher law, such as Thomas Jefferson's claim that we were "endowed by our Creator" with certain "inalienable" rights, natural rights theory became increasingly secular and influential in the West over the course of the next two centuries.[35] In addition to being thought of as inalienable, universal, and self-evident, because of their promotion as absolute values in the American and French Revolutions, natural rights also began to be seen as "imprescriptible," that is, as overriding or taking precedence over other claims and principles.

---

[31]*Ibid.*, p. 19.
[32]The logic of Locke's position far exceeded his vision in seventeenth-century England. He did not decry the restriction of rights to English men.
[33]*Second Treatise*, Ch. 19.
[34]*Ibid.*, Ch. 7.
[35]Thomas Jefferson, *Declaration of Independence* (1776).

Difficulties with natural rights

Within the tradition of Western, or Eurocentric, dialogue and debate over rights theory, numerous objections have been raised to classical natural rights. These objections can be identified as of three kinds: epistemological, logical, and practical. By considering some major points in each type of objection, we will appreciate the transition from natural rights to human rights. In the subsequent chapter we will consider criticisms—many coming from outside the tradition of Western debate—that insist that human rights are "culture-bound" and nonuniversal.

Epistemological objections are directed at claims about the way we can come to *know* that natural rights exist or that a person possesses natural rights. Ironically, natural rights theorists such as Locke appealed to God's laws of nature in support of individual rights and against religious and traditional authorities. But the weakened hold of religion and the rise of liberal democracies also undermined the Lockean conception of a state of nature with its self-evident laws. Given the rise of social diversity and toleration, some began to question the relevance of universal laws, and others doubted whether there could ever be agreement on so-called self-evident rights or on a single conception of human nature. Confidence in human knowledge was further weakened in the modern world by a number of developments including the advent of Freudian depth psychology and the rise of behaviorism. Belief in a benign "human nature" and in progress were devastated by two cataclysmic wars, the Holocaust, and a postwar world tottering on the brink of "nuclear winter."

In addition, natural rights were said to be inalienable in the sense that to deprive an individual of the right is to deprive the individual of his or her status as a person. But what is it about natural rights that really makes them *natural* in this sense? Humans do not have rights in the same way that they have natural attributes such as opposable thumbs and an upright posture. We can observe natural attributes, but we cannot observe "natural" rights in the same way. Nor do persons possess rights in the same way that they can be seen to possess an object or to have air to breath and food to eat (to the extent that they *do* have these things). By contrast, rights seem wholly *intangible:* we can observe a person *exercising* a right, for example, speaking freely to an audience, but we cannot observe the right itself.

In response, it is evident that some confusion resulted from the way that theories of human rights entered the mainstream of Western, liberal political philosophy in the seventeenth and the eighteenth centuries. Locke's way of developing natural rights theory led, not surprisingly, to the view that we possess these rights at creation, and hence, that they exist in the same way that natural attributes do. It is not reasonable, however to regard Locke as having appealed to some metaphysical theory of biological development. Instead, Locke relied on the concepts of nature and natural law to emphasize what he regarded as a special category of reasons for moral rights, as well as the critical social and political consequences of respect for these rights. Yet, the empirical insubstantiality, or "ghostliness," of these rights made it difficult for critics to regard them as quite as fundamental for social and political arrangements as rights theorists wanted them to be.

Epistemological difficulties concerning our knowledge of rights have combined with *logical* difficulties exposed in arguments for natural rights. Reasoning that natural rights are an inalienable part of personhood, some theorists attempted to derive natural rights from some set of natural capacities or qualities possessed by all persons. According to this scheme, if possession of some set of characteristics, say X, Y, and Z, can be accepted as defining personhood, and someone, say Amanda, has these characteristics, then we can conclude that Amanda is a person and possesses natural rights.

This scheme encounters two serious problems, however. Whatever natural capacity or quality is selected—for example, sentience (capacity to feel pleasure and pain), needs, rationality, or capacity for purposive activity—this capacity or quality turns out to be either too *exclusive* or too *inclusive* to serve as a criterion for holding rights. For instance, rationality is too exclusive as some nonrational beings, for example, insane persons or infants, are generally thought to have rights. And sentience is too inclusive as many animals generally not regarded as having rights are sentient beings in that they can feel pain and probably also pleasure.[36] Whether or not infants or "higher" animals are rights-holders, the point of the criticism is to show that the possession of some natural attribute is inadequate as the basis for inclusion or exclusion from the class of rights-holders.

There are other grounds as well for rejecting as defective the search for natural properties to justify the possession of natural rights. If it is conceded, as natural rights theorists must, that natural rights do not exist factually, in the way that earlobes or melanin exists, then what kind of reality do they have? Well, natural rights are claimed to be normative resources that have special moral force. If so, then natural rights are special kinds of values. But critics then point to a logical flaw in confusing facts and values. According to critics, moral values cannot be deduced from the natural capacities or potentialities of human beings. Efforts to do otherwise, say critics, involve the "is-ought" fallacy. Logically, it is no more permissible to attempt to infer moral rights from human characteristics than it is to attempt to infer a judgment about how we ought to behave from empirical data about how we do behave (i.e., often pretty badly).

---

[36]Of course, animal rights theorists have advocated a very inclusive category of rights-holders, arguing that the real problem is a failure of some humans to respond morally to the rights of animals.

Aside from epistemological and logical difficulties, *practical* difficulties concern many critics. Eighteenth-century philosopher Jeremy Bentham had practical matters in mind as well as logical problems when he attacked the assumptions underlying the French *Declaration of the Rights of Man*. "Natural rights," Bentham snorted in *Anarchical Fallacies*, "is simple nonsense: natural and imprescriptible rights, rhetorical nonsense—nonsense upon stilts."[37]

By declaring that there are no rights before and outside of society, Bentham was making a logical point: the only evidence for the existence of rights, he maintained, is that they are conferred and protected by society. The justification of rights is to be based on different considerations, namely, by demonstrating their "social utility." For Bentham social utility was the only moral basis for making decisions, and it involved identifying the outcomes of different actions and calculating which ones would produce the greatest amount of happiness for the greatest number of people.

But by referring to natural rights as "nonsense upon stilts," Bentham also suggested that talk about natural rights obscured the real issues. And some critics have followed this line in regarding the "rhetoric" of rights as an ideological ploy by which advocates of human rights attempt to achieve the adoption of their preferred values and policies. Critics have coined the term "manifesto rights" to refer to rhetorical expressions that are like rights claims except that they really express social ideals or desired objectives.[38] For instance, among the rights enumerated in the United Nation's *Universal Declaration of the Rights of Man*, one right is for periodic vacations with pay, and another is the right to participate in the cultural life of one's society. Critics have seized upon these as quite plausible social ideals but as fraudulent rights-claims.[39] They do not regard people as having entitlements to these things.

This position was strengthened in the latter half of the twentieth century by two developments. Some philosophers concluded that much of what had previously been accepted as moral judgments turned out, after analysis, to express either emotions or imperatives. Thus, for example, rather than being a moral judgment, a presumed statement about a "right" to paid vacations could be a veiled way of saying something like "I approve of paid vacations" (emotive) or "You should influence the government to give workers paid vacations" (imperative). According to such analysts, there is no real object—designated by the term "natural right"—which the discourse is about.

Another practical concern relates to the difficulty of applying vaguely formulated natural rights. As noted earlier, the more specific the entries on a

---

[37]*Anarchical Fallacies*, in *Collected Papers of Jeremy Bentham*, Vol. 2, John Bewring, ed. (Edinburgh, 1843), repr. in A. I. Melden, ed., *Human Rights* (Belmont, CA: Wadsworth, 1970), p. 32.

[38]Maurice Cranston, "Human Rights, Real and Supposed," in *Political Theory and the Rights of Man*, D. D. Raphael, ed. (Bloomington, IN: Indiana University Press, 1967).

[39]Maurice Cranston, "Are There Any Human Rights?" *Daedalus*, Vol. 112, No. 4 (Fall 1983).

list of rights, the more like dubious "manifesto rights" they seem to be. On the other hand, documents designating a few, very general rights—for example, life, liberty, and the pursuit of happiness—sound more plausible. But it is not at all clear how these general rights apply to complex social issues.[40]

The theory of natural rights does not help us find solutions to specific social problems. For instance, it may be plausible to say that natural rights to life, liberty, and the pursuit of happiness imply a further right to be self-determining and autonomous. If so, then it also seems plausible to believe that this right in turn entails a right to procreate and found a family. But it is certainly less clear that this further right entails more specific rights around which greater controversy centers. Do parents have rights, let alone natural rights, to in vitro fertilization of sperm and egg cells? If so, what kind of correlative obligations does this right generate? Likewise, do parents have rights to genetic selection, to the cloning of themselves (supposing medical technology makes this possible), and to give consent to the participation of their minor children in risky and nontherapeutic research?

As these questions show, grandly stated natural rights such as those proclaimed by Locke or Jefferson give us little direction in solving complex problems involving public choice. Note also that as we move "downward" from the more general to the more specific rights claims, the additional assertion that the right at stake is a natural right tends to lose its moral force. It is hardly surprising, therefore, that many commentators should have regarded the usefulness of natural rights as limited to inspiration for framing major constitutional documents such as the Bill of Rights, the French Declaration, and the English Reform Acts.

Because of the variety of difficulties it faced, the Lockean way of arguing for fundamental moral rights fell out of favor. But it is interesting and important that, despite weakening of the theoretical basis for natural rights in the Western and Northern hemispheres, the assumption that humans possess fundamental moral rights continued to spread. Rights-claims and correlative duties became increasingly important as ordering principles in liberal democracies.

From natural rights to human rights

There are many probable causes for the rising importance of fundamental rights during the modernization of the nineteenth and twentieth centuries in Western Europe and North America. One probable cause was the continuing abilities of states to monopolize coercive force and to exercise violence to crush individual or minority opposition. Another probable cause was the rapid advance of industrialization and the ability of market

---

[40]John Hart Ely, *Democracy and Distrust* (Cambridge, MA: Harvard University Press, 1980), pp. 48–54.

economies to penetrate all levels of society and to change many personal relationships. But simultaneously, individual liberty—indeed, the autonomy of individuals to order their lives as they saw fit—gained increasing importance. So, fundamental rights came to be seen as particularly powerful moral resources to protect individuals and minorities from overweening political and market forces. In addition, because rights-holders themselves decide whether, when, and how to exercise rights, these rights seemed consistent with the high value placed on autonomy.

Freed from the epistemological and metaphysical trappings of "nature" and "natural law," these fundamental moral rights were renamed "human rights," as they are designated, for example, in the United Nations *Declaration*. The change in terminology signified a major shift in the way that one argued for fundamental moral rights rather than the development of a new category of rights. Some recent authors prefer to dispense with the term altogether[41] but continue to discuss what they regard as the most basic or fundamental moral rights. Again, for our purposes, we can regard references to "basic" or "fundamental" moral rights as equivalent to "human rights."

The view that basic moral rights are inalienable was preserved in the transition from "natural" to "human" rights. The necessary connection between having these rights and being a human being, or a person, was carried over; or at least the necessary connection between *how we understand* what it means to be human or to have personhood and human rights was carried over.[42] This tight connection between being a person, or human, and rights—rather than God or natural laws in a state of nature—is intended to ensure that human rights are not creations of political or legal authority and not products of particular cultural traditions.

Human rights are also held to be "universal." This view involves the conceptual point about the universalizability of rights discourse, but it also involves reference to an important *ethical* point that is frequently expressed by the notion that all humans possess equal "inherent worth" or "inherent dignity." Most controversially, human rights are held to be accessible to natural reason. "Although not claiming them to be "self-evident," advocates of human rights maintain that they can be understood through the use of human reason. That is, regardless of our own culture or background, through the exercise of natural reason we can come to understand and appraise arguments for the existence of these rights and their justifications.

Finally, although human rights are not said to be "imprescriptible," or absolute, in the way that natural rights were sometimes thought to be,

---

[41]See, for example, A. I. Melden, *Rights and Persons* (Berkeley, CA: University of California Press, 1980), and *Basic Rights*.

[42]The distinction between persons and humans is important in philosophy. There is controversy over the existence, or possible existence, of nonhuman persons, and whether all persons or just all humans possess basic moral rights. Our discussion pertains only to rights that humans could have, and so I use the terms "human" and "persons" interchangeably.

human rights are nevertheless regarded as "preemptory."[43] This view means that they provide very robust reasons for respecting rights claims and protecting or facilitating the enjoyment of the objects in question. Thus, even though it is not the case that a human right can never be justly overridden by other considerations, an extremely strong case would have to be made for justly abrogating it.

Good reasons approach

Writing in the second half of the twentieth century, a group of theorists working with what I call the "good reasons approach" have had a profound effect on our thinking about human rights. They set the course for further thinking about justifications for human rights, that is, the reasons we accept for believing that certain claims are warranted and that certain actions ought to be undertaken or are rightly committed.

In contrast to classical natural law theorists, the "good reasons" theorists reject the view that the question "What are human rights?" can be answered by pointing to some attribute or property of humans. Likewise, they do not try to understand human rights in terms of some collection of "objects" (e.g., sustenance, freedom, privacy) however much people may need or want them. Instead, philosophers Ronald Dworkin, Martin Golding, and A. I. Melden, as well as social scientists Jack Donnelly, Richard Flathman, and Rhoda Howard, emphasize the need to understand human rights in terms of *social behavior* and *reasons*.[44]

In effect, the "what" of human rights consists in part of certain "behaviors": assertions of claims, expectations held, actions taken in response to claims, and attitudes and dispositions of claimants (e.g., indignation in response to perceived violations) and of respondents (e.g., respectfulness). Human rights are located within social and interpersonal arrangements as a form of principled or rule-governed behavior, which earlier I called *practices of rights*. The "what" of rights also concerns the content of communications made between the rights-claimant and others in the claimant's relevant community. These are *reasons* for believing that one is entitled to the object of a right, that others *ought* to respect one's claim, and that others ought to behave in corresponding ways. (The claimant or others or, of course, both may hold these reasons.)

---

[43]It is questionable, however, that any natural rights theorist ever believed natural rights were imprescriptible.

[44]Jack Donnelly, *The Concept of Human Rights* (London: Croom Helm, 1985); Ronald Dworkin, *Taking Rights Seriously* (Cambridge, MA: Harvard University Press, 1977); Richard Flathman, *The Practice of Rights;* Martin Golding, "Towards a Theory of Human Rights"; Rhoda Howard, *Human Rights and the Search for Community* (Boulder, CO: Westview Press, 1995); A. I. Melden, *Rights and Persons.*

But, of course, to accept these reasons for entitlement and these reasons as to why others ought to respond in certain ways *is* to accept a *justification* for the right in question. Thus, there is no real gap, or disconnect, between the existence of a right (the having of it), on the one hand, and its justification, on the other. If we accept the reasons just alluded to, then Amanda or Jorge (as two among many) has the relevant right—the right exists for her or him. But, at the same time, the right has a self-certifying or self-warranting quality. If we accept the reasons for claimed entitlements and correlative duties, then, when appropriately claimed by Amanda or Jorge, we accept the right as justified. Hence a human right cannot be specified independently of certain social behaviors and especially weighty moral reasons.

A version of this "good reasons approach" is presented by Ronald Dworkin in *Taking Rights Seriously,* in which he emphasizes the communication of moral reasons and their combination into compelling moral arguments.[45] He says flatly that "a man has a moral right against the state if for some reason the state would do wrong to treat him in a certain way."[46] And the only evidence Dworkin regards as relevant to the proof of the existence of a moral right is a persuasive moral argument—that is, the presence of persuasive reasons why it is wrong to treat the individual as he or she is treated.

According to Dworkin, rights are to be characterized by the relative strength of principles supporting that which their holder proposes to do or get (or which others propose to do or get for him or her), weighed against the strength of competing principles. Dworkin says, "the sense of rights I propose to use . . . simply shows a claim of right to be a special, in the sense of restricted, sort of judgment about what is right or wrong for governments to do."[47] Thus, for Dworkin, rights are contextually dependent upon political and moral theories concerning the type of community and polity that individuals ought to have and the goals that they ought to share.

In another major study, *Rights and Persons,* A. I. Melden also claims that rights cannot be understood independently of the social and moral practices in which discourse about rights normally occurs. Melden says, "the conception of the right of a human being is the conception of a normative status that he has with respect to others, and it is to be understood . . . only in terms of its place in the scheme of related concepts in which it has its place."[48] But, whereas Dworkin emphasizes the role of reasons, Melden focuses on the extent to which individual agents have "joined their lives together" in cooperative associations. The existence of rights is always, therefore, an aspect of this familial, communal, or social existence.[49]

---

[45]*Taking Rights Seriously.*
[46]*Ibid.,* p. 139.
[47]*Ibid.*
[48]*Rights and Persons,* p. 79. (Belmont, CA: Wadsworth, 1970)
[49]*Ibid.,* pp. 56–62, 75, 173–5, 211, 221.

Rights are *manifested* by individuals who assert themselves as moral agents. In an endless variety of ways—thoughts, actions, and feelings—persons reveal themselves as moral beings. And "what persons show about themselves by the example they provide others through their own demeanor or conduct and speech, is that they are as fully qualified as any others to employ the language of morals, to apply the concept of rights along with the conceptual structure in which it is embedded, during the course of their transactions with others."[50] Thus, for Melden, the problem of respecting rights does not hinge on discovering natural attributes. Rather, it requires attaining a deeper and richer understanding of the ways in which persons reveal themselves as the moral beings they are.

For example, in liberating herself, a woman formerly regarded as a submissive housewife, does not call attention to and achieve recognition of any attribute that has gone unnoticed by her husband, children, or neighbors. Rather, she transforms their conceptions of appropriate ways of living and interacting with her.[51] "Instead of looking for a basis for human rights," Melden says, "we need to see more clearly and in its rich and complex detail just what it is for persons to have the rights they have as human beings. It is here that all explanations come to an end."[52]

Political scientists Jack Donnelly and Rhoda Howard go so far as to assert that human rights are "socially constructed."[53] They hold that our stature as humans is strongly influenced by our biological needs but that our status as persons is also affected by norms and values that we internalize in the process of becoming social beings. Howard argues that because human rights are not "given" to us by the physical facts of life or by some supernatural power, they result primarily from our interpretations, as social and interdependent beings, of the moral significance of the facts of life.[54] Donnelly asserts that human rights result from the "reciprocal interactions of moral conceptions and material conditions of life" as these are mediated through social institutions.[55] Donnelly adds, "human rights arise from human action [and] represent the choice of a particular moral vision of human potentiality and the institutions for realizing that vision."[56]

Theorists working within the "good reasons approach" have made an indispensable contribution by identifying the importance of reasons and social practices. They turn us back from the naturalists' search into human nature to a more appropriate inquiry about the moral significance of human capacities, needs, and interests in our social and communal lives. However,

---

[50]*Ibid.*, p. 199.
[51]*Ibid.*, p. 205.
[52]*Ibid.*, p. 200.
[53]*The Concept of Human Rights*, p. 31; *Human Rights and the Search for Community*, p. 15.
[54]*Human Rights and the Search for Community*, p. 15.
[55]*The Concept of Human Rights*, p. 31.
[56]*Ibid.*, p. 35.

although the "good reasons approach" points us in the right direction, it raises its own set of concerns.

Problems with the good reasons approach

What troubles me most about this approach is that it makes having human rights entirely too dependent on changing and relative practices and conceptions of life that we presently share—or that promoters of human rights presently share. To explain the basis for my concern without extending the discussion too broadly, I will focus on some of Melden's key arguments for (and against) rights in *Rights and Persons.*

Melden argues eloquently that neonates and fetuses, as well as certain patients suffering irreversible unconsciousness, have basic moral rights because we can join our lives with them in meaningful ways. For example, although he admits that it makes no sense to speak of infants claiming or asserting their rights, nevertheless, "[t]he infant enters significantly, though passively, into the lives of its parents. They involve its life in their own lives, supplying first the hopes and interests it itself is far too immature to have. . ."[57] Furthermore, "blood parents complete their own lives by bringing a child of their own into the world and making it part of the life they share with each other from the time they first become aware of its existence in the womb, preparing for its birth, and planning for the life that lies ahead for it as the person in whom their own lives are to be continued."[58]

By contrast, Melden believes that psychopaths, or sociopaths do not have basic moral rights because they feel none or few of the moral emotions and thus have no sense of moral constraint.[59] Therefore, these human beings, who are so different from us that they must be placed in institutions, are constitutionally unable, Melden says, to "join their lives with others in such a way that they are mindful of the agency of others during the course of their own conduct."[60] But if psychopaths lack this apparently necessary capacity to participate in a moral community, then fetuses and neonates have even a greater deficiency. In addition, if, through their loving concern and planning, parents can "initiate" fetuses and neonates into the community of rights-holders, why cannot the loved ones of psychopaths? After all, their psychopathology could not have been known during pregnancy or infancy. (Are we supposed to infer that the parents or caretakers of psychopaths lacked the ability to join their lives with their children?)

Melden's view of basic moral rights as thoroughly embedded in the ways that we "join our lives with others" is especially troubling because the

---

[57]*Rights and Persons,* p. 73.
[58]*Ibid.,* p. 75.
[59]*Ibid.,* pp. 187, 209–14.
[60]*Ibid.,* p. 211.

notion of *joining lives* is both extremely vague and ambiguous. Our forms of life are often fragile and easily permeated by political, economic, and even physical forces beyond our control. Such forces may determine or strongly influence how we join our lives together. Yet these are forces that ought not to count in the moral sphere of action. For instance, the forms of life chosen by the Taliban of Afghanistan did not accord certain protected liberties to women and did not provide for certain basic needs of women. Although there was overwhelming consensus outside of Taliban-controlled Afghanistan that the human rights of Afghani women were violated, the Taliban did not accept this view. As a consequence of the "war on terrorism" waged partly in Afghanistan, the Taliban were no longer able to impose their political will on the country. But suppose that somehow they succeed in reimposing their will and restructuring repressive forms of life; should we concede that women or other Afghanis no longer have human rights? Hardly, for we should say that their human rights are being violated.

Melden also fails to acknowledge arbitrary and morally irrelevant ways in which people choose to join their lives together, even when they are not subject to gross forms of physical, political, and economic oppression or intrusion that deprives them of rational choice. We choose to commit ourselves and share plans and objectives with selected others, sometimes including fetuses. But what then of the fetus whose natural mother just does not choose to join her life with it? Does this circumstance mean that whereas some, or even many, fetuses have human rights, this fetus does not? Yes, unless Melden is willing to go further than he does in *Rights and Persons* and argue that fetuses' equal basic rights ought to be ensured by the willingness of others to join their lives with it even when natural parents choose not to do so.

In his defense, Melden can be said to maintain universalizability in his conception of basic moral rights. Also, Melden can be said to be consistently applying the concept of basic moral rights insofar as the inability of psychopaths to appreciate the moral agency of others is sufficient to exclude them form the moral community. And Melden is consistent in excluding unwanted fetuses insofar as the absence of a willing natural parent or an adoptive parent supplies a sufficient basis for this discrimination. Yet, Melden's position seems greatly at odds with deeply held moral intuitions. It is one thing to decide whether or not a fetus is a human being (or a person), or whether psychopaths have human rights. But Melden's account of personal and communal roles in endowing some beings with membership in the "community" of rights-holders, while closing others out, offends against deep intuitions about human rights. Surely *human* rights do not result from such arbitrary and contingent decisions about group membership.

The problem just discussed is symptomatic of the general inadequacy of the "good reasons approach." Although they illuminate important features of the concept of rights, analysts sharing this approach fail to specify those conditions for social arrangements or communal practices that are either necessary or sufficient for basic, or human, rights. These theorists tell us how people behave and how they talk about themselves and their behavior when they assert their rights, or recognize and accept the correlative obligations these rights may create. They dissolve the *mystery* relating to the existence of rights perpetuated by natural rights theory. They explain that rights do not exist per se, that is, that human rights do not exist as entities in and of themselves. But their accomplishments are marred by problems with the justification of human rights. Whereas natural rights theorists had tried to justify rights in terms of reasons pertaining to humans as individuals anterior to interpersonal networks and social organizations, the "good reasons approach" goes too far in the other direction. This approach tries to justify basic moral rights in terms of reasons *too relative* to particular social or communal contexts.

In summary, according to the "good reasons approach," rights are constituted, as Dworkin claims, by moral arguments contextually dependent on moral or political theories. Or as Melden claims, they are constituted by social and moral practices involved in joining our lives together. Or as Donnelly and Howard claim, they are socially constructed in various (unspecified ways). In these views, the basic, or human, rights that persons actually have are supposedly what results when someone can say that the process of arguing is over or that forms of life have been developed or that social constructions are complete. But who can say this, and when can it be said? In other words, what *criteria* do we have that any of these processes is complete?

It does not really help to claim that rights are good reasons for action or forbearance unless we have *criteria* for good reasons, that is, ways of telling what counts as a good reason. Nor is it very helpful to say that needed criteria are supplied by general moral or political theories, as Dworkin does, because these theories themselves may be the objects of contention.[61] Moreover, given disparities among situations in which rights-talk emerges and disparity among practices involving morality, it seems unlikely that we could have a clear account of the characteristics that a practice must have, or the reasons supporting it, before we could accept it as "generating" rights.

The "good reasons approach" does offer some guidance for resolving controversies that arise within the framework of commonly accepted principles. For instance, Dworkin makes valuable contributions to the resolution of public policy conflicts arising in the legal system of the United States in which the reasoned judgments of appellate court justices, especially the Supreme Court, are a final and inescapable authority.[62] But the "good reason approach" is likely to let us down just when we are in most need of it, that

---

[61]*Taking Rights Seriously*, p. 87.
[62]*Ibid.*, Ch. 4.

is, when controversies over claims for a human right are most difficult to settle. For instance, critics of liberal democracy in some East Asian societies dispute the supposed universality of human rights, maintaining instead that human rights are not relevant to their traditional ways of life. Critics of foreign aid policies in Western countries maintain that the affluent have no duty to respond to famine in the Horn of Africa because they believe that there is no human right to food. Controversies of these kinds pertain to persons of different national groups or to efforts urging application of a right that is familiar in one social context within a culture with very different practices or values.

The "good reasons approach" cannot indicate what sorts of arguments or what types of human relationships—what forms of life—are relevant to resolution of such debates. Indeed, such controversies, unlike disputes about moral rights generated under a specific practice such as civil rights in a democratic and constitutional polity, often challenge the moral and political theories, and the forms of life, which are thought to frame and ground the rights themselves. We are left with the relativism of different social practices and the relativism of differing cultural norms and ideals.[63]

Dialectical justifications

Is it possible to offer a justification for human rights that is more compelling than any justification examined up to this point? How do we persuade someone to accept human rights from "inside that person's own vantage point," as it were? This appears to be a daunting (if not an impossible) task if this person wholly rejects a morality based on human rights. But it may be possible to proceed if we can reduce sharply, if not eliminate, differences in perspective, while finding a broad enough framework for agreement on common aspects of humanity, although initially this commonality may seem to have little to do with human rights.

This is the kind of justification for human rights offered by philosopher Alan Gewirth that he calls a "dialectical" argument.[64] Rather than pre-

---

[63]The discussion so far may have raised the question whether there may be irreconcilable values and beliefs or intractable assumptions and attitudes between people situated in different cultures. This is indeed the perspective of some critics of cross-cultural efforts to promote human rights. As we shall see, assumptions and beliefs about human beings, as well as about interpersonal networks and obligations, greatly differ in Buddhist, Confucian, and West African cultures. Some commentators add that because traditional cultures do not share with the West the concepts and beliefs necessary for a practice of rights, urging these cultures to adopt such practices represents Eurocentric chauvinism, or—if threats are made or enticements tendered—a form of ideological imperialism. In Chapter 2 we consider arguments that human rights are inapplicable or meaningless in such traditional, non-Western societies.

[64]Alan Gewirth, *The Community of Rights* (Chicago: University of Chicago Press, 1996). Philosopher H. L. A. Hart was a predecessor in the use of a "dialectical" argument for a natural right to be free. See "Are There Any Natural Rights?" *Philosophical Review,* Vol. LXIV (April 1955), pp. 175–91. Gewirth has produced the most thorough justification, however.

senting an argument and then asking us—as readers—to evaluate and accept it as persuasive (as do the theorists considered so far), Gewirth seeks to draw out from us reasons that we would use to justify claims that we make and our behaviors. Gewirth's dialectical argument can also be regarded as "transcendental" because, rather than presenting us with an external argument, Gewirth asks us to "transcend" what we believe and do by reflecting about the reasons we would use as a justification. Another key to Gewirth's approach is to start with commonalties we share as moral agents. Gewirth has us consider questions such as "How do I understand my agency as an individual?" and "Whatever I regard as necessary or good, how would I justify getting or having it?"

Gewirth asserts that we must concede that as active agents, we ascribe to ourselves both voluntariness and purposiveness, or intentionality. We assume both that we can control our behavior by unforced choice and that we aim to attain some end or goal that explains why we are acting. Next, it is easy to accept Gewirth's conception of *well-being* as the substantive conditions necessary for acting at all and for having general chances of success in achieving one's purposes.[65] Now rights-claims and rights "arise logically and fundamentally out of the concern of all human beings, as purposive prospective agents, that the . . . necessary conditions of their action and generally successful action be protected."[66]

Gewirth's argument then proceeds to establish these two theses: (1) every agent must accept that he or she has rights to freedom and well-being; and (2) every agent must accept that all other agents also must have these rights equally with his or her own, that is, he or she must accept the existence of universal moral rights, and thus of human rights.[67] Let us look more closely at each of these theses.

First, for whatever you select as your ends or objectives, you must accept that those ends are good or have value sufficient to your attempts to attain them. However, since freedom and well-being are necessary conditions for your acting to attain any end, you must also accept the belief that "my freedom and well-being are necessary goods." This belief logically implies the practical prescription "I must have freedom and well-being." If you maintain this, then you must also believe that it would be wrong for others to destroy or interfere with your freedom and well-being. But it also follows that others have obligations to you with respect to your freedom and well-being. In other words, you must also agree that "all other persons at least ought to refrain from removing or interfering with my freedom and well-being."[68] And this is equivalent to your accepting that you have *rights* to freedom and well-being.

---

[65]*The Community of Rights*, p. 14.
[66]*Ibid.*, p. 16.
[67]*Ibid.*, p. 17.
[68]*Ibid.*, pp. 17–8.

Gewirth emphasizes that every agent must accept that he or she has rights, even if he or she seeks to reject this claim. He says, "All action is necessarily connected with the concept of rights. For every agent logically must hold or accept that he has rights to the necessary conditions of action and successful action in general."[69] Yet, these rights-claims are so far only prudential rights-claims. The argument for Gewirth's second thesis involves the transition from prudential to moral rights.

It has been established that, simply because you are a purposive agent, you must acknowledge that you have prudential rights to freedom and well-being. Now suppose that you claim that you have these rights in virtue of your possession of some special quality or qualification (e.g., wealth or nationality) rather than simply because you are a purposive agent. But if so, you would be contradicting your own claim that you must possess freedom and well-being as necessary conditions for your action. For instance, you would be consenting to the view that others could strip you of your prudential rights should you lose the quality or qualification in question (e.g., being forced to flee your country or losing your wealth). But because we have already established that you must claim freedom and well-being as conditions for purposive action, you could not consent to these restrictions.

It follows that you cannot regard the conditions necessary for your freedom and well-being as things you possess fortuitously or as gifts or privileges. You must regard them as rights. And every purposive agent is in exactly the same position as you are. Logically, therefore, you and every other agent must accept that "all purposive agents have rights to freedom and well-being." Gewirth points out that accepting this principle of universality requires that we recognize the rights in question as moral rights "because the agent is now committed to taking favorable account of the interests of other persons as well as of himself."[70] Moreover, since all humans are actual, prospective, or potential agents, these generic rights are human rights.[71]

It should be noted that if an agent denies that other humans have moral rights as purposive agents, then he is not just being inconsistent. The agent, in fact, is denying the inherent worth of human beings, an inherent worth that is based, as Gewirth says, on having the abilities of a rational and volitional agent.[72] He denies the inherent worth of others if he claims that, although he possesses rights, others do not possess equal rights, and he denies the inherent dignity of himself if he claims that no one, including himself, possesses human rights. To deny the inherent worth of humans is to

---

[69]*Ibid.*, p. 18.
[70]*Ibid.*, p. 19.
[71]*Ibid.*
[72]*Ibid.*

violate a moral principle very widely recognized as fundamental. Jesus and Confucius expressed this principle as the Golden Rule. One Western formulation was given by the philosopher Immanuel Kant as the Categorical Imperative that requires us to treat others as well as ourselves as ends in themselves and never merely as means.[73]

Gewirth provides a far-reaching and powerful justification for human rights. His argument does not require that we accept some conception of individuals in a "state of nature" or of various forms of life, as the natural rights or the "good reasons approach" required. It requires only a minimal recognition of ourselves as volitional and purposive agents. Gewirth shows that human rights are indeed universal. They are not dependent on any restrictive condition, whether natural or social and cultural; and they must be accepted logically by all persons who concede that they are actual or prospective purposive agents—and it is impossible for any *rational* agent to avoid that conception. To be sure, an individual could deny that he or she is a purposive agent. But such a claim would be wholly irrational for it would be tantamount to having no interests in acting whatsoever, even insofar as acting is conducive to the preservation of one's life, or even ending it. Justifications can be addressed only to those who are rational.

It is also important to appreciate that because the justification is made "from the standpoint of the agent," it has a special kind of persuasiveness. Any agent who denies equal human rights is denying (self-contradictorily) the claim that others ought not to remove or interfere with her own freedom and well-being. Hence, if this agent does violate the rights of others and in turn, if interference with her freedom or well-being is necessary to protect human rights, then she has no basis for complaint about that intervention. In the process of violating the human rights of others, the rights-violator continues to be a purposive agent and thereby continues to affirm the necessity of the conditions for purposive agency. To be sure, because she acts contradictorily, the rights-violator is being irrational. But the point is not just logical. *Morally*, we must regard the rights-violator as willingly denying for herself the restraint and noninterference she also denies to others through her rights-violations. Morally, then, the rights-violator must be understood as authorizing whatever minimum level of restraint or interference is necessary to protect others' rights from her infringements.

There are a number of ways of distinguishing among the objects that purposive agents seek as goods.[74] Gewirth identifies a hierarchy of three

---

[73]Immanuel Kant, *Grounding for the Metaphysics of Morals* [1785], trans. James W. Ellington (Indianapolis, IN: Hackett Publishing, 1981).

[74]There is also increasing concurrence over the most basic examples of these goods. Compare Diana Myers, *Inalienable Rights*, p. 53; Henry Shue, *Basic Rights*, pp. 20–3; with Alan Gewirth, *The Community of Rights*, pp. 14–5.

different levels: *basic, nonsubtractive,* and *additive* goods. Those goods that are basic provide the essential preconditions for purposive action. Thus, among basic goods are those necessary for life, freedom, physical integrity, and mental equilibrium. In speaking of "nonsubstractive well-being," Gewirth says that these goods "consist in having the general abilities and conditions needed for maintaining undiminished one's general level of purpose-fulfillment and ones's capabilities for particular actions . . ."[75] In other words, certain goods are "nonsubtractive" for all of us, for to be with-out them, is to be diminished in our capacities, as human beings, to act as purposive agents. Included among these goods are shelter, clothing, med-ical care, employment, welfare assistance, social security, private property, and access to information necessary to pursue one's objectives. (Gewirth notes that this last good entails the right not to be lied to.) Gewirth appreci-ates that as autonomous and purposive agents, our strivings do not cease when our most basic and nonsubtractive needs are met, however. On the contrary, such states of stasis would not befit human beings. Consequently, we have, in addition, human rights to "additive" goods needed to increase one's level of purpose-fulfillment and one's capacities for particular actions. Examples of additive goods include education, self-esteem, opportunities for acquiring wealth and income, and community, both as solidarity through association and participation in a stable political order.[76]

One might question the way Gewirth has distributed the goods, or ob-jects, of human rights into three different levels, or categories; for instance, education might be regarded as a nonsubtractive good rather than as addi-tive. A more serious objection is that Gewirth's dialectical justification is based on Western conceptions of reason and logic, and certainly his presen-tation of the argument follows an analytic pattern of reasoning perhaps most familiar to educated Western readers.

This objection raises a more general question about the possible cul-tural relativity of reason itself.[77] This is an issue that is considered in Chapter 2. Here it needs to be emphasized that Gewirth's justification makes very minimal and seemingly uncontroversial demands on our capac-ity for reason and logical thought. Indeed, it requires only that we under-stand ourselves as volitional and purposive agents. It is quite unlikely that moral agents anywhere lack this understanding even if, in fact, many have not reflected logically about its implications.

---

[75]*The Community of Rights,* p. 14.
[76]*Ibid;* pp. 14–15. Specific examples of these three "levels" of goods and the human rights they entail can be found throughout *The Community of Rights.*
[77]It may be possible that although the mode of presentation of Gewirth's "dialectical" ar-gument is culture-bound, there are other patterns of reasoning by which persons of other cul-tures may reach the same conclusions.

3. Application: The Anikwata Case[78]

Virginia Anikwata is the mother of 12-year-old Chenidu. She is terrified that she and her daughter will be sent back to Nigeria. Virginia came to the United States with her husband, who had a visa to study as a graduate student. Tragically, her husband died from unexpected but aggressive cancer just weeks after the birth of Chenidu. With the death of her husband, Virginia's immigration status went from legal to illegal. Since then Virginia has educated herself, earned her nursing certification, and supported herself and her daughter as a single mother. Virginia has fought for years against the Immigration and Naturalization Service (INS), but she has been denied both asylum and hardship relief, and she is now on the verge of being deported.

Virginia has every reason to expect that if forced to return to her village in Nigeria, she and Chenidu will face bleak prospects. According to tribal traditions of the lbo clan of her in-laws, she and her daughter will be regarded as nothing more than the property of her deceased husband's family. Widows are commonly blamed for a husband's death, and they are expected to serve as a second or third wife for another male relative. Virginia is most terrified, however, about the fate awaiting her young daughter at the hands of her father's family, especially the practice of female "circumcision," frequently referred to as "female genital mutilation" (FGM) in the United States where the practice is outlawed.

Female "circumcision" is a traditional "operation" in the community into which Virginia was born, as well as in much of the rest of Africa. Women perform this procedure on girls and teenagers to ensure their "cleanliness" and suitability for marriage by suppressing a woman's sexuality. The procedure generally involves cutting away the clitoris and labia minora with a razor blade, knife, or piece of glass. Rarely are such tools sterilized, or is anesthesia used. Profuse bleeding, infection, infertility, and death can result.

Virginia is grateful that she cannot remember her own circumcision, which occurred when she was a baby. She knows that it would be traumatic—physically and psychologically—for twelve-year-old Chenidu, however. This view is shared by the World Organization Against Torture USA that has attempted to use the International Convention Against Torture to shield the Anikwatas from deportation.

Law in Nigeria certainly does not give Virginia any rights empowering her to avoid the consequences of extreme patriarchy nor to protect Chenidu from circumcision. INS rulings have found that the "threats" of

---

[78]This case study is based on a newspaper story by Susan Levine, "Determined to Spare Their Daughters: Mother Faces Deportation Despite Mutilation Fear," *The Washington Post*, May 17, 2000, B1.

circumcision to the daughter and sexual servitude to the mother do not constitute "persecution." The law applied by the INS does not recognize persecution within a family or an extended family. Thus, Virginia has no legal right to asylum in the United States.

One INS lawyer wrote that Chenidu would not have to go to Nigeria unless her mother took her there. But the expectation that a deported mother should abandon her child runs counter to the principle of family unity. The INS took extreme measures to reunite a young Cuban boy with his father in the well-publicized Elian Gonzalez case.

Do the Anikwatas Have a Right to Asylum?

Although we feel concern for Virginia and Chenidu as real people and are interested in the morally best outcome, our focus here is on the case as *heuristics*. We need to concentrate on how this case may illuminate *reasoning* about human rights. There are two issues. First, is it meaningful to talk of the Anikwata case in terms of human rights, and if so, how and why? Second, if the answer to the previous question is affirmative, then how might we justify either a judgment that the Anikwata's have a human right to asylum in the United States or a judgment that they do not?

No doubt, many readers will regard what Virginia and Chenidu may be required to suffer as wrong morally. Indeed, the Anikwata case is one in which the language of rights and rights-claims seem to arise easily. It seems natural to consider whether the deportation of Virginia and her daughter or the separation of mother and daughter will result in the violation of their moral rights. Domestic law in the United States, international law, and rulings of the INS do not provide Virginia with a legal right to asylum. Yet, relying on the distinction between legal rights and moral rights, it may be meaningful to inquire whether Virginia has a moral right to asylum. So, is it the case that Virginia and Chenidu have moral rights that are or will be violated?[79]

There are a number of complex issues that might be discussed in terms of moral rights. We might consider whether Chenidu has a right not to be subjected to "circumcision" or the right not to suffer the threat of such "mutilation" while remaining united with her mother. We might consider whether Virginia has a right not to be forced into sexual servitude, to be able to make decisions regarding her child's welfare, to be free from psychological anguish, and to receive asylum in the United States. In order to add clar-

---

[79]A detractor might object that analysis of this case study cannot be "neutral" because readers in North America and Europe will presuppose that deportation would violate the moral rights of Virginia and Chenidu Anikwata. This must be admitted. Nevertheless, the case is extremely valuable because it helps readers clearly see aspects of the case that relate to the concept of rights, and therefore, the way that a moral right is "found" in the case.

ity and specificity to this illustration, we should settle on or identify one issue or concern as a "candidate" for recognition as a moral right. But which one should be selected?

In its rulings, the INS has denied that persecution can come from other family members, even if they are in-laws in an extended family. Likewise, the INS has questioned the gravity and proximity of the claimed dangers to Virginia's and Chenidu's well-being. They question Virginia's claims not because they deny that sexual servitude or "circumcision" of a twelve-year-old girl would be real harms, but because they believe that these harms are not as likely to occur as Virginia believes. We are not in a position to settle this factual issue. On reflection, however, even if there is *some* risk of harm, should not the person who might be subject to a violation of bodily integrity and loss of freedom, and who is a mother, be left to decide whether the risks shall be run? Answers to this question involve efforts to *justify* claims about rights or nonrights in the case.

But the question also points in a helpful direction. Whatever the real likelihood of the harms that Virginia and Chenidu might suffer if they are deported, they will suffer no risk of these harms if they are given asylum. Likewise, whether or not we believe that they should receive asylum, asylum would preserve Virginia's capacity as single parent to decide for Chenidu's welfare, and asylum would do so without straining the bond between mother and child. In addition, if the issues identified before reveal any real moral rights, then the INS will meet its correlative obligations by granting asylum. Hence, the most cogent issue for discussion seems to be this: does it make sense to think of Virginia as having a moral right to asylum? Let us be clear about the question. We are asking whether it is *credible* to treat Virginia's case as involving a moral right to asylum in the United States.

Virginia Anikwata's claims have two identifiable parts, or "levels." At one level, the claims communicate that there are objects, or substances, of the claimed rights that would be good for Virginia and her daughter. At this level Virginia's claim is based on several critical values: security against mutilation and psychological trauma, Virginia's freedom from sexual servitude, the psychological benefit of the mother's ability to protect her child from harm, and the benefits to both mother and daughter in maintaining family bonds.

At a second level, Virginia's claim is also one of *entitlement*. At this level she communicates a conception of herself and her daughter as persons and appeals to us to respect these conceptions. Virginia communicates the view that the violation of her right to asylum would be a grave wrong, and not just because she and Chenidu would be deprived of the objects in question. We can understand her as believing that the violation of her right also would diminish her humanity. It would deprive her of the respect and dignity due to a rational agent who is capable of deliberating about and making her own decisions about the most important issues in life.

Whether or not we agree that Virginia has the entitlement she has claimed, we can understand her message as involving ideas about both the *objects* of rights and the *entitlements*. Our ability to understand Virginia's claims are related to—and perhaps largely dependent on—the fact that we share with her a *social context* in which her position and her claims are highly intelligible. Also we share an ability to comprehend references to the granting of asylum as fulfilling *correlative obligations* and an ability to understand what is meant when one speaks of Virginia's assertions as the *self-administrative* aspect of rights. In general, modern Western societies have well-developed practices of rights in which individuals do take stands and make moral demands on one another as matters pertaining to their autonomy and their dignity as persons.

Of course, there may be no similarly developed practices of rights in Ibo tribal societies in Nigeria. There might be concern, therefore, that reasoning about human rights cannot meaningfully apply to a problem that involves the Anikwata's return to the society of Virginia's birth. *Cultural relativists* believe that what is true is relative to a particular culture or society. Are Virginia's self-identity as a rights-holder and the value that she places on autonomy merely transient and culturally contingent products of socialization? Are her objections to what traditional Nigerians might regard as her "familial duties" simply a result of her socialization? These are important issues that relate to the debate over *cultural relativism*. In Chapter 2 we shall consider the consequences of this debate for human rights.

The critical question at present is whether the absence of a relevant social context in traditional Ibo society is sufficient to overcome reasonable presumptions that the discourse of rights is appropriate for the Anikwata case. In this connection, two points seem decisive. First, the requisite understandings and social responses are certainly possible *in principle*. We have no difficulty thinking of Ibo Nigerians accepting such rights (just as we have no difficulty imagining Friday in *Robinson Crusoe* learning rights language). But second, supposing that, even in principle, Ibo villagers could not understand the possibility that Virginia might have objections to FGM and her prospective sexual servitude, it seems most reasonable to evaluate the facts in the social context we share with Virginia. The decision must be made in the United States and not in Nigeria, and Virginia is not a person who is half-allegiant to Ibo culture. In the twelve years since the death of her husband, Virginia has become entirely "Americanized," adopting goals and values familiar to American families and raising her daughter in the same manner as Chenidu's classmates.

It might be objected that the preceding discussion misses the significance of the context dependence of the concept of rights. Suppose that Ibo villagers find the concept of individual rights wholly inconceivable. This possibility suggests that cultural relativists might be right after all and that values true for us in the United States or the West are incommensurable

·with values in some traditional African societies. But does this mean that we cannot think about the Anikwata case in terms of rights? Hardly. If the cultural relativist is correct, then no culture's values can be privileged over another's. Traditionalist African views of individual identity formed through allegiance to the group cannot be preferred over Western individual rights. In fact, from the relativists' perspective, the most cogent consideration is the place or location at which an ethical decision must be made. The Anikwata case must be decided in the United States, and it is therefore proper that the values consulted be those that are salient in twenty-first century American society.

Next, consider the feature of *universalizability*. If we imagine ourselves in situations relevantly similar to Virginia's, we must concede that, when pressed, we would defend the protection we enjoy against similar threats as a matter of rights. This tendency is not the same thing as saying something like "if I were in Virginia's shoes I would not want it to happen to me or to my daughter." We are not concerned with contingent issues such as what people prefer and want, but rather with *logical* issues. Because we would defend ourselves from similar threats by claiming asylum as a right, we must recognize Virginia's claim as a rights-claim.[80] Note that Virginia's gravest concerns involve the physical harm and psychological trauma her daughter would suffer as well as her own loss of autonomy and degradation. We can reasonably expect that, although Ibo villagers disagree over the facts—they do not regard FGM and polygamy as harmful—they would demand protection, including claiming asylum as a right, against severe threats (e.g., claiming sanctuary during a civil war). In this event, the Ibo would claim as a right protection from a threat comparable in severity to the threats from which Virginia seeks security. The consequence of treating one's own claim as a rights-claim but failing to treat Virginia's claim as a rights-claim is logical inconsistency. And logical inconsistency signifies irrationality in a system of beliefs or worldview. Hence, when we universalize what we would say if we faced similar threats, we find it very easy to interpret the Anikwata case as involving rights.

Given the analysis of rights in Section 1, we should have no difficulty in thinking of a moral right to asylum as central to the Anikwata case. Reasoning about the case has shown how and why we can bring it clearly within the scope of discourse about moral rights. At this stage it seems natural to ask, "Well, how *much* of a right does Virginia have, or how strong and significant is it?" Questions such as this probe for the strength and relevance of *arguments* that Virginia has the entitlement claimed and that she and Chenidu should receive the goods that are the objects of a right to

---

[80]This principle is true even if Virginia did not make her appeal for asylum in terms of rights. Often the principle of universalizability leads us to recognize that others have rights deserving of respect even if they do not assert those rights or even if they are not aware of those rights.

asylum. Exploring such questions implicates us in arguments over the *justification* of Virginia's claim to a right.

Considering justifications

Our objective in this concluding subsection is to consider how to construct and evaluate justificatory arguments as to the strength and relevance of moral reasons. Our focus therefore will be on what needs to be considered in completing such an argument rather than on examining a completed argument as a specimen. Two other points should be noted. First, since the claim in the Anikwata case is for a moral right, a counterargument seeking to show why there is no justifiable right must respond to moral considerations. A counterargument must contend with the moral reasons offered for the right, or it must show why, despite the right, it should be outweighed by other moral concerns. Second, as noted in Section 2, whether or not a moral right should also be described as a *human right* depends on how basic, or fundamental, it is for our existence as purposive agents.

It should not be surprising therefore that an indispensable requirement for a persuasive justificatory argument is its ability to present reasons that indicate why a right to be recognized and assigned to an individual is very basic. The more basic a right, the more indispensable it is to one's agency and prospects for attaining any of one's goals. Thus, the most basic rights have as their objects goods that are indispensable prerequisites for action. And the *strength,* or weight, of moral reasons can be assessed in terms of success in establishing connections between basic goods and the rights to be justified.

In developing and assessing arguments for and against a moral right that Virginia may have for asylum, it is important to consider how the right is related to basic, nonsubtractive, and additive goods as discussed earlier. The reasons establishing a connection between an entitlement and basic goods will be much stronger than the reasons establishing connections with only additive goods, other things being equal. In other words, a justification is more persuasive if it shows that denying a rights-claim will result in the deprivation of basic goods. Much about the Anikwata case depends therefore on the centrality of asylum for Virginia's access to enjoyment of the basic goods that are necessary for her agency and the nonsubtractive goods that are necessary for her purpose-fulfillment.

In assessing justificatory arguments, we should also consider the *relevance* of the reasons offered. Clearly, reasons are not sufficiently relevant if an intended conclusion does not follow from them. This would be the case, for example, if one attempted to establish a right to life by referring only to the additive goods that would be lost with death. There are subtle but important ways in which reasons may have greater or less relevance, however. One of these involves the link between the claimed right and a basic or nonsubtractive good.

Many people would not consider buses equipped with a lifting entrance (known as "kneeling" buses in Washington, D.C.) a basic or nonsubtractive good. For people with certain physical disabilities, however, such buses may be necessary to enjoy certain goods (e.g., freedom of movement, freedom of association) that are taken for granted as basic or nonsubtractive by the nondisabled. In general, because of the correlation between rights and duties, we ordinarily recognize that if a person has a right X, then that person must have a further right Y to whatever means are necessary for the enjoyment of right X. Thus, although possibly irrelevant to your enjoyment of rights, the presence or absence of "kneeling" buses in public transportation is highly relevant to the enjoyment of very basic and nonsubtractive rights for a person who must use a wheelchair.

In arguing about the Anikwata case, therefore, we also should consider whether, given Virginia Anikwata's position, asylum is or is not necessary for her enjoyment of basic and nonsubtractive rights, and whether or not the right to asylum is itself a right to a basic or nonsubtractive good. It is helpful in this connection to consider the *proximity* between nonprotection of a right, on the one hand, and the loss of a significant good, on the other. It is also helpful to consider both the *effectiveness* of asylum in negating threats to significant goods and its *indispensability* in protecting from harm. As previously noted, Virginia believes that asylum would be very effective in protecting Chenidu and herself from very proximate, or likely, harm should she be deported. An effort to provide a moral defense of the impending INS decision to deny asylum might question whether the feared harm is as likely as it is believed to be or whether asylum is actually necessary to avert harm.

Our assessment of the strength and relevance of reasons should be as responsive as possible to the Personal Worldview Imperative (PWI) articulated by philosopher Michael Boylan.[81] The PWI requires each of us to "develop a single, comprehensive, and internally coherent worldview that is good and that we strive to act out in our daily lives."[82] Thus, for instance, although it is reasonable to expect widespread, intersubjective agreement over what counts as a basic good, personal worldviews will influence individual judgments about the significance of these goods and certain threats to them. No doubt, Virginia's observations concerning what is conducive to her daughter's thriving physically and psychologically reinforce her judgment that "circumcision" would be a serious evil. Of course, what counts as "thriving" is determined in part by Virginia's personal worldview. The same consideration may well be true for her view of her responsibilities as a parent.

---

[81]Michael Boylan, *Basic Ethics* (Upper Saddle River, NJ: Prentice Hall, 2000).
[82]*Basic Ethics*, p. 27.

Sensitivity to personal worldviews comes into play when an individual at risk (possibly Virginia Anikwata) and those who are assessing the case "rank" goods differently, emphasize differently the connections between goods and rights, or evaluate differently the proximity of a harm or the effectiveness or indispensability of protection given by a right. When there is disagreement over the gravity or proximity of some harm, for instance, it is reasonable to give the benefit of doubt to the rights-claimant when there is evidence that he or she is fulfilling the duties required by the Personal Worldview Imperative. On the other hand, it may be reasonable to discount some claim if there is evidence that a worldview is seriously inconsistent or is exploitative. For instance, consider how differently we would think of Virginia if we found out that after obtaining asylum, she intended to place her daughter in a foster home so that she can pursue a lucrative career in pornography.

Up to this point, our focus has been on the strength and relevance of reasons connecting rights-claim with significant goods. Our concern has been with ways of assessing the quality of arguments offering a justification for a moral right. We should turn our attention, even if briefly, to one final issue: the relative strength of an argument justifying a rights-claim versus contending ethical arguments. In the long run, we want not just to justify the rights-claim (or to counter it) but also to argue for (or against) acting in ways that respect for the right would require. For this purpose, we need to show that respecting the right is morally required or morally the best course, even though an alternative ethical theory might dictate a contrary action.

In general, a moral judgment, including the conclusion of an argument justifying a right, is said to be *defeasible* if it can be overcome or set aside by other moral considerations. Thus, an argument for a rights-claim may be sufficient to establish a human right but may fail to compel action if countervailing moral considerations outweigh it. Should the rights-claim be defeasible, then it is not void in the sense that it has no basis after all. Rather, as a result of weighing all relevant moral considerations, it is set aside or annulled as a prescription for action in the present case.

One way to test for the defeasibility of a rights-claim is to examine the circumstances in which it would be applied and enforced. No human right is "absolute" in the sense that there are no logically possible conditions in which it could be annulled. Indeed, it is always a moral issue, informed by facts, whether a human right should be observed. It is easy to think of hypothetical situations in which it would be morally correct to annul a right. Imagine, for example, that a terrorist has used a computer chip to set a code that will cause a nuclear device to explode in two hours and thus to kill a million innocent people. The same computer chip is needed to decode the nuclear device so that it will not detonate. The terrorist has swallowed the computer chip to keep it hidden, but he was observed doing so just before he was apprehended. Certainly the terrorist has the human right to physical integrity, but given the "facts" of this imaginary case, could we seriously doubt that it is morally permissible (if not morally required) to force the captured terrorist to undergo a surgical procedure to recover the computer chip?

The "facts" of the hypothetical case involving the terrorist show that the consequences render the terrorist's rights-claim to physical integrity defeasible. Challenges to rights-claims, as well as to moral judgments more generally, are often based on disputes over morally relevant facts. Thus, it is helpful to view the case from an ethical perspective that emphasizes different facts, such as that offered by utilitarianism. Utilitarian ethical theorists discount people's interests in dignified treatment and equal regard (for instance) in favor of the consequences of action.[83] Looking at the Anikwata case through a utilitarian "lens," we would attempt to foresee the consequences of the INS granting asylum versus the consequences of deportation. As far as we can tell, however, the only persons who would experience serious and negative consequences are mother and child. Possible long-term consequences relating to consistency in INS rulings, following precedent, the effects of "striking a blow against FGM," and so forth, are entirely remote and speculative. The consequences for all of us who have read about the case are very hard to measure and are perhaps incalculable. For the Anikwata case, then, the available facts do not sustain a utilitarian challenge.

As this book goes to press, Virginia Anikwata and her daughter Chinedu (or Sharon) continue to live in the United States, as their deportation becomes less likely. With the assistance of several NGOs, Virginia reasserted her case for asylum under Article 3 of the Convention against Torture and Other Cruel, Inhuman, or Degrading Treatment or Punishment. Shortly thereafter, on February 15, 2000, Representative Constance (Connie) Morella (MD-8) introduced in the House of Representatives a bill "For the Relief of Virginia, and Daughter, Sharon, Anikwata," that would grant them permanent resident status. The bill was referred to the Committee on the Judiciary and then to its Sub-committee on Immigration and Claims where it remains. The INS is now adverse to proceed against Virginia and women similarly threatened. To deny such petitions would be tantamount to denying that FGM and sexual servitude, if (arguably) not torture, is not cruel, inhuman or degrading, as well as to cause Congress to bestir itself. On the other hand, finding in Virginia's favor would open the door, in the view of the INS, to a snowballing number of asylum requests from persons whose own societies or cultures do not regard the treatment for which they claim relief as cruel, inhuman, or degrading. In the meantime, both Virginia and Chinedu are prospering from their reprieve. Virginia recently purchased a home in Montgomery County, Maryland with state assistance and she has become active in women's rights organizations. Chinedu is an honor roll student at Paint Branch Elementary School.

---

[83]See Michael Boylan, *Basic Ethics*, Ch. 3.

chapter two

Debating the Universality of Human Rights

Claims about the *universality*, or *universalism*, of human rights maintain that every human being everywhere, regardless of features such as race, gender, class, or ethnicity, has human rights simply in virtue of his or her humanity. Documents such as the Universal Declaration of Human rights (UDHR) enumerate human rights that are claimed to apply universally as moral norms. The UDHR's claims of universality are evident in the first sentence of the Preamble, which asserts the "inalienable rights of all members of the human family" and by the inclusive language of its following thirty Articles. Inclusivity is assured by the use of words such as "everyone" as in the statement "Everyone has the right to life, liberty and security of person," and "no one" as in "No one shall be subjected to torture or to cruel, inhuman or degrading treatment or punishment."

The international community has reaffirmed the universality of human rights in a number of international human rights instruments. For instance, 172 states, more than the 53 states represented during the UN General Assembly's adoption of the UDHR in 1948, sent delegates to the UN sponsored World Conference on Human Rights at Vienna in 1993. The conference resulted in the preparation and the adoption by consensus of the Vienna Declaration and Programme of Action. This document reaffirmed the universality of human rights articulated in the UDHR, asserting that "the universal nature of these rights and freedoms is beyond question. . . . Human rights and fundamental freedoms are the birth rights of all human beings; their protection and promotion is the first responsibility of Governments." By the beginning of the twenty-first century, a whole network of normative expectations, supported by an extensive body of international law, centered on the premise that human rights are universal.[1]

1. UNIVERSALISM VERSUS EXCEPTIONALISM

Universalism has a very strong intuitive appeal for many people. After all, despite great diversity among us, as human beings we all have basic needs that must be met in order to survive, and we must be protected from certain well-recognized dangers, or "standard threats," to our well-being if we are to have a chance to thrive. And it seems plausible to suppose that there could be agreement on at least a minimum of needs for a "good life" for human beings. Philosopher Stuart Hampshire identifies a list of the "great evils of human experience" that he says are "re-affirmed in every age and in every written history and in every tragedy and fiction." This list contains familiar items: "murder and the destruction of life, imprisonment, enslavement, starvation, poverty, physical pain and torture, homelessness, friendlessness."[2] The universalist's sentiment is put well by political scientist Rosalyn Higgins:

> I believe, profoundly, in the universality of the human spirit. Individuals everywhere want the same essential things: to have sufficient food and shelter; to be able to speak freely; to practice their own religion or to abstain from religious belief; to feel that their person is not threatened by the state; to know that they will not be tortured, or detained without charge, and that, if charged, they will have a fair trial. I believe there is nothing in these aspirations that is dependant upon culture, or religion, or stage of development. They are as keenly felt by the African tribesman as by the European city-dweller, by the inhabitants of a Latin American shanty-town as by the resident of a Manhattan apartment.[3]

Despite widespread approval of human rights, there are many who object to the international human rights regime. As spokespersons for their

---

[1]For a brief overview of the body of covenants, international law, courts, international human rights organizations, and human rights NGOs comprising the international human rights regime, see Appendix A. For an extensive collection of documents, data and interpretations, see Henry J. Steiner and Philip Alston, eds., *International Human Rights in Context*, 2nd ed. (Oxford: Oxford University Press, 2000), esp. pp. 557–983. See also Jack Donnelly, *International Human Rights*, 2nd ed. (Boulder, CO: Westview Press, 1988).

[2]Stuart Hampshire, *Innocence and Experience* (Cambridge, MA: Harvard University Press, 1989), p. 90.

[3]Rosalyn Higgins, *Problems and Process: International Law and How We Use It* (Oxford, UK: Oxford University Press, 1994), p. 96.

own cultures, societies, or states, objectors usually do *not* deny that there is some (sometimes variable, sometimes nebulous) core of goods needed by all human beings. (These goods are what we identified as the objects of rights in Chapter 1.) In fact, they usually assert that their own cultures or societies value these goods and have devised traditional means of providing them for members. Critics object, instead, to what might be called the "assumptions and implications" of international human rights and the practices of rights that they involve.[4] Thus, some object to the view that human rights require that one standard be applied equally to all cultures and societies, without regard to traditional and cultural differences in the way that the goods, or objects of rights, are valued, or to the needs of developing states. Many detractors are concerned with the ways in which the practices of rights, which emphasize individual entitlements rather than duties to the community, thrust aside traditional values. In addition, although some critics regard many of the articles of international human rights instruments as enumerating genuine human rights, they object to others as fraudulent or as less important than vital interests of the group or state.

Among critics of universalism are Mahathir bin Mohamad, prime minister of Malaysia for over thirty years. In 1997, Mahathir urged that the UN mark the fiftieth anniversary of the UDHR by revising or even repealing it because its human rights norms focus excessively on individual rights while neglecting the rights of society and of the common good.[5] Former Australian Prime Minister Malcolm Fraser has dismissed the declaration as reflecting the views of the Northern and Eurocentric states, and even former German Chancellor Helmut Schmidt claims that the UDHR reflects the philosophical and cultural background of its Western drafters.[6] Among American objectors, Michael Sandel in *Democracy's Discontent* criticizes what he sees as the elevation of personal rights above the common good and the corresponding emphasis on individualism. Sandel believes that the ethos of individual rights undermines the civic virtues that sustain Americans' sense of communal responsibility.[7]

So-called "reservations" to the international treaties, or covenants, on human rights reflect the interests of some states in picking and choosing among human rights norms. For instance, in ratifying the International Convention on Civil and Political Rights (ICCPR) in 1992, Congress added a

---

[4]Raimundo Pannikar, "Is the Notion of Human Rights a Western Concept?", in *International Human Rights in Context*, 2nd ed., Henry J. Steiner and Philip Alston eds. (New York: Oxford University Press, 2000), pp. 383–9.

[5]On Mahathir see Peter Van Ness, "Introduction," in *Debating Human Rights*, Peter Van Ness, ed. (London: Routledge, 1999), p. 11.

[6]Thomas M. Franck, "Are Human Rights Universal?," *Foreign Affairs*, Vol. 80, No. 1 (January/February, 2001), p. 196.

[7]Michael J. Sandel, *Democracy's Discontent: America in Search of a Public Philosophy* (Cambridge, MA: Harvard University Press, 1996). See also Thomas M. Franck, "Are Human Rights Universal?," *Foreign Affairs*, Vol. 80, No. 1 (January/February, 2001), pp. 191–204.

reservation to the effect that it would not recognize Article 6 prohibiting capital punishment of those under the age of 18. In agreeing to the Convention on the Rights of the Child (CRC) (which has not been ratified by Congress), Malaysia stipulated a reservation against the protection of children against discrimination (Art. 2). A total of 67 states parties to the Convention on the Elimination of All Forms of Discrimination Against Women (CEDAW) had entered reservations or declarations.[8] For example, Egypt entered a reservation against Article 9, paragraph 2, maintaining that, in marriages among partners of different nationalities, the nationality of any children of the union would be determined by the nationality of the father rather than the mother.[9] As these examples suggest, much heated debate arises over conflicts between the universal reach of human rights norms and the particular values or interests of members of a particular culture, society, or state. In such cases the all-human rights-are-equally-applicable-to-all-people approach usually maintained by advocates of international human rights norms is pitted against a pick-and-choose approach to human rights.

We can understand most critics of the human rights regime as presenting versions of *exceptionalism*. That is, the critics allow that although some groups—whether cultures, societies, or states—may choose to observe human rights norms—their group, or other groups' values or vital interests create exceptions to the application of human rights norms.[10] Exceptionalists thus argue against the presumption that human rights are universal. If any version of exceptionalism is correct, then universalism is wrong, at least in the strong form presumed by the international human rights regime. But is any version of exceptionalism correct? We can begin to answer this question by distinguishing among different versions of exceptionalism, and the best way to identify exceptionalist positions is to look at differences among the *reasons* proposed for rejecting universalism. We can then assess these reasons.[11] Although exceptionalist arguments may combine (or confuse) various reasons, an analysis that disentangles these reasons enables us to identify six positions. They are listed here together with a name or brief characterization that we shall employ for ease in referring to them. (The reason is underlined and the name, or characterization, is given in italics.)

1. <u>Contrary to universalism, it is not possible for human rights norms to be truly universal. The claim that such norms are universal is logically inconsistent</u>

---

[8] As of June 2004 CEDAW had been ratified by 62 states' parties without reservation.

[9] *International Human Rights in Context,* p. 442.

[10] "Are Human Rights Universal?," pp. 191–3.

[11] Note that it is important to classify exceptionalist positions based on the reasons offered to justify the position rather than the *attitudes* of those who reject human rights norms. For instance, there are "rejectionists," such as the former Ayatollah Khomeini of Iran, who completely rejected human rights as valueless. But we cannot respond intelligently to such charges unless we know the reasons for asserting them. See Jay Drydyk, "Globalization and Human Rights," in *Moral Issues in Global Perspective,* Christine M. Koggel, ed. (Peterborough, Ontario: Broadview Press, 199), p. 34.

with well-established truth about the relativity of all norms, or values. As this challenge depends on a doctrine known as *ethical relativism*, we may call it the *ethical relativism challenge*.

2. As products of Eurocentric, or Western, culture, human rights cannot be properly integrated into non-Eurocentric cultures or societies. Because human rights norms are incommensurable with the values and beliefs of these communities, the latter must rely on traditional values and practices. To claim that concepts and norms are *incommensurable* is to claim that they cannot be transferred from the one culture to the other, or that they cannot be introduced into a different culture without an irretrievable loss of meaning. As criticism (2) depends on such a claim, it is the *incommensurability claim*.

3. Human rights norms represent means by which powerful and developed states in Europe and North America attempt to politically control and to dominate economically the weaker and lesser-developed countries of the world. As it reflects a concern with unjust domination and exploitation, this criticism may be called the *imperialism charge*.

4. The introduction of foreign human rights norms and rights practices will destroy values native to a culture or society, or lead to disrespect for its traditionally valued practices and ways of life. As this criticism asserts a causal connection between human rights norms and the decline of traditional cultures or societies, it is the *causal complaint*.

5. Human rights norms are really irrelevant, or beside the point. The values and practices indigenous in a community or society already afford better access to or protection of the objects, or human goods, the international human rights regime intends to protect. This charge is most appropriately characterized as the *irrelevancy criticism*.

6. The immediate implementation of some human rights norms would be politically or socially dislocating and would thus undermine the state's progress in protecting or advancing other human rights. As this position maintains that some human rights must be suppressed in order to protect or promote other human rights, it is commonly known as the *trade-off argument*.

These six charges against universalism can be organized in a number of ways. As just presented, they proceed from the strongest, or most extensive, reasons for rejecting universalism to those that are comparatively less hostile to the international human rights movement. The strongest reason for rejecting universalism, and conversely, accepting exceptionalism, is presented by (1)—the *ethical relativism challenge*. This view holds that there are no universal normative standards because all values are relative to a particular society or group. Ethical relativism will be considered in more detail in a moment, but note that if it were true, the international human rights movement would be stopped in its tracks. The universalist claims for international human rights norms would clearly fail because they would involve *logical inconsistency*. If nothing can have value except relative to a particular society or particular groups, then necessarily, human rights norms that are claimed to be relevant everywhere cannot be valid.

Moreover, two other important consequences would follow from the conclusion that there are no universally valid or transcultural human rights norms. First, no one would be justified in criticizing other cultures or states for giving priority to their own native, or indigenous, values over human rights norms. For instance, as long as a practice is supported by a culture's or a group's own values and norms (say China's), then there would be no justifiable basis for foreigners' objections to that practice (for example, a government crackdown on free expression and religious belief). Second, if criticisms made by persons outside a state are unjustified, then efforts to hold government leaders of that state accountable for rights abuses would (if they go beyond mere exhortation) constitute interference and harassment. Military intervention to end massive rights violation, as in genocide, would exemplify the principle that "might makes right" rather than a vindication of universal and fundamental moral norms. Likewise, perpetrators of crimes against humanity who are hauled before international tribunals such as the International Criminal Court might be regarded as victims of "victor's justice."

In contrast to the ethical relativism challenge, most of the other complaints against universalism do not raise issues about the logic or coherence of universal human rights. Those who make the imperialism charge and the causal complaint object to the view that international human rights norms are fundamental values. Even if these norms are universal, the critics claim that they are not of significant value. Indeed, these critics decry what they see as the destructive or unwanted effects of these norms. Likewise, the irrelevancy criticism regards the *issue of universality* in a different light. Although these critics do not question the logical consistency or coherence of human rights norms, they are concerned with the universal *application* of those norms. They claim exceptions for their own cultures or states because, in their view, human rights norms are irrelevant: as far as their societies are concerned, human rights offer no improvement in protecting human dignity or promoting human agency. The trade-off argument does not deny the existence of universal human rights norms. Rather, its advocates base their claims for exceptionalism on "political realities" that require that governments limit individuals' exercise of rights.

One other criticism in our list does challenge the possibility of universal human rights norms, however. Advocates of the incommensurability position join ethical relativists in maintaining that values derived from particular cultures cannot be universal, or transcultural. Whereas ethical relativists base this claim on the inconsistency of universalism with what they regard as the truth about the relativity of value, advocates of incommensurability charge that universalism is conceptually incoherent. In their view, values supporting the international human rights movement and concepts implied by human rights discourse cannot be transcultural because they cannot be transferred or translated into cultures different from those of their origin. Thus, despite other differences between them, the ethical relativism challenge and the incommensurability claim pose the most serious challenges. If they were credible, then universalism would have to be abandoned. Consequently, we must begin a defense of universalism by examining these two challenges.

2. Is It Possible for Human Rights Norms to Apply Universally?

Ethical relativism begins with observations about *cultural relativism*. It is noted that values and norms are relative to the particular culture or society in which they occur. Cultural relativists assert that what is considered morally right or wrong varies from society to society, so that there are no values, or moral norms, accepted by all societies. But, of course, it does not follow that a practice is morally justified from the mere fact that a culture or social group accepts it. After all, persons may commit *moral errors* as well as factual errors. Just as people were wrong to believe, for example, the heliocentric theory—that the Sun revolved around the Earth—so too, they may be wrong in believing that the punishment of death for apostasy (renouncing one's religion) saves the soul of the victim from perdition or safeguards the community. Thus, because a significant objection to universalism does not arise from the mere anthropological observation that moral values and norms vary from society to society, to oppose universalism, ethical relativists make a stronger claim. This is the claim that the empirical evidence of diversity tells us something critical about the way norms are created or are adopted as valid standards by peoples. It is maintained that there are no universally valid moral norms because all moral norms *derive their validity* from acceptance within particular cultures or societies.[12]

As stated in item (1), ethical relativism directly contradicts universalism by claiming that universal human rights norms are *impossible*. It tries to put advocates of the international human rights movement on the defensive and to require them to prove that there are universal human rights norms. But when set in these terms, the controversy becomes extremely and needlessly difficult to resolve because the different sides are prone to disagree just as vehemently over what could count as a "proof." Furthermore, as we

---

[12]Ruth Benedict, *Patterns of Culture* (Boston: Houghton Mifflin, 1934), Chs. 1–3; Clifford Geertz, *Local Knowledge: Further Essays in Interpretive Anthropology* (New York: Basic Books, 1983); Samuel P. Huntington, "The Clash of Civilizations," *Foreign Affairs*, Vol. 72, No. 3 (Summer 1993), pp. 22–49; Samuel P. Huntington, *The Third Wave: Democratization in the Late Twentieth Century* (Norman, OK: University of Oklahoma Press, 1991); John Ladd, ed., *Ethical Relativism* (Belmont, CA: Wadsworth, 1973); Nancy Scheper-Hughes, "Virgin Territory: The Male Discovery of the Clitoris," *Medical Anthropology Quarterly*, Vol. 5, No. 1, pp. 25–8; Edward Westermarck, *Ethical Relativity* (Highland Park, NJ: Humanities Press, 1960).

saw in Chapter 1, just because human rights are special kinds of moral resources, advocates of universal human rights norms must presuppose what ethical relativist have already rejected, that is, that certain moral concepts and principles can be equally understood by persons of different societies and cultures.

It seems equally pointless to try to shift the burden of proof back onto the shoulders of the ethical relativists. Suppose that ethical relativists succeed in demonstrating that some values and norms derive their validity from the way they are accepted within a particular culture or community. This outcome does not prove that *all* values must be validated in this way, that is, that *no* values are universal or that no value could become universal. Indeed, as ethicists and analysts point out, the attempts of ethical relativists to argue that no values are universal become ensnared in contradiction or inconsistency. For instance, it would follow from the argument that all values are culturally specific that it is wrong for any group to criticize the values of a different group. Each group must be tolerant of the values of others. But what, then, is the status of this principle of toleration if it is not universal?[13]

Fortunately, as it turns out, ethical relativism does not pose such a serious challenge after all. In the first place, in attacking universalism, ethical relativists often confuse universalism with *absolutism.* Second, they mistakenly regard universalism as incompatible with *value pluralism,* a thesis that ethical relativists approve of. Third, they are inclined to suppose that universalism is an ideological prop for oppressive regimes. When they understand that there is no necessary, indeed, no special, relationship between universalism and any of these three, then ethical relativists often admit that they had the wrong thing in their gun sights.

Absolutism is the view that certain values are absolute; that is, that these values must be given precedence over all other competing values. By contrast, universalism is the view that human rights norms apply to everyone. If human rights advocates were also absolutists, then they would argue—implausibly—that human rights norms can never be set aside or subjected to any other values or considerations, no matter how pressing. But advocates of human rights do not make such an unreasonable claim. Human rights norms prevail over most competing claims in most circumstances; that is why they were said in Chapter 1 to be peremptory in character. But it was also noted in Chapter 1 that human rights are *defeasible,* meaning that in certain circumstances human rights legitimately might be limited or set aside. For instance, the right to life is a good candidate for being the most peremptory of all human rights. But there may be circumstances in which, tragically, the loss of a human life might be necessary if there is no other way to avert a terrible catastrophe, such as in thwarting a

---

[13]Elvin Hatch, *Culture and Morality: The Relativity of Values in Anthropology* (New York: Columbia University Press, 1983), p. 8.

terrorist's intent to detonate a powerful bomb in an urban center, thus murdering hundreds of people.[14]

In the human rights movement, commentators often make use of the distinction between *derogable* and *nonderogable* rights, as well as defeasible and nondefeasible rights.[15] In ordinary circumstances, a human right is nonderogable or nondefeasible; to say that it cannot be derogated is to say that it cannot be set aside or overturned. But this does not mean that a human right is absolutely nonderogable. In some extraordinary cases, a right must yield against rights of greater priority (e.g., yielding on the right to move freely after dark (under curfew) to secure greater fulfillment of the right to bodily security). Other extreme cases involve the same right held by a larger number of people (e.g., the right to life in the preceding terrorism case). As expected, there is much controversy over which rights are the most "basic" in the sense of being least derogable. Philosopher Henry Shue has made a powerful argument for the overriding priority of rights to security, subsistence, and liberty as most basic in the sense that, without enjoyment of these, there can be no enjoyment of any other rights at all.[16]

Note that commentators do speak of human rights as "applying *equally* to everyone everywhere." But the reference to equal application does not mean that human rights are nonderogable; rather, it means that all humans are *equal* in their possession of rights. Return to the hypothetical example of the terrorist who has created a situation such that he or she cannot be prevented from committing mass murder except by ending his or her life. We would not say in this case that the terrorist had lost or somehow forfeited or waived the right to life. From a human rights perspective, all human lives are presumed to be of equal value. Rather, the terrorist's right to life was, under the circumstances, derogable, because his or her death was causally necessary for the survival of a larger number of persons whom, except for the terrorist's actions, would not be endangered.

Critics who find ethical relativism attractive also may falsely assume that if a norm or value is presumed to be universal, then one would have to believe that there can be no variation from culture to culture or society to society in the way that the right is applied. Consider that for very many people, the intuitive appeal of international human rights is strongest when we

---

[14]Note that because the right to life is peremptory, we would require the most stringent restrictions in a case such as this one. These conditions would be similar to those specified by Just War Theory for the permissible use of deadly force, including last resort, and proportionate use of force. Killing the terrorist would not be justified if he or she could be disarmed in a way that would preserve his or her life. See James P. Sterba, in "Terrorism and International Justice," in *Terrorism and International Justice,* James P. Sterba, ed. (New York: Oxford University Press, 2003), 206–28.

[15]See "General Comment No. 24 of Human Rights Committee," *International Human Rights in Context,* pp. 1044–7.

[16]Henry Shue, *Basic Rights: Subsistence, Affluence, and U.S. Foreign Policy* (Princeton: Princeton University Press, 1980).

have in mind the sorts of human rights identified earlier by Hampshire and Higgins. For many people, intuitions about the universality of human rights begin to wane when they read in the text of the Convention on the Rights of the Child that "The child shall have the right to freedom of expression" (Art. 13.1) and weaken further with the UDHR's declaration of "periodic holidays with pay" (part of Art. 24) and the right "freely to participate in the cultural life of the community" (part of Art. 27). These examples do not seem nearly as "basic," or "fundamental," and it is hard to know what a right to cultural participation entitles one to do or to get. It is not surprising that the intuitive appeal of ethical relativism is strongest at precisely this point. The relativist position itself loses intuitive appeal, however, when we consider the most basic issues of life. Even those willing to consider that group choice validates the norms for the group that chooses them might find their intuitions quailing at the suggestion that the freedom not to be tortured or the freedom to have good health are valuable only because they are chosen by this or that group. But why should this be the case? What are our intuitions telling us?

Our intuitions strongly suggest that initial impression of the terms of disagreement between ethical relativism and universalism were *artificially* extreme. It seemed, in the view of the relativists, that univeralists were committed to the unreasonable position that the same human rights apply *universally in exactly the same way,* regardless of other conditions. But, as we saw in Chapter 1, human rights as moral resources involve reasons that have the same moral weight in *relevantly similar circumstances.* An illustration will make this matter clearer. Consider the UDHR identification of periodic holidays with pay as a human right. This provision has often been criticized as being applicable only in countries that are industrially developed but not in countries that are largely agrarian or in economic transition. How can this human right be thought to exist in Mali, for example, where a majority of the population maintains itself through subsistence agriculture and herding?

But the criticism is misplaced. It is not that the human right does not exist, but rather that at present it has no scope for application in Mali. The Dogon peasant in Mali has exactly the same human rights as any other person. Therefore, a Dogon peasant who migrates to an urban center and works in an industrial occupation morally must be given the same moral consideration as any other worker regarding the substance of human rights. As we recall from Chapter 1, human rights protect humans from certain standard threats, but where those threats do not occur or do not arise, there are no relevantly similar circumstances for application of the human rights.[17]

---

[17]Jack Donnelly, *Universal Human Rights in Theory and Practice,* (Ithaca, NY: Cornell University Press, 1989), p. 27.

In Chapter 3 we will discuss a very helpful set of distinctions introduced by political scientist Jack Donnelly. These distinctions—between the
core of a human right, *interpretations* of it, and respective *forms* of the right—
will help us see how the international human rights regime can accommo-
date a great deal of global cultural diversity.[18] Until then, it is important to
remember that a human right does not come into play—it is not claimed as
a moral resource in a practice—if the human flourishing it is intended to
protect or to promote is not disrupted or threatened. This does *not* mean
that the human right does not exist or could not apply in the society or culture in which the disruption or threat is presently absent. It does mean,
however, that we must consider carefully the actual conditions within a particular society or culture and then assess whether or not there are disrup-
tions or threats, that is, whether or not relevantly similar circumstances
justify claims that human rights are being violated.

We have reached a point at which it is appropriate to comment on another common confusion. Some advocates of ethical relativism have confused their position with *value pluralism,* and they regard universalism as
hostile to value pluralism. Both ethical relativism and value pluralism maintain that there is a diversity, or pluralism, regarding conceptions of the good
life, or the good for human beings. Value pluralism does not commit one to
challenging the view that human rights norms are universal, however. Likewise, value pluralists need not argue, as do ethical relativists, that ethical
values derive their validity from their origins in particular communities or
cultures. Value pluralists maintain the less ambitious view that human nature "conceived in terms of common human needs and capacities, always
underdetermines a way of life, and underdetermines an order of priority
among values . . ."[19] Hence, although social and biological needs, common
to all human beings, provide the foundations for universal human rights,
needs, interests, and preferences that are not common to all human beings
explain the great diversity in ways of life on the globe. So as lawyer Michael
Perry notes, universalism and value pluralism are not incompatible. "A conception of human good can be, and should be, universalist as well as plural-
ist: It can acknowledge sameness as well as difference, commonality as well
as variety."[20] It follows, therefore, that ethical relativists are simply mistaken
in believing that value pluralism—ether as a descriptive or normative
claim—refutes universalism.

Some ethical relativists are motivated to oppose universalism for political reasons. In their view, by seeking to apply human rights norms universally around the globe, the international human rights movement seeks to

---

[18]*Ibid.,* pp. 109–24.
[19]Stuart Hampshire, *Morality and Conflict* (Oxford, UK: Basil Blackwell, 1983), p. 155.
[20]Michael J. Perry, *The Idea of Human Rights: Four Inquiries* (New York: Oxford University
Press, 1998), p. 65.

impose values that originated in Western societies on non-Western societies. They thus regard universalism as an ideological ploy by which Western societies attempt to maintain their domination, or hegemony, over less developed areas of the globe. This view was given some support by an early response of the American Anthropological Association to the UN Commission on Human Rights.[21]

Because it implicates the *imperialism criticism*, this charge will be discussed in more detail in Section 3. Note in passing, however, that the charge itself raises a number of problems. By assuming that human rights norms are Western and "imposed" on non-Western societies, ethical relativists who make this charge are begging the question. The relativity of human rights norms versus their universality *is* the subject of debate; hence, relativity cannot be assumed in an effort to advance the ethical relativists' claims. Furthermore, critics who take this view confuse the truth or falsity of universalism with the uses, legitimate or illegitimate, which may be made of it. Ill-advised or abusive tactics on the part of those who advocate human rights norms do not demonstrate the falsity of these norms any more than a teacher's cruel humiliation of his or her students demonstrates the falsity of mathematics.

A discourse and the norms or principles within it have no mystical ability to impose themselves or to "colonize our consciousness." We may of course use a discourse unreflectively and thereby perpetuate certain beliefs and judgments. Too often we are unaware that discourse conveys ideas and judgments disproportionately shaped by those most likely to gain from their use. Feminists and "deconstructivist" philosophers working in the late twentieth century have revealed the extent to which various discourses reinforce the power of those with privilege.[22] As beneficiaries of their analyses, we have a legitimate concern with the tendency of any "universalizing" discourse to promote class, gender, or ethnocentric interests.

Yet, the insights of feminists and deconstructivists apply across the board. No discourse is immune from political influence, the discourse of ethical relativism no less than that of universalism. Some critics have

---

[21]American Anthropological Association, Statement on Human Rights, *International Human Rights in Context*, pp. 372–5.

[22]The literature on both feminist and deconstructivist critiques is very large. On the former, see Mary Daly, *Beyond God the Father: Toward a Philosophy of Women's Liberation* (Boston: Beacon Press, 1973); Carol Gilligan, *In a Different Voice: Psychological Theory and Women's Development* (Cambridge, MA: Harvard University Press, 1982); Alison M. Jaggar and Paula S. Rothenberg, eds., *Feminist Frameworks: Alternative Theoretical Accounts of the Relations Between Women and Men*, 2nd ed. (New York: McGraw Hill, 1984). For brief introductions to deconstructivist views see Michel Foucault, "Excerpt from *Discipline and Punish*," in *Violence and Its Alternatives: An Interdisciplinary Reader*, Manfred B. Steger and Nancy S. Lind, eds. (New York: St. Martin's Press, 1999), pp. 70–6; Jacques Derrida, "Excerpt from. *Force of Law: The Mystical Foundation of Authority*," in *Violence and Its Alternatives*, pp. 77–83.

pointed to the ways that ethical relativism can be used for exploitative purposes, including justifications for not assisting developing nations in the
South or East.[23]

The discussion so far has presented reasons for rejecting the ethical relativist's claims that universalism is false. Universalism is not to be confused
with the untenable position known as *absolutism*. Contrary to entailing the
falsity of *value pluralism*, universalism is logically compatible with value
pluralism. There is, in addition, no logical reason why universalism is more
likely to be a prop for repressive regimes than is ethical relativism.

So far we have been turning back the charges made by relativists. But
as we need to consider the reasonableness of both positions overall, it is fair
to take the battle to the relativists' home ground. We can begin by noting
that ethical relativists take the position that values and norms are valid relative to some *specified* group but not that their validity constantly varies.
Thus, the ethical relativist, if American, might say that the ethical values of
Americans are relative to the U.S. Constitution or to the morals taught by his
or her church, synagogue, or mosque. A relativist in Kenya might claim that
ethical values are relative to the tribal mores of the Masai or Kiyuku or perhaps to some intertribal consensus within Kenya. A similar position seems to
be taken by some defenders of so-called "autonomy regimes" by which the
domestic and family affairs of members of different religious or ethnic
groups within a single state—for instance, Israeli Jews and Palestinian Muslims in Israel—are governed by separate courts and systems of law. As these
examples show, ethical relativists seek to defend the particular values that
they favor (or that are favored by groups for which they speak) from alien
values not seen as relevant to them. Universal human rights norms are not
relevant, it is claimed, because they are not relative to the traditional practices, beliefs, and ways of life "inside," or indigenous to, the group.

So the ethical relativist asserts that there are certain community, as
well as group, or traditional *realities*, that establish the relevance of some
values rather than others. These realities distinguish the Buddhist culture of
Thailand from the culture of the Ibo in Nigeria, for instance, as well as from
the cultural values of the Timorese. Ethical relativists must make this move
to avoid an empty, merely negative position. After all, ethical relativism
usually arises in resistance to claims that other norms, such as universal
human rights norms, ought to prevail locally. How can it even be claimed
that a particular group or community ought to be permitted to honor its
own beliefs and values if there are no definitive beliefs and no "content" to
its values?

[23]See Yash Ghai, "Human Rights and Governance: The Asia Debate," in *International Human Rights in Context*, pp. 550–2; *Universal Human Rights in Theory and Practice*, pp. 118–19; Inoue Tatsuo, "Liberal Democracy and Asian Orientalism," in *The East Asian Challenge for Human Rights*, Joanne R. Bauer and Daniel A. Bell, eds. (Cambridge: Cambridge University Press, 1999), pp. 27–59.

So, at a minimum, an ethical relativist must be committed to the view that there is some set of beliefs and values that are so important for the people who share them that they must be defended against universal human rights norms. But how, then, do they defend their own norms and values from other relativist claims? *Relativism is itself always relative.* In other words, any identifiable set of group values or beliefs can be challenged on relativist grounds. The values of the national group might be challenged by the values of a separatist ethnic or religious movement, the values of the latter by a sect or cult, and values of all three by nonconformist families. The ultimate form of relativism is really *subjectivism,* the claim, in the words of the ancient Greek philosopher Protagoras, that "man is the measure of all things."

We need to ask, relative to what? What is the standard or criterion to which judgments must be relative? Ethical relativists' standards reveal that they make the questionable assumption that there is such a thing, or an entity, as *the* culture, *the* community, or *the* group. That is, they suppose that there is some one, definite, fairly clear and permanent thing to which standards are relative rather than to some other thing, such as some other (perhaps larger) community. This is very definitely the view of some fundamentalist Muslims, for instance, who believe that the *Qur'an* and *shari'a,* the body of legal interpretation and commentary informed by the *Qur'an* and the example (*sunna*) and sayings (*hadith*) of Mohammed, constitute a complete and an exhaustive guide to human life.[24] The difficulty, of course, is that the values of conservative Muslims are challenged by reinterpretations of basic texts and that some progressive Muslims argue that values derived from scripture and religious law pertain only to certain areas of life.[25]

How then does the relativist defend the selection of one set of values over any others? Controversies about the "genuine" values of this or that group or community have sparked many historical, anthropological, and hermeneutical debates. In some cases, historical or anthropological research has shown that values regarded as traditional within the group were actually introduced fairly recently and sometimes by former colonial powers.[26] Often values touted as traditional were imposed through custom and therefore cannot be defended as accepted by consent. Arguments about implicit consent seem especially suspect when large minorities, such as the Dalit, or "Untouchables," in Hindu society of India seek an end to the oppressive caste system. In other cases, the values that are trumpeted as indigenous to

---

[24]See, for example, Abu Al'a Maududi, *The Islamic Human Rights* (Leicester, UK: Islamic Foundation, 1980).

[25]Ustadh Mahmoud Mohamed Taha, *The Second Message of Islam* (Syracuse, NY: Syracuse University Press, 1987).

[26]See the examples in Section 3 of caning school children in Sub-Sahara Africa and of discrimination against women among the Maliseet of New Brunswick, Canada.

the culture and as expressive of traditional virtue and character, are often the preferred values of an autocratic elite.

To be sure, ethical relativists can retort that they certainly recognize the realities of social and cultural change. As long as there is change there will be continual controversy, often healthy, over which values are "genuine," or deserving of respect, within the group. This outcome is surely the case, but it is also beside the point. Ethical relativists have not shown how the way a group acquires its values (e.g., as emerging from consensus, the result of tradition, or impositions of earlier generations, copied from other groups) qualifies them for adoption or *disqualifies* a set of values, including human rights norms. Because ethical relativists do not offer a justifiable account of how values derive their legitimacy from the culture or society in which they are native, their cry against human rights norms that "they are not ours" is a form of prejudice. Ideas and values belong equally to everyone although they certainly may be discovered, articulated, described, and respected in one part of the globe before spreading elsewhere. On the other hand, however, if relativists insist that there are features internal to their culture that legitimate values, then their version of ethical relativist cannot maintain a consistent position; they are "essentialists" rather than relativists.

We are now in a position to see that the exceptionalists' first criticism (1) of universalism fails. The *ethical relativism criticism* maintained that it was impossible for human rights norms to be universal. But as we have just seen, this charge falls flat on two counts. First, various false or unacceptable positions, such as absolutism, are neither the same as universalism nor implied by universalism. Second, relativists cannot endow the values of a particular culture with superiority over other values, or norms, including human rights norms, because this treatment implies a standard or validating source that is itself not relative, which is impossible given the premises of ethical relativism. As we have also seen, the ethical relativist offers no compelling reason for believing that all values must derive their legitimacy from some particular culture or other. Let us therefore conclude our examination of ethical relativism and move on to assess the second main reason for rejecting universalism: *the incommensurability claim.*

Exceptionalists who claim that cultural values are incommensurable usually embrace one or more positions reflected in the remaining criticisms on the original list. In particular, they often embrace the *irrelevancy criticism* by asserting that traditional values inherent in their culture already provide the protections or the access to goods for which advocates of human rights norms say they are needed. In fact, most of those who advance the remaining criticisms (2) through (6) share the view that human rights norms are based on values that are basically Eurocentric and North Atlantic and are thus impositions on cultures and societies outside that geopolitical sphere.

It is worth examining the factual basis for the claim that human rights norms are *alien* because this widespread belief strongly influences attitudes.

Moreover, as the claim arises in connection with each of the remaining criticisms, it is a good idea to deal with it now. To start with, it cannot be denied that, *historically,* liberty and civil rights, such as those articulated in the ICCPR, were publicly recognized and defended in tandem with the growth of political liberalism in Western Europe and North America. The legitimacy, or validity, of a belief or a value does not depend on its ontological status or historical genesis, however. The possibility that it could depends upon the plausibility of relativism, which as we have just seen, is a most dubious position to maintain. In the absence of good reasons for supposing that truth or validity is derived from the process of discovery or origination, the claim that it does is a version of the *genetic fallacy.* It is not reasonable to believe that because geometry originated among the ancient Greeks, it was valid only for ancient Mediterranean cultures. And it is no more reasonable to suppose that because conceptions of human rights emerged first in Europe and North Atlantic societies that they are valid only for cultures in those regions.

We must also be cautious not to assume greater cultural difference than actually exists. In a classical analysis of colonial ideology, the scholar Edward Said explained the development of "Orientalism" among students of Asia.[27] For Said, "orientalism" referred to scholarship in the West that, by assuming a rational and an objective approach, and hence, superiority for their own cultures, assumed a corresponding inferiority for the Asian cultures studied. According to Said, these Western scholars maintained that the concepts and categories employed to understand the societies and cultures of their own West were irrelevant and inapplicable in Asia and vice versa.[28] Western scholars studying the "Orient" regarded Asian cultures as monolithic and static, while assuming an objective and rational approach that implied the superiority of their own, defining cultures. Although it was an ideology among intellectuals, orientalism was easily associated with the efforts of citizens within colonial powers to differentiate their own sense of identity from that of the peoples they dominated. Hence, "Orientals" became regarded as distinctly "other," as "the inscrutable Chinese," for example, who were so different psychologically and culturally to be virtually unintelligible to most Westerners. In addition, the West was seen as complex and progressive, and the East as largely monolithic and static.

Some commentators are concerned that the tendency of human rights critics to think in terms of stark differences and categories poses dangers of orientalism in reverse.[29] Some who charge that human rights norms are "alien" make the same ideological mistake in assuming mistakenly that

---

[27]Edward D. Said, *Orientalism* (New York: Georges Borchardt Inc., 1978).

[28]Elizabeth Ann Mayer, *Islam and Human Rights: Tradition and Politics* (Boulder, CO: Westview Press, 1999), p. 7.

[29]See "Liberal Democracy and Asian Orientalism," esp. pp. 38–42.

there are absolute differences between cultures or by imagining that cultures present a kind of static quality, undergoing relatively little change from century to century. This tendency is decried by Fouad Zakaria who believes that Islamic fundamentalists tend to freeze the basic concepts of the tradition, thereby hampering Islam's ability to respond to emerging social and political realities such as the advanced military power of states. "It is non-historical, or rather, it freezes a certain moment in history and holds fast to it till the very end, thus doing away with dynamism, mobility and historical development."[30]

In any event, many advocates of international human rights consider irrelevant claims that conceptions of human rights are "culture-bound." Even if many of the first human rights, or rather, natural rights, notions emerged in Eurocentric cultures, these are *not* the human rights conceptions and constructs enshrined in the UDHR and in other international human rights instruments. Historian Mary Glendon records the genuinely transcultural efforts of the framers of the UDHR to achieve a universal consensus on human rights.[31] Their work was informed by a massive study by the "philosopher's committee" sponsored by UNESCO and chaired by the eminent French philosopher Gabriel Marcel. The philosopher's committee surveyed the opinion of religious, philosophical, and cultural leaders around the world and involved an extensive study of major documents from all of the world's major cultures. It documented the compatibility of human rights with fundamental liberties, norms, or concepts of human dignity essential to the cultures examined.[32] Moreover, the drafters of the UDHR were themselves individuals of great intellectual breadth and sensitivity, and before its adoption, the members of the General Assembly subjected the UDHR to extensive debate.[33]

It is sometimes argued that the adoption of the UDHR by states in Africa and Asia with non-Eurocentric cultures should be discounted because the UN representatives of these states had already been "westernized." This response ignores the fact, however, that 191 countries were represented at the Vienna Convention in 1991 that reaffirmed the universality of human rights as expressed in the UN's major instruments. The view that human rights norms are strictly Western in content is also inconsistent with the view of some exceptionalists who disagree with universalists over which rights humans do or do not have. For instance, although they regard some international human rights norms as inapplicable within their countries, the authors of the Universal Islamic Declaration of Human Rights of

---

[30]Fouad Zakaria, "Human Rights in the Arab World: The Islamic Context," *Philosophical Foundations of Human Rights* (Paris: UNESCO HighCom Paper 237, 1986).

[31]Mary Ann Glendon, *A World Made New: Eleanor Roosevelt and the Universal Declaration of Human Rights* (New York: Random House, 2001).

[32]*Ibid.*, pp. 73–8.

[33]*Ibid.*, pp. 143–71.

1981 claim that human rights have been understood and justified in Muslim countries all along. "Islam gave to mankind an ideal code of human rights fourteen centuries ago," they declare.[34]

What does seem characteristically modern, of course, and to have its vanguard in the West, is a discourse that emphasizes human rights over other sorts of values. Why has this phenomenon come about? Although the values protected and advanced by human rights have deep and global cultural roots, a discourse in which rights are prominently asserted and practices of rights are well developed is a late twentieth century phenomenon. A human rights discourse came to prominence earliest in North Europe and North America where modernizing trends—now referred to as globalization—were first perceived as threats to individuals. Thus, lawyer Thomas Franck argues that human rights are grounded not in any particular culture but in modern trans-cultural social, economic, and scientific developments. Franck says, "far from being deeply rooted in Western culture, [human rights] are actually the products of recent developments—industrialization, urbanization, the communications and information revolutions—that are replicable anywhere, even if they have not occurred everywhere at once."[35]

Although major transformations such as increased personal autonomy in religion, speech, and equal legal rights for the races and sexes have occurred at different rates in different areas of the globe, they were not caused by factors inherent within cultures. Instead, Franck argues, they were brought about "by changes occurring, at different rates, everywhere: universal education, industrialization, urbanization, the rise of the middle class, advances in transportation and communications, and the spread of new information technology."[36] These forces also include globalizing fiscal, commercial, cultural, and informational forces. "These changes were driven by scientific developments capable of affecting equally any society," Franck adds. "It is these trends, and not some historical or social determinant, that—almost as a byproduct—generated the move to global human rights."[37] Human rights are thus the consequences of modernizing and globalizing forces that are not culturally specific.[38]

Rights theorists often distinguish between "first generation," "second generation," and "third generation" rights. The first generation corresponds roughly to the human rights in the ICCPR, the second corresponds to the human rights in the ICSER, and the third refers largely to the most recent

---

[34]Quoted by Jay Drydyk, "Globalization and Human Rights," p. 31.
[35]"Are Human Rights Universal?," p. 198.
[36]*Ibid.*, p. 200.
[37]*Ibid.*
[38]Franck points to certain developmental parallels between Western culture and other cultures. For instance, Franck claims that for most of its first two millennia, Western Christianity maintained most of the same prohibitions against religious freedom as does fundamentalist Islam today.

human rights presently being recognized in multiparty declarations and international covenants, especially the rights of "self-determination" and "self-development." These distinctions are instructive, for they identify (very roughly) the major advocates of the three different kinds of human rights. Although the liberal democracies of Europe and the North Atlantic were major champions of the first generation, members of this cohort (especially the United States) did not give much support to human rights of the second generation. Socialist states, social democracies in Europe, and an increasing number of state parties in the Southern hemisphere were major champions for rights in the second group. It is not surprising that major champions of third generation rights have been the newest UN members from Asia, Africa, and Latin America, and the South Pacific. This development supports the claims of Franck and others that discourse about rights gained prominence with the advance of modernizing forces. Moreover, various critics of human rights in the United States and the countries of Western Europe recognize, at least implicitly, the irrelevance of the *historical* origins of human rights. Libertarians criticize second and third generation rights even though these rights were inspired by the concept of equal liberty that had its origins in the West. Other conservative and communitarian critics in the United States and Western Europe even believe that overemphasis of first generation rights endangers other important values.[39]

It is time to pause and take stock. We began to consider the incommensurability claim by assessing the view that human rights are basically Eurocentric and Western concepts. A contrary view can now be seen to be more reasonable. This is the view that, despite some antecedents and precedents in Western cultures, human rights concepts are modern, having been formed out of the consensus surrounding the development of the UDHR and other major human rights instruments. The historical *origin* of these concepts and values is not really significant; rather, what is important is the international *consensus* over them. And even if this international consensus is characterized as some super multinational culture, we have as yet no reason for believing that the concepts and values originating in that super multicultural setting cannot be integrated into more particular, insular cultures in which they at first might seem alien. (It is the task of those asserting incommensurability to make this case.) Thus, the discussion so far has exposed the implausibility of asserting that human rights norms are incommensurable simply because their origination was in a cultural setting different from one's own.

The next issue is whether or not there is some *conceptual* reason for believing that values and concepts brought into play by human rights norms

---

[39]For a discussion of the range of criticisms and a lively response, see Michael Ignatieff, *Human Rights as Politics and Idolatry* (Princeton: Princeton University Press, 2001).

cannot be understood by, or cannot be employed by, persons inculcated with different cultural values. Pointing to the *absence* of human rights values and concepts within a cultural framework is not enough to show that such a conceptual difficulty exists. The questions to ask, then, are first, can values and concepts be so "culture-bound" that they become unintelligible and meaningless for others outside their culture of origin or meaning? Second, if there are any values or concepts that truly fail to be culturally transmissible, are concepts of human rights in this category?

Philosopher Kenneth Inada asserts, "It is incorrect to assume that the concept of human rights is readily identifiable in all societies in the world."[40] Inada asserts that Buddhism has an entirely different ontology, or view on the manifestation of human nature, than does the Western view supporting human rights. He characterizes this more specifically as a difference between an emphasis on "soft relationships" rather than on "hard relationships" in the West.[41] By drawing on notions of humans as basically separate, or atomistic, agents who act in mechanical, self-interested ways, hard relationships are based on self-assertion, rigid roles, and superficial egoistic interests. By contrast, in drawing on views of human nature as open, extensive, and flexible, soft relationships are characterized by patience, humility, tolerance, compassion, deference, and nonaction.[42]

Inada's analysis may well show why human rights notions, if they require relationships as "hard" as he claims, did not arise within Buddhist cultures. But this analysis cannot be interpreted as an argument that human rights concepts and values are incommensurable with Buddhist culture. There are two good reasons for reaching this conclusion. First, there is no reason why some "soft" aspects of a culture cannot be compatible with other, quite different cultural elements. Consider, for instance, that human rights are an important, perhaps even necessary, part of liberal democracies within which value pluralism flourishes. There is no incompatibility within liberal societies between human rights and "soft relationships" or ways of life based on these relationships. On the contrary, respect for human rights within liberal democracies makes it possible for people to *choose* to nurture "soft relationships."

Second, many predominately Buddhist societies have been penetrated by concepts and values that are certainly hard, or *harsh*, but not in the way intended by Inada. Some of these are genocide (in Cambodia or Kampuchea), brutal repression and exploitation (the Chinese occupation of

---

[40]Kenneth K. Inada, "A Buddhist Response to the Nature of Human Rights," in *Applied Ethics: A Multicultural Approach,* 3rd ed., Larry May, Shari Collins-Chobanian, and Kai Wong, eds. (Upper Saddle River, NJ: Prentice Hall 2002), p. 112.
[41]*Ibid.,* p. 115.
[42]*Ibid.,* pp. 116–21.

Tibet), autocratic rule and the suspension of fundamental liberties (in Myanmar or Burma), and economic exploitation of the needy and vulnerable (in Thailand). It is, of course, the view of rights activists that human rights are necessary resources against such terrible onslaughts. In some cases Buddhists are making valiant, even heroic, efforts to protect themselves from forms of repression and exploitation previously unknown in their societies. Tibetan resistance illustrates this effort, and Inada himself refers to the movement in Thailand that was led by the monk Buddhadāsa "to keep a steady course on traditional values."[43] In Sri Lanka, by contrast, the Buddhist Tamils have used elements of the Buddhist worldview to focus ethnic demands for secession and to promote violence, even against the traditional nonviolent ethos of Buddhism. The point is that in all of these cases, if Buddhists can come to understand and to resist, or to adapt, socialist, democratic, autocratic, or capitalists concepts and values, then there is no reason to suppose that this effort cannot be done with human rights as well. Again, the absence of human rights norms as salient features of the culture provides no reason for supposing that they cannot become fixtures within such cultures.

Indian philosopher Raimundo Pannikar argues that no value is transcultural, since it must originate in one culture.[44] Certainly, insofar as values and concepts are conceptually distinct (that is, that distinctions mark real differences), they must have arisen somewhere. But this perception does not support the view that they cannot be absorbed by other cultures—that they must remain incommensurable. Canadian philosopher Charles Taylor believes that there can be an "overlapping consensus" through which different peoples and different cultures reach agreement on human rights.[45] Sudanese lawyer Abdullahi Ahmed An-Na'im argues that even for traditional Islamic cultures, whose traditions do not contain human rights discourses, it is possible to reinterpret key parts of customary and religious laws to make human rights cognizant with indigenous traditions. Indeed, An-Na'im believes that modern human rights concepts and values can be given "cultural legitimacy" through correct reinterpretations of the cultural traditions of societies in which they are not now accepted.[46] Even Pannikar believes that concepts and values can become cross-cultural when they become what

---

[43]*Ibid.*, p. 117. Further examples of peaceful Buddhist social activism—much of it seeking to extend protection of human rights—can be found in David W. Chappell, ed., *Buddhist Peacework: Creating Cultures of Peace* (Somerville, MA: Wisdom Publications, 1999).

[44]Raimundo Pannikar, "Is the Notion of Human Rights a Western Concept?," in *International Human Rights in Context*, pp. 383–9.

[45]Charles Taylor, "Conditions of an Unforced Consensus on Human Rights," in *The East Asian Challenge for Human Rights*, pp. 124–44.

[46]Abdullah Ahmed An-Na'im, "Human Rights in the Muslim World," *International Human Rights in Context*, pp. 389–97.

Pannikar calls *homeomorphic equivalents*. Pannikar points out that the words "Brahmin" and "God," although not equivalent in meaning, are homeomorphic equivalents because "They perform a certain type of respectively corresponding function in the two different traditions where these words are alive . . ."[47] To illustrate further, Mahatma Gandhi claimed that he had been influenced by each of the world's great religions. Consequently, when Gandhi wrote about "God" in referring to his conscience, or "the still small voice within," he was confident that readers, whether they were Hindus, Buddhists, Christians, Muslims, Jews, or Jains, would understand him with equal clarity.

Pannikar's notion of homemorphic equivalents should help us see that cross-cultural understanding cannot be measured by the presence or absence of a certain vocabulary, terminology, or discourse. Key elements of a shared concept of human rights are the recognition that some types of actions and unmet needs are threats to safety and subsistence, the acknowledgment that humans ought not to be subjected to such threats, and agreement that others are responsible to afford some protection. In referring to basic threats to human agency, philosopher Jay Drydyk notes, "However human rights language may be used, it must refer to the presence, absence, or violation of social protection against standard threats exemplifying some type of danger to humans."[48] Drydyk adds the following:

> These dangers will be recognized differently, with different language, and under different descriptions, in different cultural contexts. Protections against them will also be justified differently. But as long as this kind of protection can be described within a culture, no matter how it is conceived or described, then we cannot say . . . that the concept of human rights is foreign to this culture."[49]

It is of course true that some societies may choose to protect some human rights but not others, or that the priority they assign to certain rights may differ greatly from the priority assigned by other groups. As we shall see in considering the *trade-off argument* in the next section, some governments and commentators believe even that the realization of some rights requires, at least temporarily, suppressing other rights. Adamantia Pollis and Peter Schwab claim that human rights are meaningless in most of the world.[50] Insofar as they may be advancing the incommensurability claim,

---

[47]"Is the Notion of Human Rights a Western Concept?," p. 384.
[48]"Globalization and Human Rights," p. 33.
[49]*Ibid.*
[50]Adamantia Pollis and Peter Schwab, "Human Rights: A Western Construct with Limited Applicability," in *Cultural and Ideological Perspectives*, Adamantia Pollis and Peter Schwab, eds. (New York: Praeger Publishers, 1979), pp. 1–15.

they are confusing the *significance* that persons assign to certain conceptions of human rights with those *conceptions* in and of themselves. They should be understood as objecting to ways that human rights can be construed in biased ways to favor individualism over communalism, for example, or private property over the group commons, or nuclear over extended families.[51]

Persons of different cultures may understand very well the concepts involved in a right to property or a right to form a family. At the same time, they may disagree vehemently over whether or not these respective rights mean a right to form a nuclear family (in addition to an extended family) or a right to the use of communal property (instead of private property). We must remind ourselves that rights are no more determinate in meaning, no less susceptible to varying interpretations and disputes, among individuals and groups, than other moral and political concepts—for example, "liberty," "justice," "authority," or "national interest." The fact that interpretations and meanings are contested does not show that different parties in a debate cannot share the same understanding of basic concepts, such as human rights. On the contrary, such concepts cannot be intelligibly contested, as they are, unless one could grasp others' meanings and unless agreement is (at least potentially) possible.

So far we have found that those who have advanced the incommensurability claim have been mistaken about what their arguments show. Nor does it seem that a plausible case can be made for accepting the incommensurability claim. It does not follow from a concept's having originated in a particular society, or from its being absent from a society (or from its being contested) that it cannot be cross-cultural. What would be required to make the case that a concept is *unintelligible* to a group of persons? If one wants to support this radical claim—and precisely this support is required for incommensurability—then one would have to bear the burden of showing that people on different parts of the globe are so different from one another that some are incapable of understanding how others think. It will not do to say that the language they speak has no words for human rights or that their practices are unlike those of the "civilized" (for example, that they were once headhunters such as the Yanomamo). Nor will it do to say that they cannot understand our concepts unless they understand our social practices, or "forms of life." This may all be true, but it refers to *contingent* features of human life that can be changed.

No, an argument for incommensurability must maintain some version of *cultural* or *social determinism.* Moreover, the thesis would have to maintain that once a group had acculturated a person, no change in his or her beliefs or values could result from contact with persons of a different culture who believed in human rights. But is it plausible to accept a determinism so com-

---

[51]Jay Drydyk commenting on the view of Pollis and Schwab, "Globalization and Human Rights," p. 34.

plete that it would have to override all possible biological and psychological similarities among persons, including intelligence, perception, empathy, curiosity, creativeness, and imagination? Is it plausible to accept a view that is not supported on empirical grounds? Indeed, it is ironic that some exceptionalists have wanted to employ the incommensurability claim as a way of defending their own native cultures from the "encroachments" of a modern human rights regime. The irony lies in the fact that theses spokespersons for exceptionalism cannot intelligibly claim that human rights concepts and norms are incommensurable with the concepts and values of their own cultures, unless they can also *know* what human rights concepts mean and what the norms require.

Some people delight in pointing out that we cannot really *know* that the Yanomamo tribespeople have the same understanding of human rights as we do no matter how similar our discourse or our practices. Insofar as acquiring this knowledge would require access to mental events that are not (at least not now) available for inspection, we have to agree. But this situation is not really different from the confidence we have that other drivers (leaving aside the small population of those who are colorblind) experience the colored lights of traffic signals in the *same way* as we do. The experience of color is subjective and therefore possibly different for each of us. But what is important is that experiences of green and red occupy relatively the same "logical spaces" in other drivers' thoughts or habitual behaviors. This is not unlike the way in which concepts of human rights can become homeomorphically equivalent cross-culturally. Some groups may not have the concept, just as some persons in societies in which automobiles are right now becoming indispensable means of transportation may not understand the meaning of traffic lights. But this condition does not mean that human rights cannot become a viable concept for them.

We have now concluded our responses to charges that universalism is impossible either because it involves logical inconsistency or because it is conceptually incoherent. In the next section, we proceed to consider exceptionalist objections that are based on views that human rights norms should not be applied universally. Although these critics may be understood as conceding the possibility of universalism, for various reasons they maintain that a specific state, society, or culture (usually their own) constitutes an exception. It is an exception in the sense that we ought not to expect them to observe international human rights norms, or, more frequently, that we ought to accept their disregard of the human rights these states, societies or groups regard as unimportant.

Before proceeding, however, it must be emphasized that cultural diversity and the difference between human rights norms and locally preferred values and practices is a subject requiring careful attention. Persons who seriously defend values that they regard as important deserve our respect, not our ridicule. Likewise, the problem of integrating human rights norms and applying them within an indigenous culture must be approached with sensitivity and diplomacy. These are issues that Section 4 touches on briefly and that are addressed at length in Chapter 3. As will be seen in these discussions, a sensitive and an intelligent application of human rights norms is compatible with the integrity of morally defensible traditions and particular values.

3. Should Human Rights Norms Apply Universally?

If human rights norms are conceded to be universal, and yet one is still opposed to their application, then—provided that the opposition is rational—this must be the case because one discounts their importance. After all, many universals have very little significance.[52] And several critical claims might be made, as represented by the next four positions. It can be said that human rights norms are thinly disguised tools of imperialist powers, the *imperialism charge,* or that they are destructive of more important traditional values and ways of life, the *causal complaint.* In addition, it might be charged that human rights norms are simply irrelevant to a particular culture, the *irrelevancy criticism,* or that some can be set aside by more important considerations—*trade-off arguments.*

We turn first in this section to an assessment of the imperialism charge. Are universal human rights norms means by which powerful and wealthy states seek to extend their political power? Some exceptionalists aver that the international human rights regime represents a continuation of the efforts of powerful states in the North Atlantic and western hemisphere to exert political domination, or hegemony, over the rest of the world. Nikhil Aziz explicitly criticizes human rights as a means of Western control and domination:

> Human rights have become another weapon in the arsenal of western countries in their efforts to bring recalcitrant Third World nations to heel in their "New World Order." Western nations are increasingly using the very narrow interpretation of human rights as a yardstick with which to judge Third World governments.[53]

Another critic who maintains this view is Malaysian social activist Chandra Muzaffar.[54] In Muzaffer's eyes, enthusiasm for human rights on

---

[52]This observation is true of abstruse mathematical formulas, and even of norms, such as the near universal norm that one should drive on the right side of the road.

[53]Nikhil Aziz, "The Human Rights Debate in an Era of Globalization: Hegemony of Discourse," in *Debating Human Rights: Critical Essays from the United States and Asia,* Peter Ness, ed. (London: Routledge Publishers, 1999), p. 39.

[54]Chandra Muzaffar, "From Human Rights to Human Dignity," in *Debating Human Rights,* pp. 25–31.

the part of Westerners is belied by extensive deterioration of the family and the community in the West as well as a general spiritual degeneration:

> The dominant West's violations of human rights in the non-Western world, coupled with its inability to uphold some of the fundamental rights of its own citizens, has raised some important questions about the very nature and character of Western human rights . . .[55]

In response, we should note two interesting points about the imperialism charge when it is lodged against the states that promote rights discourse. First, Muzaffer seems to believe that moral decay and spiritual degeneration in the West, especially in America, are proof that the real motivation to "push" human rights norms is to advance its own interests. But this charge is beside the point. It is analogous to the *ad hominem* fallacy; it does not follow from motives to profit by advancing a human rights agenda, if this is indeed the case, that the human rights on that agenda are bogus. It speaks, on the contrary, to the unseemliness of the profiteers and to the need of others to remember to draw some careful distinctions. Second, what should we say about the complaints made by many states and groups about rights abuses in the United States, including the complaints of Muzaffer's own government? Are these countries behaving in an imperialistic way?

The United States has made its own exceptionalist arguments, including its own versions of the irrelevancy *claim,* sometimes on the grounds that rights already protected by the U.S. Constitution "go beyond the protections of international treaties." It makes these arguments to exempt itself from living up to certain international human rights norms. As noted earlier in this chapter, this is the point of the United States's reservation to the ICCPR regarding capital punishment of minors.[56] Self-serving national interests in avoiding national responsibilities on rights to adequate housing and rights to adequate food seem to explain the failure of the United States to ratify the ICESCR.[57]

Other state parties signing human rights covenants can and do criticize the United States for its shortfalls in observing international human rights norms, regarding both U.S. domestic and U.S. foreign policy. They object to the imposition of capital punishment on minors and to an inadequate safety net in the United States against poverty, illness, and homelessness. The Reagan administration was widely criticized for flouting the decision of the International Court of Justice regarding the illegality of the mining of the harbors of Nicaragua in its support of the U.S.-sponsored Contras'

---

[55]*Ibid.,* p. 28.

[56]*International Human Rights in Context,* pp. 1029–48.

[57]The United States strongly opposed all references to the right to adequate housing and the right to food. Since the Covenant was signed by President Carter and sent to the Senate, which took no action, no other presidential administration has presented it to Congress. See "Comment on Governmental Ambivalence," in *International Human Rights in Context,* pp. 249–51.

war against the Sandanistas. Examples of this kind can be multiplied. The point here is that it would be odd to suggest that, in reproaching the United States for failing to live up to human rights standards, these states attempt to impose their will on the United States.

To be sure, citizens of many countries may still be smarting from the after effects of colonial legacies. They may therefore have grounds for suspicion when demands to observe human rights norms are made by former colonial powers, especially if strings seem to be attached. For the most part, however, and except for gross violations of the most basic rights, for example, genocide and "ethnic cleansing," the issue is one of moral suasion, not coercion. Some states may use pressure to coerce another state to improve its human rights record, for instance, by withholding "most favored nation" (MFN) trading status or membership in the World Bank (WB) or International Monetary Fund (IMF). And certainly some states may benefit in some way from another's compliance with human rights norms. (Sadly, it is much more common for states to compromise on observance of human rights norms when doing so is perceived to be to their advantage, as states did in disregarding human rights in trying to take advantage of China's burgeoning economy.)

It remains an open question, of course, whether and when coercive measures might be justified to protect human rights. But note that even when the motives for urging or coercing compliance are self-interested or unjustified, such morally unworthy motives must be distinguished from the moral requirements for observing human rights norms. In other words, the *imperialism charge* confuses two different issues and therefore does not constitute a good challenge to universalism. It confuses concern with the *validity* of universal human rights norms with questions about the *means* and *motives* occasionally used to advance the international human rights regime. The latter are concerns with the ways that state parties may abuse discourse over human rights and human rights instruments to advance their own interests. They do not establish a defect in universal human rights, however. To see this, we need to ask such critics, "What would be your objections to international human rights if the pressures for observance came not from the North and West but from 'Third World' states that are politically weaker and that have no prospects of becoming hegemons?" Since objecting parties could not fear imperialism from these states, this exercise shows that any remaining objections to the international human rights regime, if they are genuine, must be based on other reasons altogether, that is, on the causal claim, the irrelevancy criticism, or the trade-off argument.

The fourth of the initial charges against universalism—the *causal claim*—maintains that some human rights norms are destructive of values indigenous to the cultures or groups onto which critics say the "foreign" values are imposed. Pannikar uses the colorful analogy of a Trojan horse for the effects of international human rights norms. In his view, once members of a traditional society have adopted the apparent gift from the West, they will find that human rights involve assumptions and implications that undermine the mores and ways of life of traditional cultures.

Pannikar and other critics do not regard human rights norms as destructive in and of themselves. Indeed, it is hardly plausible that they could do so, since human rights, as certain kinds of moral resources (see Chapter 1), have no *effects* unless people make claims, fulfill obligations, and develop schemes, or practices, by which basic goods are protected or provided. Hence, critics focus on the "assumptions and implications" of human rights norms. Most often, critics claim that human rights norms promote personal autonomy, and self-interested individualism that is destructive of social responsibility, duties, and communal loyalties.[58] These ill effects are often associated with the spread of market economies (capitalism) and other features of modernity, industrialism, and urbanization, as well as the "homogenization" of a global culture in which blue jeans, rock and rap, and McDonald's have become prominent symbols.

Again, it is important to separate *attitudes* from empirical issues. There may be dislike for human rights norms because of "guilt by association" with other disparaged changes. Disliked features of modernity and globalization are highly variable, however. There is much less opposition to modern forms of communication, media, and transportation, (such as the TV, the internet and the jet airplane) which have probably had a far greater effect on changing traditions than have human rights norms. It should be clear that critics assume a *causal* relationship between encroaching rights practices and other destabilizing forces; in their view, it is the adoption of human rights norms that *leads to* the destruction of traditional culture.

Does the spread of practices centering on human rights norms cause, or lead to, the disintegration of traditional cultures? In response it must be said that it is simply false that all of the beliefs and values associated with human rights conflict with traditional views, despite critics' tendencies to refer to stark and absolute oppositions. For instance, the complaint that human rights emphasizes individualism and entitlements at the cost of duties to one's community ignores the fact that human rights impose correlative obligations (Chapter 1) and that fulfilling these obligations will limit the freedom of others.

---

[58]Claude Ake says of human rights in the African context, "we do not allow that the individual has any claims that may override that of the society," "The African Context of Human Rights," in *Applied Ethics: A Multicultural Approach*, pp. 94–5. Jomo Kenyatta states that, among the Gikuyu, "An individualist is looked upon with suspicion and is given a nickname of *mwebongia*, one who works only for himself and is likely to end up a wizard." "Facing Mount Kenya: The Tribal Life of the Gikuyu," in *International Human Rights in Context*, p. 347. See also Chandra Muzaffar, "From Human Rights to Human Dignity," pp. 28–9.

Citizens of states that take seriously the social and economic rights of persons recognize that they must bear considerable obligations—usually in the form of high taxation—to ensure that all receive a decent and equal response to their needs. Citizens of Denmark, Sweden, the Netherlands, and Norway (for instance) consent not to dispose freely of a significant portion of their income, in striking contrast to the preference of the majority of citizens of the United States. The unwillingness of Americans to shoulder these obligations explains, in part, the greater popularity of civil and political liberties in the United States and the unwillingness of Congress to ratify the ICESCR.

The point of this brief discussion is to show that an increase in respect for human rights does not necessarily entail a diminution of responsibility and duty. It is possible, however, that those who hold the contrary view worry that human rights norms will upset the structures of duty from which they benefit. For example, high caste Hindus in India benefit from the rigidity of the caste system in India and thus feel threatened by the interests of the downtrodden Dalits or "Untouchables" in improving their lot. Likewise, men in many traditional societies feel threatened by changes of patterns of recognized obligations that would end their patriarchy and domination of women, just as many religious leaders are concerned that individual choice may lessen conformity and the clerics' control over social life.

The situation is far more complex than the critics perceive it to be, however. It appears that at least some features of modernity have proved adaptable to, even beneficial for, traditional cultures. Consider, for example, the recent combination of rock and rap music and fundamental Christianity in the United States, or the shrewd use by traditional Muslim *imams,* or religious leaders, of modern mass media—leading, in the view of Muslim feminist Fatima Mernissi, to "a monstrosity: the all powerful, unchallengeable media imam."[59]

Still, it cannot be denied that globalization, capitalism, urbanization, and increased state power have broken down social and cultural structures that permitted the persistence of more traditional, communal ways.[60] So, returning to our question, is there evidence of a *causal* connection between the advance of human rights norms and the decline of traditional cultures? It seems far more probable that rather than a causal connection, there is a *cor-*

---

[59]Fatima Mernissi, *Islam and Democracy: Fear of the Modern World,* trans. Mary Jo Lakeland, rev. ed. (Cambridge, MA: Perseus Publishers, 2002), p. 23. Mernissi's point is that the authority of the *imam* developed in a society in which the religious authority's interpretations of holy texts took place in a face-to-face community of peers. An *imam* could have an influence on the masses only by first gaining the consent of these peers. With modern mass media, however, an *imam* such as Khomeini could directly reach a mass audience, thereby weakening the authority of intermediaries. Thus, through modern media the *imam* is able to assume an autocratic power.

[60]Jack Donnelly, "Human Rights and Asian Values: A Defense of 'Western' Universalism," in *The East Asian Challenge for Human Rights,* pp. 60–87, esp. p. 69.

relation, or *coincidence,* between the advance of rights practices and the decline of traditional cultures. Since the international human rights movement itself emerged in the late twentieth century, it is very plausible that both the human rights movement and the transformation of traditional societies are consequences of the same forces. In fact, given the rapid increases in state power, urbanization, industrialization, capitalism, and globalization, it is hardly surprising that there is a correlation between the international human rights movement and the decline of traditional, communal forms of life.

Exceptionalists oversimplify the complexities of global changes. They seem to believe that human rights norms are so inextricably combined with the degrading trends of modernity and globalization that, if only they can staunch the spread of human rights norms, they will be able to preserve cultural values and practices.[61] But by failing to conceive of how human rights norms may be separable from other aspects of modernity, exceptionalists fail to consider that human rights norms might actually *bolster* aspects of traditional cultures that are worth preserving.

Political scientist Rhonda Howard observes that because they are based on ascribed and face-to-face relations in small pastoral or agricultural groups, communally oriented systems of social justice cannot be transferred to modern, large-scale states.[62] Her point, however, is that the decline of communal systems of justice in Africa has resulted from the increasing domination of African societies by states possessing a monopoly of power and an interest in centralizing their authority. Jack Donnelly questions the assumption of the continuing relevance of traditional practices in modern conditions.[63] Should one transfer the traditional tribal or communal values of leadership to an authoritarian leader who is backed by modern military forces? Can traditional local autonomy exist in the village in the face of the commercial penetration of the countryside and the economic and political integration in a modern nation-state? Can practices developed for rural societies with little social mobility or demographic change protect persons from exploitative commercial practices in modern urban life?[64] Traditional cultures and ways of life often do not prepare their members to protect themselves from forms of power and exploitation introduced in modern societies.

The seriousness of these issues is illustrated by the expanding sex industry in Bangkok, Thailand. Because of Bangkok's increasing popularity as a tourist destination and business center and because of the government's choice to "look the other way" in order to promote business, the flesh trade

---

[61]It is an open question whether some traditional beliefs and practices ought to be preserved. We return to this issue later.

[62]Rhoda E. Howard, *Human Rights and the Search for Community* (Boulder, CO: Westview Press, 1995), p. 90.

[63]"Human Rights and Asian Values: A Defense of 'Western' Universalism," pp. 60–87.

[64]*Ibid.,* p. 81.

has grown greatly despite the fact that it involves a systematic violation of human rights. As Thai philosopher Suwanna Satha-Anand says, "the right to freedom from slavery and servitude, the right to work and free choice of employment, the right to just remuneration ensuring an existence worthy of human dignity, and the right to a standard of living adequate for health and well-being are being violated on a regular basis."[65] Already by the early 1980s, prostitution counted for the largest percentage of women employed in any occupation in Thailand outside of farm work.[66]

In examining this phenomenon, Satha-Anand notes that because poverty in the provinces of Thailand is so much more severe than it is in Bangkok, young women and children are lured to Bangkok in great numbers to become prostitutes. Satha-Anand points out that although Thai women are heavily burdened with their families' financial responsibilities, life in the provincial villages offers inadequate economic and social support for women.[67] More serious, however, is the lack in the provinces of cultural protection in the form of models of virtue for women or as principles upholding the dignity of women.[68] In Satha-Anand's view, in predominantly Buddhist Thailand, feminist reinterpretations of key Buddhist passages would help to change the cultural conditions that contribute to the pervasive problem of female prostitution.

Similar problems arose regarding the exploitation of women and children working in Nike factories in India, and regarding working conditions comparable to slave labor in China that result in products imported for sale in the United States, such as blue jeans made for the Gap. Consider that within some forms of African communalism, the dignity of the person was insured by membership within the group, whether family, lineage, or tribe. One could feel secure of one's status as long as he or she fulfilled a prescribed role. When security within the group can no longer be assured, however, then individuals need the protection of human rights against the standard threats associated with arbitrary uses of power. This phenomenon was illustrated dramatically in Somalia by the ceaseless fighting among warlords; the resulting collapse of social order; widespread starvation and disease; and attacks on humanitarian NGOs, making it impossible for them to deliver relief. Ultimately, the UN approved forceful humanitarian intervention into Somalia, and the United States first undertook this task (not with much success) in 1992, to be followed by the continuing efforts of the UN.

Numerous examples such as these support the claims of Donnelly and Howard that because traditional, communal societies are increasingly in decline, human rights norms are now needed to protect fundamental needs

---

[65]Suwanna Satha-Anand, "Looking to Buddhism to Turn Back Prostitution in Thailand," *The East Asian Challenge for Human Rights*, pp–193–211.

[66]*Ibid.*, p. 201.

[67]*Ibid.*, p. 200.

[68]*Ibid.*, pp. 204–11.

and human dignity that were formerly protected by traditional values and ways of life. Insofar as individuals, families, and societies in developing states face threats from modern market forces and centralized power that are the same as those within Western societies, they need the same protections provided by a robust human rights regime.

Moreover, although human rights norms are needed to protect persons formerly protected by traditional means, rights practices based on human rights norms also protect some *traditional* values and ways of life from disintegrating forces. Human rights are crucial in protecting minorities seeking to pursue their own ways of life from domination by central governments and majorities. This need is most evident in extreme cases in which humanitarian intervention is vindicated—as it was in Bosnia and Kosovo and as it would have been in Rwanda—to stop genocide, "ethnic cleansing," and forced migrations. It is also apparent in the protection of the freedom of religious or ethnic minorities to worship as they deem fit, to use a native language, or to teach their children their own customs and folkways. Protecting human rights can also promote other values of community; for instance, families and communities can be protected by promoting the right to have food, and by protecting individuals from arbitrary arrest, abuses of power, and torture, especially when the individuals protected are spokespersons for traditional cultures.

A good illustration of the way that human rights norms might protect traditional ways of life can be drawn from the international movement against the global trade in small firearms. The relatively low cost, portability, and worldwide availability of these arms has led to a dramatic increase in murder and terror around the world. At present, widespread opinion in the international community supports the view that human rights norms require a covenant restricting the international trade in small firearms. (The United States, which leads all other states in revenue from the sale of arms abroad, has not indicated a willingness to be a part to such a treaty.) The availability of small firearms also has had a devastating affect on traditional systems of authority among some African tribes. Whereas in the past, tribal members looked to revered elders to resolve disputes, with easy access to firearms today, hot-blooded young men have brushed aside the mediating skills of their elders. An unprecedented increase in the rate of murder has resulted from the efforts of teenage perpetrators to enforce their own "solutions."[69] Another disastrous consequence of the international trade in small arms is the way in which inexpensive and light firearms have accelerated the tendencies of rebel and guerrilla factions to recruit children as soldiers. Insurgents frequently attempt to assassinate the tribal elders and thereby to

---

[69]Karl Vick, "Small Arms' Global Reach Uproots Tribal Traditions," *Washington Post,* July 8, 2001, p. A19.

undermine belief in traditional authority, sometimes by requiring the youngest child-soldier to "execute" the tribal chieftain.[70]

The effects of modernization and globalization, which are usually thought by traditionalists to be destructive of traditional ways of life, may actually have some positive consequences for diversity. Studying the cases of Taiwan and Singapore, law professor Kevin Tang from Singapore argues that the effects of globalization, through greater prosperity, education, and international communications, have positive effects on the advancement of civil and political rights.[71] Exercises of the latter are indispensable to the health of democracy that, in turn, helps to ensure the freedom of people to select others with whom they wish to share their lives and form communities. A similar view is taken by Thomas Franck, who believes that, freed from unnecessary communal constraints, "individuals will not retreat into social anomie but, on the contrary, will freely choose multi-layered affinities and complex, variegated interpersonal loyalties that redefine community without the loss of social responsibility."[72] Instead, Franck claims, ties autonomously chosen and respect for human rights can strengthen traditional cultural ties:

> Modern human rights-based claims to individual autonomy arise primarily not out of opposition to community, but from the desires of modern persons to use intellectual and technological innovations to supplement their continued traditional ties with genetically and geographically based communities. Liberated from predetermined definitions of racial, religious, and national identities, people still tend to choose to belong to groups.[73]

Freedom of choice threatens states and traditional groups only insofar as they are no longer able, on their own, to respond to some of the most difficult global problems facing humanity: epidemics, trade flows, environmental degradation, or global warming.

Note that so far in considering the exceptionalists' charge that human rights norms are destructive of traditional cultures, we have been proceeding on the presumption that all and every traditional value or practice is worthy of preservation. But, of course, this presumption is highly dubious. Human rights norms do conflict with some historically sanctioned practices and values. For instance, human rights norms cannot be squared with the acts of stoning adulterers to death, chopping off the limbs of thieves or pickpockets,

---

[70]"Kalashnikov Kids," *The Economist,* July 10, 1999. Reprinted in *International Human Rights in Context,* pp. 533–6.

[71]Kevin Y. L. Tan, "Economic Development, Legal Reform, and Rights in Singapore and Taiwan," *The East Asian Challenge for Human Rights,* pp. 264–84.

[72]"Are Human Rights Universal?," p. 201.

[73]*Ibid.*

the beating of wives, the exposure of female infants, or the sale of children.[74] Thus, when human rights norms clash with traditional values and practices, it is always an open question whether the latter are *worth* preserving.

It is important to understand that charges of the destructiveness of human rights norms arise most frequently and shrilly in response to challenges to traditional family and domestic practice or to challenges to religious authorities or governing elites. In Kenya, for example, controversy centered around the first woman of the Masai tribe who went to court to stop her husband from beating her with a club. Physical beatings of wives and the view of wives as being property was widely accepted among the Masai.[75] In India, Shah Bano, a destitute and divorced Muslim woman, sued her former husband for support (alimony). Although she won her case on appeal, public outcry and disturbance led her to refuse payment and to renounce the judgment in her favor.[76]

A practice's pedigree as traditional, or long-standing, is not sufficient to justify its continuation. To believe that time justifies practice is to commit the *ad verecundiam*, or "to custom," fallacy. There are two inescapable questions: How is a decision to be made? Who is to make it? Since our concern is with what *ought* to be done, then the decision should be made as rationally as possible. Thus, the tradition is justifiable if it gives sufficient protection to the basic goods necessary for human agency. Of course, the tradition may do so in a way that gives expression to distinctive cultural values. And this possibility is what is most to be hoped for in a world rich with cultural plurality. The noncoerced consent of the people who will live with the practice must be an important part of this process.

The concept of "official culture" helps us understand how some practices that may seem to express the traditional values of a people may be relatively recent imports to serve the self-interests of a privileged class or power elite. For instance, the beating of children by schoolteachers is accepted without question as traditional in much of sub-Saharan Africa even when it results in serious harm. Yet corporeal punishment—justified as tradition— was a relatively late import from British colonialist educational practices.[77] Franck relates the case of Sandra Lovelace of the Maliseet Indians in New

---

[74]These abuses are but some of thousands reported on a regular basis by human rights organizations including Amnesty International USA, *www.alusa.org;* Human Rights Watch, *www.hrw.org;* and Madre: An International Women's Human Rights Organization, *madre@igc.org.*

[75]"Kenyan Tradition Confronted: A Beaten Wife Goes to Court," *New York Times,* October 31, 1997, p. A5. Reprinted in *International Human Rights in Context,* pp. 11–2.

[76]*Mohammed Shmen Khan v. Shah Bano Begum,* Supreme Court of India (1985), 2 Sup. Ct. Cases 556. Reprinted with "Comment on Aftermath of Shah Bano" in *International Human Rights in Context,* pp. 503–11.

[77]Human Rights Watch, "Spare the Child: Corporal Punishment in Kenyan Schools," *International Human Rights in Context,* pp. 524–6.

Brunswick who lost her right to live on tribal land when she "married out" of the tribe.[78] When her right to reoccupy her land was disregarded by her tribe and the Canadian government, Lovelace made an appeal to the ICCPR's Human Rights Committee. Lovelace claimed that the tribal law requiring forfeiture of her land was discriminatory because the Maliseet did not apply it to male members of the tribe. The Committee found in her favor and pressured the Canadian government to repeal the law.

For our purposes, the most important thing about the Lovelace case was what anthropological research revealed. Far from being a traditional requisite of tribal unity, research showed that discrimination against women by the Maliseet had been copied from male-dominated Victorian society. "As with much that passes for authentic custom, the rules turned out to have been imposed, quite recently, by those who stood to benefit."[79]

This outcome highlights the need for opportunities to exercise real choice among people who are aware of possible alternatives. Donnelly notes (wryly) that there is no evidence that Asians value protection from arbitrary government less than do Westerners or that they value less highly the opportunities for families and individuals to make important choices about their lives and futures.[80] Asian peoples may want to organize their social life around values and principles different from those that predominate in the West. But can they have good government without human rights? Donnelly notes that liberal democracy is the best way for Asian values to be protected: if Asians truly do value family over self, they will exercise their personal rights with the consequences for the family in mind.[81]

Rhoda Howard reports that for many peoples in Africa, "unequal allocation of responsibility and privilege according to age, gender, or social status is still a fundamental and valued way of ordering the world."[82] This view demands respect, because as Howard adds, "For such people, to assert their human rights as individuals would be unthinkable, as to do so would be to undercut their dignity as group members."[83] Conceptions of human dignity also are closely connected with a certain structure of relationships. "African communalism stresses the dignity of membership and fulfillment of one's prescribed roles in a group (whether family, lineage, or tribe). This is how they see their personal relationships to society."[84]

Because group membership so completely determined personal identity, it may have seemed inconceivable that individuals needed protection against the group. Groups themselves undergo changes, however: some-

---

[78]"Are Human Rights Universal?," pp. 197–8.
[79]*Ibid.*
[80]"Human Rights and Asian Values: A Defense of 'Western' Universalism," p. 76.
[81]*Ibid.*, p. 80.
[82]*Human Rights and the Search for Community*, p. 90.
[83]*Ibid.*
[84]*Ibid.*

times in ways that diminish the lives and dignities of individuals within them, and sometimes because forces that threaten members in new ways penetrate the life of the group. When these changes occur, individuals must be allowed to take responsibility for their own choices, as they must when they come to believe that some values within their traditions must be abandoned. In such cases human rights practices, by restoring to persons greater control over their own lives, will help them make new affiliations, join alternative groups or communities, or otherwise help them reverse the deterioration of communities that they truly value.

Howard and Donnelly argue even that persons should have a guaranteed right to "opt out" of traditional practices.[85] In many cases opting out may require nothing more than a right to abstain from participating in a cultural practice. And one major advantage of an "opt out provision" is that in the absence of strong wishes to take advantage of the provision, it creates a presumption in favor of the cultural norms or practices according to which human rights norms are said to be irrelevant. It is a measure, however imperfect, of consent. But because it implicitly recognizes freedom of individuals to choose to "opt out," such provision will be unacceptable to those who maintain autocratic or authoritarian "traditional" systems.

The *irrelevancy criticism,* to which we now turn, can be characterized bluntly as maintaining the following position: "We do not need human rights; our laws, courts, values and traditions do a better job of protecting fundamental interests and human dignity." In some cases, human rights norms may be regarded as irrelevant because of the claimed superiority of national or cultural practices. In other cases, it may be conceded that human rights norms have value but that they are not needed and that they may be set aside for more pressing interests, such as "national interest."

It is helpful to recall the earlier discussion of the incommensurability claim. There we noted that although a culture or society may lack a discourse of human rights, it did not follow for that reason alone that human rights were disregarded. What is essential is the recognition of certain standard threats to human survival and well-being, the fact that these human threats pose an affront to human dignity, and the obligation of a group or society to respond appropriately. In addition, not all social groups recognize the same relevant priorities among rights or the various ways societies might organize in response to standard threats. Some societies have conceptions of human rights or concepts homoeomorphically equivalent with human rights that are "incomplete."[86] They fail to recognize a whole category of rights, such as the rights of women or the rights of children.

---

[85]Rhoda E. Howard, "Women's Rights in English-Speaking Sub-Saharan Africa," in *Human Rights and Development in Africa,* Claude E. Welch and Ronald I. Meltzer, eds. (Albany, NY: State University of New York Press, 1984), pp. 66–8; *Universal Human Rights in Theory and Practice,* p. 124.

[86]"Globalization and Human Rights," p. 32.

Appreciating these complexities helps us see that some claims about the irrelevancy of human rights are really claims about the nonrecognition or the insignificance of certain types, or categories, of rights. This perception is illustrated by some controversies within Muslim societies. Some Muslim leaders who claim that international human rights are irrelevant are actually opposed to the inclusion of some protections among human rights. Consequently delegates of Muslim countries meeting in Cairo could simultaneously adopt the Universal Islamic Declaration of Human Rights and yet omit from the document women's and children's rights recognized in the Convention on The Elimination of All Forms of Discrimination Against Women (CEDAW) and the Convention on the Rights of the Child (CRC).

The preceding comments reflect the fact that charges of irrelevancy do not really challenge the universality of human rights norms. Rather, they challenge the view that some putative rights ought to be included among human rights. These critics want to adopt a pick-and-choose approach rather than the "holism" on which international human rights activists insist. Often conflicts of this kind are best approached by processes of "cultural diplomacy, or cross-cultural negotiation," discussed at length in Chapter 3.

Claims about the irrelevancy of human rights are themselves subject to challenge, however. We first need to consider whether those criticizing human rights have the authority to represent the persons on whose behalf they claim to speak. It is often assumed that leaders who are selected by time-honored traditional means or who are put into office through populist movements have a better understanding of the communal good and are therefore the proper spokespersons for their societies. On the contrary, however, sometimes they do not genuinely and legitimately represent those on whose behalf their claims are made.[87] In general, the more autocratic or authoritarian the spokesperson, the more diverse the society or group, or the greater the apparent resistance or suffering of groups within the regime, then the more dubious is the claim that the view expressed was truly representative. The Taliban of Afghanistan were notorious for their claim to speak on behalf of the Afghan people even though they silenced half of their population.

As noted already, Donnelly, Franck, and Howard are wary of the ways that autocratic leaders and an elite attempt to maintain their power or to sanction oppressive practices by arguing that human rights are irrelevant for their societies. In her study of Islam and human rights, Ann Elizabeth Mayer points to the difficulty of distinguishing between "official culture" and authentic manifestations of indigenous and traditional culture.[88] She notes, "the most serious and pervasive human rights problems afflicting the

---

[87]Franck, p. 196.
[88]*Islam and Human Rights: Tradition and Politics*, p. 37.

Middle East are . . . policies and laws that are designed by elites for implementation by modern state systems at the expense of the rights and freedoms of individuals."[89] Norani Othman, of the Sisters of Islam in Malaysia, refers to the "monopoly of the clergy" and the need to reclaim "the right of the community to be the living frame of interpretation for their own religion and its normative regime."[90] An-Na'im makes the important point that "people in nations whose elites reject human rights have never had an opportunity to develop consensus by re-examining their cultural traditions in terms of universal and international human rights."[91] Even prominent voices in non-Western societies reject the claims of exceptionalists who supposedly speak for their regions of the world. Sri Lanka's president, Chandrika Kumarantunga, dismisses talk about "a conflict of values" as "an excuse that can be used to cover a multitude of sins."[92] Radhika Coomaraswami, the UN special rapporteur on violence against women, draws attention to the question whether those who are said to be "enjoying their cultural attributes are doing so voluntarily."[93]

It is not surprising that the evidence suggests, over and over again, that when people are free to choose, they do not find human rights to be irrelevant. One variation of the irrelevancy criticism is pressed by powerful states that claim to act with popular approval. Perhaps the most egregious example is the United States itself. The United States's record on the ratification of international human rights instruments is among the worst in the world. One major reason for this is the greater popularity in the United States of first generation, or civil and political rights, over second generation, or economic and social rights.[94] In addition, in the mind of many voters, a public responsibility to protect the social and economic rights of all Americans, such as rights to work and to receive adequate housing and food, would require undesirable restrictions of freedom in the form of increased taxes and government regulations. Of course, the voices of those who are marginalized in America, such as the homeless and chronically unemployed, do not have as much impact in our electoral system as do the wealthy and those relatively well-off.

---

[89]*Ibid.*, p. 17.

[90]Norani Othman, "Human Rights as Universal Concepts in Islam," High Commissioner's Seminar on *Enriching the Universality of Human Rights: Islamic Perspectives on the UDHR*" (New York: UNESCO, n.d.), p. 374.

[91]Abdullahi Ahmed An-Na'im, "Islam, Islamic Law, and the Dilemma of Cultural Legitimacy for Universal Human Rights," in *Applied Ethics: A Multicultural Approach*, pp. 83–93.

[92]Quoted in "Are Human Rights Universal?," p. 197.

[93]Quoted in "Are Human Rights Universal?," p. 198.

[94]The United States has been a key dissenter on ICESCR and UN-sponsored world conferences in 1996 on human settlement (Istanbul) and food (Rome). See *International Human Rights in Context*, p. 251.

The human rights of individuals should not be overridden by the will of a majority, let alone by the will of powerful or wealthy minorities (see Chapter 1). So, what possible arguments can be made to justify the status quo in America? It is not surprising that such arguments are one or another version of the irrelevancy criticism. In explaining the objections of Senator Jesse Helmes (R-N.C.), until recently the chair of the Senate Committee on Foreign Relations, to the Convention on the Rights of the Child (CRC), a spokesperson said, "There is only one court that matters here. That's the U.S. Supreme Court. There's only one law that applies here. That's the U.S. Constitution."[95] At the 1979 Senate hearings on the ICCPR, Phyllis Schlafly, a nationally recognized antifeminist, testified against ratification by proclaiming, "the treaties do not give Americans any rights whatsoever. They do not add a miniscule of benefit to the marvelous human rights proclaimed by the Declaration of Independence, guaranteed by the U.S. Constitution, and extended by our Federal and State laws."[96]

The irrelevancy criticism arises frequently in connection with a state's preferences in pursuing its own "national interests." The meaning of "national interest" is subject to volumes of debate into which we cannot enter here. Suffice it to say that a nation-state's interests can be whatever its leaders or citizens choose as important for its foreign policy. So, for example, former president Jimmy Carter attempted, largely unsuccessfully, to organize United States foreign policy around the protection of human rights. By contrast, with an equal lack of success, the administration of former president Ronald Reagan sometimes identified the national interest of the United States with the supporting of repressive dictators who would sign up as "friends" of the United States in its global struggle against communism. Regarding long-term benefits to Americans in respect to global stability, William Schulz, executive director of Amnesty International USA, makes the persuasive case that global policies to protect human rights are in the national interest of Americans.[97]

From the moral perspective advocated in this book, promoting the human rights of people abroad only because of the advantages to be gained for Americans smacks of immorality. If, for example, we are motivated to support the health of Mexican peasants only because they are less likely to infect U.S. citizens if they immigrate to the United States, then we treat them merely as the means to our ends. We fail to respect them as persons with inherent dignity or worth of their own. Yet this treatment occurs with great regularity whenever the government decides to abandon, suspend, or

---

[95]Quoted by William L. Schulz, *In Our Own Best Interest: How Defending Human Rights Benefits Us All* (Boston: Beacon Press, 2001).
[96]Quoted in *International Human Rights in Context*, p. 1037.
[97]*In Our Own Best Interest: How Defending Human Rights Benefits Us All.*

avoid a policy in protection of human rights just because it is not seen as promoting the economic or political benefits of the United States. In other words, what happens to these people, so the argument goes, is just *irrelevant* for us.[98]

Both China and the United States are among nation-states that egregiously invoke the irrelevancy claim when international human rights norms are perceived to go against their own "national interest." Despite its relatively poor record on civil and political rights, China seeks to improve its political and economic influence in international affairs. In its efforts to deflect international criticism and to avoid sanctions for its poor record on rights, China invokes the concept, traditional in international law, of *national sovereignty*. According to this concept, most, if not all, of what occurs within the geopolitical boundaries of a nation-state is a matter for its exclusive discretion. Thus, according to official spokespersons, international human rights norms are irrelevant when they would restrict the way that the Chinese government deals with its own citizens. This outlook explains why Chinese officials often assert that critics who decry the frequency of torture, imprisonment without trial, and lack of freedom of press and speech in China are trying to violate the country's national sovereignty.[99]

The difficulty with this position is that the extreme version of national sovereignty invoked by China to protect its interests is no longer recognized in international law. In fact, China itself is signatory to the majority of international covenants that have restricted and redefined what a government may permissibly do to its own citizens. These covenants and laws are now understood to circumscribe the sovereign authority of the state.

In contrast to China, the United States rarely resorts to cries that its national sovereignty has been infringed. The United States does not need to do so because it has ratified relatively few of the international human rights covenants. It thus seeks to protect a privileged position that matches its view of its vaunted power (but diminishing moral authority). This position was evident, for instance, in the decision of the United States not to support the International Court of Justice (a position shared only with Somalia). This decision was based on the grounds that the United States would not subject its military personnel to the same standards of moral responsibility required

---

[98]See Jack Donnelly, *International Human Rights,* 2nd ed. (Boulder, CO: Westview Press, 1998); Geoffrey Robertson, *Crimes Against Humanity: The Struggle for Global Justice* (New York: New Press, 1999); Nicholas J. Wheeler, "Enforcing Human Rights," in *International Human Rights in the 21st Century: Protecting the Rights of Groups,* Gene M. Lyons and James Mayall, eds. (Lanham, MD: Rowman & Littlefield, 2003), pp. 169–99.

[99]The White Paper on Human Rights, *Human Rights in China,* Information Office of the State Council (Beijing: Foreign Languages Press, 1991). See also Rosemary Foot, *Rights Beyond Borders: The Global Community and the Struggle Over Human Rights in China* (Oxford, UK: Oxford University Press, 2000), pp. 19, 121–2, 144, 186, 242, 257, 262–3.

of all other military personnel. In addition, in more recent years, the policy of the United States government seems to be to withdraw from international treaties, such as the Kyoto Accord that would reduce degradation of the environment (and hence protect the right to health), or to refuse to participate altogether. This general position is taken when the international accords advancing human rights are regarded as irrelevant to (narrowly defined) national interests. It should not be surprising, therefore, why millions of persons worldwide regard leaders of the United States as duplicitous when the latter charge foreign countries with human rights violations.

In conclusion, we can see that the irrelevancy criticism faces two major problems. First, claims about the irrelevancy of human rights never provide sufficient reasons for ignoring international human rights norms. In fact, as we have seen, such claims are often made when human rights norms are most needed and are therefore highly relevant. This is the case when the claim is made by self-serving autocrats seeking to maintain their power or the privileges of an elite. It is also the case when a government, whether or not it is representative of its people seeks to pursue policy objectives inconsistent with human rights. In these cases human rights norms are relevant precisely because they are at risk of being violated. Thus, the irrelevancy criticism is made to distract attention from exactly how relevant human rights norms really are. Second, *if* there is a legitimate basis for the claim that a human rights discourse is irrelevant, then this can be the case only because critical needs and fundamental freedoms are already well protected within a traditional society. Thus, we should point out that what is said to be irrelevant in such cases is best understood as foreign *discourse* about human rights, not the human rights themselves. We should be prepared to inquire whether, if the discourse and practice of rights were adopted, the conceptions of rights would be, in the terms used by Drydyk, neither *incomplete* nor *defective.*[100]

In some cases there may be grudging recognition of human rights norms, yet apologists for a government's actions, such as that of China, may say that these norms must be set aside for the greater good of society. In such cases an effort is made to defend the suppression of some human rights by arguing that repressive policies are necessary to promote other human rights. For instance, representatives of the Chinese government say that it must first promote the social and economic human rights of its billions of people; that doing so requires stability and control; and that these conditions would be destroyed by millions exercising their political and

---

[100]Conceptions of human rights are "incomplete" if they overlook certain protections that persons are due and they are "defective" if protections are limited to in-groups. See "Globalization and Human Rights," p. 32.

civil rights.[101] Because such arguments concede that human rights are relevant but maintain that some human rights must be suppressed for the realization of others, they are best understood as *trade-off* arguments. With this recognition, we advance to a consideration of the last of the major arguments that human rights norms ought not to apply universally.

Advocates of trade-offs among types of human rights (and these usually involve the categories of first generation for second generation or vice versa) take advantage of two facts about human rights norms. First, as we observed in response to ethical relativism, all human rights norms are defeasible, or derogable. Second, although international human rights norms form a consistent set, the norms often do conflict in particular applications. The difficulty with trade-off arguments, however, is that they attempt to take advantage of these two facts to support unjustified assumptions about the supposed *necessity* of trade-offs among human rights. There are three different ways in which these attempts are made. Each deserves to be examined in turn.

In the first place, trade-off arguments often assume falsely that there is a conflict between whole categories, or types, of rights.[102] Consider, for instance, conflicts that may arise between interests in protecting freedom of speech and the right to life. Plausible examples range from the prohibition against falsely giving an alarm by yelling "Fire!" in a crowded theater (which would put persons' safety at risk) to a case involving a court order preventing a newspaper from publishing a story identifying persons in a witness protection plan. Other real or hypothetical cases easily come to mind. What is novel about some trade-off arguments, however, are their efforts to characterize a whole category of human rights as defeasible in order to advance protection of another category. The government of China hopes that we will adopt its view that in China, defeasibility applies to the *whole range* of civil and political rights, as well as the rights of physical security (such as security against torture) virtually anywhere and at any time. The implausibility of this position is staggering. For even when the argument is made in good faith, it betrays a failure to understand the complex issues involved in applying human rights norms so as to minimize conflicts.

---

[101]Michael J. Sullivan, "Developmentalism and China's Human Rights Policy," in *Debating Human Rights,* pp. 120–43; Xiaoqun Xu, "Human Rights and the Discourse on Universality: A Chinese Historical Perspective," in *Negotiating Culture and Human Rights;* Lynda S. Bell, Andrew J. Nathan, and Ilan Peleg, eds. (New York: Columbia University Press, 2001), pp. 217–41.

[102]"It is necessary for a developing society to succeed *first* in economic development before it can attain the social and political freedoms found in the developed societies"; Kishore Mahbubani, "An Asian Perspective on Human Rights and Freedom of the Press," in *Debating Human Rights,* p. 92.

Advocates of human rights have always been aware that, because of the nature of certain cases, some conflicts in the application of human rights are quite predictable. But notice that the Chinese government does not characterize rights conflicts in terms of conflicts among correlative obligations in particular circumstances. Nor can these conflicts be characterized as occurring as a result of the nature of the case and independently of the ruling party's own judgments. On the contrary, conflicts between applications of human rights norms exist for however long and under whatever circumstances the Chinese government judges them to conflict with its own efforts to promote social and economic development.[103]

We might give the government of China (and others making similar trade-off arguments) the benefit of the doubt in supposing that the arguments are made in good faith. Other issues may actually be of greater concern. One of these is a second unexamined assumption underlying trade-off arguments. Dictators or authoritarian regimes sometimes assume that allowing citizens to exercise their human rights will lead to a "slippery slope." This term refers to an imagined scenario in which allowing even the smallest exercise of rights will lead to an inevitable and irreversibly disastrous outcome.[104] The disastrous outcome is pictured as one in which all social order is gone, the economy collapses, and chaos reigns, followed by tragedies generally as grim as the proverbial Four Horsemen of the Apocalypse (war, famine, disease, and death).

Concerns about such slippery slopes might be based in part on dubious beliefs about causal connections. Research does not support the view that societies governed by liberal or liberalizing regimes—those that do not violate human rights—disintegrate into chaos and a war of all against all. When societies governed by liberalizing regimes have collapsed, as did the Weimar Republic in prewar Germany or Lebanon in the 1970s, the collapse has occured not because of human rights but rather their absence—as reflected by deep social inequality or racial and ethnic discrimination—or by economic crisis. The slippery slope may capture one part of reality, however. Because they purport to provide a "totalism" that provides all answers to all problems of life, it is not surprising that authoritarian governments feel threatened by any exercises of individual rights. Anything that diverges from the party line is seen as an attack on the party's monopoly. And although liberalization does not by itself lead to an end to dictatorship, it is

---

[103]"The PRC interprets the right to development as only implying the right of a nation's development rather than the right of individuals to control their own destiny"; Michael J. Sullivan, "Developmentalism and China's Human Rights Policy," in *Debating Human Rights,* p. 121.

[104]The former president of China, Jiang Zemin, employed this argument: "Without social stability it will be impossible to achieve economic development, without economic development there will be no social progress, and without progress for the whole society it will be impossible for human beings to take their destiny in their hands." Quoted in "Developmentalism and China's Human Rights Policy," p. 132.

understandable why authoritarian governments might perceive an increase in the exercise of human rights as a slippery slope.

Such cases represent the unjustified attempts of a dictator, a clique, or a party to maintain the agent's own interests even when this involves terrible violations of citizens' rights. Yet, some state leaders argue that it is not the self-interest of the regime but rather the realities of economic and social development that require the postponement of civil and political rights. This argument is made, for instance, by Kishore Mahbubani, permanent secretary in the Ministry of Foreign Affairs in Singapore, and by Lee Kuan Yew, former prime minister of Singapore.[105]

It is asserted that the historical evidence from Western Europe and North America supports this causal connection. That is, advocates of trade-offs like to refer to the history of the industrialization of Western Europe and North America. They point out that civil and political liberties emerged slowly, and in most cases, long after significant industrial and commercial development. Civil and political liberties are associated with the emergence of a relatively affluent middle class capable of participating in public life. And the latter is dependent on economic development and the accumulation of capital.

There are a number of problems with this argument, however. In the first place, there is no compelling evidence for this kind of historical causation. Nobel prize–winning economist Amartya Sen is among those who, after careful studies, have shown that the expectation of such a simple causal connection is unrealistic.[106] The actual complexities of the situation in Western states do not fit the simple model of trade-offs. Some political rights emerged relatively late; for instance, women in most Western "democracies" continued to be disenfranchised well into the twentieth century. Other political liberties emerged very early, such as the rights involved in owning property, in making contracts, or in having access to information. In some states, economic development did not readily lead to concern for and protection of economic and social rights. In the United States, for instance, economic development has consistently tended to associate with political rights. In Germany, by contrast, a relatively extensive recognition of social and economic rights emerged earlier as social welfare legislation and just at the beginning of large-scale industrial and economic development.

---

[105]Kishore Mahbubani, "An Asian Perspective on Human Rights and Freedom of the Press," in *Debating Human Rights*, pp. 80–97; Fareed Zakaria, "Culture Is Destiny: A Conversation with Lee Kuan Yew," *Foreign Affairs*, Vol. 73, No. 2 (March/April, 1994), pp. 109–26.

[106]See Amartya Sen, *Development as Freedom* (New York: Alfred A. Knopf, 1999); Amartya Sen, *Human Rights and Asian Values* (New York: Carnegie Council on Ethics and International Affairs, 1997); Dan Rodrik, *The New Global Economy and Developing Countries: Making Openness Work* (Washington, DC: Overseas Development Council, 1999). For a dissenting view, see Michael W. Dowdle, "How a Liberal Jurist Defends the Bangkok Declaration," in *Negotiating Culture and Human Rights*, pp. 125–52.

(Millions of Germans were denied these rights by subsequent German governments, the most notorious being the Third Reich.)

Development first, rights second. This is the rallying cry of Singapore's Lee Kuan Yew. And it is a popular slogan among many business corporations that seek good investment opportunities abroad. But extensive material prosperity in both Singapore and Malaysia has not led to a corresponding increase in citizens' enjoyment of civil and political rights. In addition, given the absence of controlled experimental conditions, there is no way to test the claim that social stability, and hence, political repression, was necessary for the level of material prosperity presently enjoyed in those countries. It is entirely possible that they could have achieved the same, or even greater, prosperity and economic stability with less repression of civil and political human rights. In fact, the cases of Taiwan, and especially South Korea, offer some reason for supposing that prosperity and stability develop most soundly when political and civil rights are respected.[107] It has become so dubious that development will lead to liberalization among repressive authoritarian regimes that recently the International Monetary Fund (IMF) and the World Bank, although not traditionally known for their interest in promoting human rights, have argued that governments seeking loans must take steps to ensure the protection of certain fundamental liberties.[108]

In summary, advocates of the trade-off argument fail to make a persuasive case. They argue that the suppression of some human rights is necessary for or justified by greater gains in protection of (or enjoyment) of other rights. On the contrary, however, repression of civil and political rights does not automatically lead to greater enjoyment of economic and social rights among those whose civil and political rights are suppressed. Moreover, there is no necessary causal connection between advancement or suppression of civil and political rights, on the one hand, and economic and social rights, on the other. Empirical studies reveal many complexities but also show that advocates of trade-off arguments are mistaken in believing that (1) it is necessary to suppress civil and political rights in order to advance economic and social development, or that (2) economic development must precede the enjoyment of civil and political rights, or that (3) "premature" enjoyment of civil and political rights will result in economic stagnation or social instability. Causal "arrows" may go in other directions, depending on the case; for instance, citizens' exercise of political rights might enhance a country's economic development. Finally, because of these multiple complexities, advocates of trade-offs are prone to engage in erroneous "categorical" thinking when they regard a whole category of rights as defeasible. As Donnelly notes, blatant trade-offs of civil and political rights

---

[107]*Universal Human Rights in Theory and Practice*, pp. 163–202.
[108]*In Our Best Interest*, pp. 83 and 143.

unjustifiably ignore the great diversity of these rights and the multiple ways that rights (of each "generation") interconnect in developing societies.[109]

4. DIVERSITY, HUMAN RIGHTS, AND CROSS-CULTURAL NEGOTIATION

Returning to the discussion in Chapter 1, we understand that all human beings have human rights. We have these rights because we are beings with agency, that is, because we are capable of action based on choice and self-direction, and because the world is a place such that, except for assistance from their fellows, persons' agency often can be hindered or destroyed. In the previous two sections, we considered and rejected arguments against the view that human rights are universal—that is, that all humans possess these rights at all times in all places. These exceptionalist objections failed to provide adequate reasons for rejecting the universalist claim. It can now be asserted that the arguments of Chapter 1 and Chapter 2 together establish a very strong case for the universality of human rights. This is more than a mere presumption or even a prima facie argument. It is true that demonstrating the failure of the exceptionalist arguments against universalism does not establish the truth of universalism *conclusively,* or beyond the shadow of a doubt. We would commit the fallacy of negative proof to believe otherwise, for it is still *logically* possible that a convincing argument against universalism can be found. We can now regard the universality of human rights as very well grounded, however.

It will be asked, nevertheless, "What do human rights require here and now, that is, what does Abdul's right to speak entitle him to do today and in Saudi Arabia?" Such questions—and they are innumerable—are perfectly sensible, because as moral resources, universal human rights prescribe norms, but how these norms are to apply in particular circumstances is a subject of reasonable disagreement. The next question for consideration, therefore, is not whether human rights ever cease being universal (they do not, as this chapter has shown) but what the specific ways are in which prescribed norms apply, that is, what goods or activities they entitle rights-holders to receive or to do, and exactly what they require of the persons who have correlative obligations.

A beginning can be made by remembering that protections of human rights are *morally required* when these are the only effective protections that persons have against standard threats to their agency. Consequently, we can expect arguments that certain standard protections and practices *are not* morally required when (1) standard threats to human agency do not arise or

---

[109]*Universal Human Rights in Theory and Practice*, p. 201.

(2) there are equally adequate alternatives or means by which conditions potentially defeating human agency can be overcome. But given opposition (as shown by the arguments refuted before) to certain human rights in some states or within some groups, *rational* debate about the actual *application* of human rights norms must presuppose that everyone, including former detractors, engage willfully and reflectively in dialogue about his or her perceptions of the appropriate range of human rights. This is the subject of Chapter 3 on cross-cultural negotiations. There I introduce strategies designed to assist parties, presently or recently at cross-purposes in the human rights debate, to reach new, synthetic positions satisfactory to all sides.

chapter three

Human Rights and Cross-Cultural Negotiations

The subject of this chapter is cultural negotiation or, in other words, how a greater "cross-cultural consensus" can be developed regarding human rights. My position, established in Chapter 1 and supported throughout, is that all human beings have basic human rights. As demonstrated in Chapter 2, there is no longer a contest between those who advocate the universality of human rights standards and others, such as some in the Asian values debate, who maintain that human rights norms are invalid or inapplicable in their own societies or cultures. As we have seen, arguments against the universality of human rights fail. Hence, our focus now shifts to ways in which greater respect for, and further observance of, human rights can be promoted or advanced in places where the human rights record has been weak or inadequate. For instance, in many societies where the Muslim law of *shari'a* is imposed, it is illegal to commit apostasy, that is, to renounce one's belief in Islam as the correct religion. Apostasy is often severely punished in Islamic societies, even though this constraint on conscience directly violates freedom of religion as understood in Article 18 of the Universal Declaration of Human Rights (UDHR) and Article 18 of the International Covenant on Civil and Political Rights (ICCPR).

Given, then, that there is resistance to certain human rights in some societies or within certain groups, what might be the best ways to persuade or to encourage people to reconsider their reasons for opposing rights norms? As international jurist Abdullahi Ahmed An-Na'im has observed, the advance of human rights norms in traditionalist Islamic regimes will be undermined, if not totally repudiated, by the appearance that extracultural values and norms (e.g., equality of women before the law) are being imposed from without.[1] Guardians of tradition and the status quo will want to seize on any pretext to undermine the credibility of proponents of change. From the perspective of cultural negotiation, then, the task of rights advocates is to avoid a head-on collision with *shari'a*, or religious law. Instead, rights advocates need to foster an "internal discourse" within traditionalist cultures that will lead to changes in the content of religious laws, thereby bringing them closer to human rights standards, but without challenging the perceived legitimacy of *shari'a*. In this way, human rights norms could attain internal validation within a culture even though, initially, powerful religious leaders had been quite hostile to them.

This strategy for cultural negotiation, which I shall call *internal validation*, will be discussed in greater detail in this chapter, along with three other strategies. As will be seen from the preceding brief illustration, *cultural negotiation* can be understood as *methods of extending respect for human rights, by engaging others, and especially those reluctant to embrace human rights, to reflect dialectically about their cultural values in creative tension with human rights norms*. Several preliminary points need to be made about cultural negotiation. First, for the purposes of this discussion, a culture may be understood as a worldview shared by members of a group. A worldview can be understood in terms offered by American philosopher Michael Boylan as "a network of beliefs that together express values concerning the critical concerns of life: ethics, politics, religion, aesthetics, and so forth."[2] Thus, for instance, liberals who advocate human rights can be seen, on this account, to have a different culture, or worldview, from traditionalists who believe that religious laws should control human interactions, whether or not these two groups live under the same regime.

Second, negotiations between cultures should be *dialectical*; that is, without shirking real, often strong, differences, all sides should adopt the objective of attaining an agreement, or synthesis, that will be more satisfactory to everyone involved.[3] On the way to this synthesis or in the event that

---

[1]Abdullahi Ahmed An-Na'im, "State Responsibility under International Human Rights Law to Change Religious and Customary Law," in *International Human Rights in Context,* Henry J. Steiner and Philip Alston, eds. (New York: Oxford University Press, 2000), pp. 426–8.

[2]Michel Boylan, *Basic Ethics* (Upper Saddle River, NJ: Prentice Hall, 2000), p. 24.

[3]Dialectical reasoning, from the Greek *dialectos* for "discourse" or "debate," was developed by Zeno, Socrates, Plato, and the Sophists as a means of exposing inconsistent beliefs and bringing contradictions to light. Much later Fichte and Hegel used the concept to refer to the emergence—through the contrast of opposites—of a new stage, or synthesis. See "Dialectical" in W. L. Reese, *Dictionary of Philosophy and Religion* (Atlantic Highlands, NJ: Humanities, 1980), pp. 129–30. The concept, as used here, also includes the notion developed in Mohandas K. Gandhi's *Satyagraha*, or "soul force," of a victory over the conflict situation rather than the perceived adversary. For discussion of the Gandhian conception of dialectic in conflict resolution,

it cannot *yet* be achieved, each side must commit to critical reflection about its own worldview and to defending its position through reasoned argument. Because cultural negotiation is committed to the promotion of human rights through rational argument—and the belief that principles such as critical self-reflection and logical consistency will extend respect for rights—cultural negotiation differs significantly from other types of rights advocacy. An alternative kind of advocacy is well-known from organizations such as Amnesty International and Human Rights Watch that publicize abuses of human rights and engage in traditional "pressure politics" methods of aiding political prisoners or prisoners of conscience, or of ending some other abuse.[4] (See Appendix B for a selected list of human rights NGOs.) These organizations are often very effective, and they do a great deal on behalf of those whose rights are violated; thus, in calling attention to the differences between cultural negotiation and their methods of pressure politics, I mean only to note the difference and not to make a judgment on the former.

Third, and finally, it has to be admitted that many human rights, as recognized in the international covenants and treaties, are described in broad and general terms. The generality of these conceptions is, in part, the basis for their broad appeal. Because of their widespread acceptance across diverse cultures, conceptions of human rights embedded in the International Bill of Rights, as well as subsequent conventions giving them effect (e.g., CEDAW), can be presumed to have achieved a very high degree of consensus.[5]

But rights stated vaguely or in general terms in a covenant might be open to various interpretations. Consider, for instance, diverse interpretations of the ICCPR prohibition of "cruel, inhuman or degrading treatment or punishment" (Art. 7). At one extreme, officials in Saudi Arabia deny, against vociferous criticism, that the legally prescribed amputations of limbs for a thief is not proscribed, whereas as in Sweden and most of Europe (unlike in the United States), the death penalty for even the most serious crimes is considered cruel and degrading. Of course, part of the project of cultural negotiation is to engage these differing interpretations. At the same time, however, we need to be open to some possibly permissible variations in the way that human rights norms are applied, depending on local, or culturally specific conditions and practices.

see Joan V. Bondurant, *Conquest of Violence: The Gandhian Philosophy of Conflict*, rev. ed. (Princeton, NJ: Princeton University Press, 1988), pp. 189–99. Also see Mark Juergensmeyer, *Gandhi's Way: A Handbook of Conflict Resolution* (Berkeley, CA: University of California Press, 1984).

[4]See Thomas Risse, Stephen C. Ropp, and Kathryn Sikkink, eds., *The Power of Human Rights: International Norms and Domestic Change* (Cambridge: Cambridge University Press, 1999). Also see Margaret E. Keck and Kathyrn Sikkink, *Activists Beyond Borders: Advocacy Networks in International Politics* (Ithaca, NY: Cornell University Press, 1998).

[5]As Ann Elizabeth Mayer notes, consensus can be measured not just by recognition, consent, and compliance, but also by defensiveness in response to criticism. See *Islam and Human Rights: Tradition and Politics* (Boulder, CO: Westview, 1995), p. 29.

In what follows I shall consider four different strategies for cultural negotiation. The first to be considered is a *transformational strategy*. The second may be called a *strategy for accommodation;* the third, as I noted before, is a strategy of *internal validation,* and the fourth to be considered is *worldview integration*. Although for purposes of clarity these strategies are here presented as alternatives, they are far from being exclusive; on the contrary, they might be combined in important ways. All but one of these approaches—worldview integration—was developed in connection with controversies over human rights, although I will be extending their usages here. And although, as of yet, none of these strategies has been fully developed or extensively employed, they are discussed here as offering the most promising future directions for cultural negotiations.

1. A Transformational Strategy

The *transformational strategy* was developed by Canadian philosopher Jay Drydyk. Drydyk begins his exposition of this strategy by making two specific points.[6] The first point is that "Properly understood, human rights are justifiable from within all cultures."[7] But, second, although all cultural groups have or have had conceptions of human rights, their conceptions may be either "defective" or "incomplete," or both. This tendency is as true for European or North American cultures that have had longer historical discourses about rights, as it is of cultures that have newly emerged. In all cultural traditions, at some time or other, some people have employed conceptions that are *defective* in the sense that "they limit human rights protections to in-groups, excluding out-groups."[8] By contrast, an *incomplete* conception of human rights is, Drydyk claims, "one that overlooks certain protections that people are due."[9] In other words, defective conceptions give rise to discriminatory practices whereby some people in a society are not regarded as rights-holders. By contrast, incompleteness involves an inadequate "list" of human rights, one in which there are no protections due to persons against some standard threats.

To illustrate how conceptions of human rights can be defective, Drydyk explains that even John Locke, who is lauded as one of the formulators of human rights theory, had a defective conception of human rights. It is

---

[6]Jay Drydyk, "Globalization and Human Rights," in *Moral Issues in Global Perspective,* Christine Koggel, ed. (Peterborough, Ontario: Broadview, 1990), pp. 30–42. For an extended version of Drydyk's position, see *Global Justice, Global Democracy,* Jay Drydyk and Peter Penz, eds. (Halifax, Nova Scotia: Fernwood, 1997), pp. 159–83. Unless otherwise noted, all references to Drydyk are to the excerpt in Koggel, *Moral Issues.*

[7]*Ibid.,* p. 31.

[8]*Ibid.,* p. 32.

[9]*Ibid.*

notorious that Locke did not conceive of equal rights for women, and Locke was the second largest shareholder in the Royal Africa Company, "explicitly a slave trading enterprise."[10] Locke's defective, and hence exclusive, conception of rights is similar in its defectiveness to the view of rights of the Akan people of West Africa who, as described by Kwasi Wiredu, understand protections to be based on group membership.[11] Nor do the Lockean and Akan views of rights as exclusive differ that much from the situation of the Dinka of the Sudan who, according to Francis Deng, recognize as persons only those members of the society who accept its culture, its responsibilities, and their place within it.[12] Against those who would claim that the Dinka lack a conception of the individual necessary for human rights, Drydyk argues that the problem is not that Dinka culture lacks respect for individuals. "The problem is that it respects too few individuals; what is missing is not individualism, but universality."[13] Drydyk adds that if Locke, the Akan, or the Dinka lacked conceptions of human rights, "then they would be unable to pick out any communities in which such social protection is warranted. But they can pick out at least one such community, namely one that includes themselves and people 'like them.' What they cannot so easily do is to pick out others. Their knowledge of how to use the language of human rights is not absent; it is more accurate to call it 'defective'."[14]

In other words, although Drydyk believes that all cultures have moral and political experience sufficient as resources for human rights conceptions, he does not believe that it is necessary that a society or cultural group have human rights laws on the books, or even that they have a public discourse about human rights. It is enough, Drydyk believes, that the society or group justifies the protection of members against standard threats that exemplify fundamental dangers to humans.

> These dangers will be recognized differently, with different language, and under different descriptions, in different cultural contexts. Protections against them will also be justified differently. But as long as this kind of protection can be described within a culture, no matter how it is conceived or described, then we cannot say . . . that the concept of this human right is foreign to this culture.[15]

Drydyk's view of the conditions for a conception of human rights is not without difficulties. Is it sufficient that members of a society believe it good and right that they be protected from standard threats? One problem

---

[10]*Ibid.,* p. 34.

[11]Cited by Drydyk, p. 34. See Kwasi Wiredu, "An Akan Perspective on Human Rights," in *Human Rights in Africa: Cross-Cultural Perspectives,* Abdullahi Ahmed An-Na'im and Francis M. Deng, eds. (Washington, DC: Brookings Institution, 1990), pp. 361–89.

[12]Cited by Drydyk, p. 34. See Francis M. Deng, "A Cultural Approach to Human Rights Among the Dinka," in *Human Rights in Africa,* pp. 261–89.

[13]*Ibid.,* p. 34.

[14]*Ibid.*

[15]*Ibid.,* p. 33.

is that conceptions of human rights include notions of *entitlement* and socially supported *guarantees* against abuse. (See Chapter 1.) Assuming, as Drydyk claims, that all cultures have "deep moral resources that block giving priority to interests that would violate protection" of human needs, are these moral resources enough to support a conception of human rights?[16] This concern might arise, for example, in connection with a social group whose members believe that the kinds of protections needed and the conditions for their application are to be determined by a dictator or an authoritarian government and cannot be claimed by the group or its members as a matter of entitlement. Nevertheless, we can concede that a socially accepted view that persons ought to be protected against standard threats is at least some basis for a conception of human rights. We can concede further that the resources for such concern, based on what Drydyk calls "knowledge of care, neglect, and abuse," probably are common for every social group.[17]

Of course, Drydyk acknowledges that, for any particular culture, there may be cultural beliefs that argue for other priorities. When other interests conflict with human rights standards, are there ways of settling these issues? Drydyk believes that when such conflicts occur, there are deeper resources in the culture that enable its members "to know that needs protection is not to be overridden by other norms or considerations."[18] These are the resources already identified—*knowledge of care, neglect, and abuse*—available in every culture. What this knowledge *ought* to do, Drydyk claims, is to block the use of other cultural norms to justify or condone neglect or abuse. Hence, Drydyk believes that human rights conceptions that are incomplete, because they overlook protections that people are due, can be extended once members of the society confront one another, and give proper weight to knowledge of care, neglect, and abuse. Likewise, we can presume that there is knowledge of the way humans are fundamentally the same that ought to block practices of discrimination and exclusion. Both kinds of knowledge would be applied to overcome the incompleteness and defectiveness of conceptions of human rights and move these revised conceptions closer to impartiality and universality.

But just how can we expect knowledge of care, neglect, and abuse to prevail against entrenched interests that infringe human rights? In response, Drydyk emphasizes features of cross-cultural dialogue that overcome privileges, entrenched power, and nonparticipation leading to discrimination and exclusion. Moreover, this cross-cultural dialogue can build on the moral resources, which are available in all cultures, that strongly argue against incompleteness.[19] Drydyk is strongly influenced by what he sees as the success of a *dialogic process*, though imperfect, in producing a remarkable

---

[16]*Ibid.*, p. 37.
[17]*Ibid.*
[18]*Ibid.*
[19]*Ibid.* p. 32.

degree of consensus on the international level. Indeed, there is a presumption among the hundreds of IGO's responsible for humans rights issues and NGO's that lobby on behalf of human rights that there be a dialogic and participatory process on the international level. In other words, nations resisting implementation of human rights as defined in the International Bill of Rights and in other treaties are expected to make their case in public and in international forums, and by attempting to persuade the world community. And to a very large extent, countries do accept this responsibility, although there is room for skepticism about sincerity. Second, it is commonly believed that dissenting nations or social groups must meet certain tests. It is generally believed that the dissenting state or group explain why they believe that there is an irreconcilable conflict between the right(s) in question and other norms or values that they regard as deserving higher priority *and* that (1) the good or object of the right is sufficiently provided for in some other way, or (2) the good or object of the right is not something valued by members of the group, *and in addition* that (3) rejection of the right is not an affront to human dignity.[20]

Without this dialogic process on the international level, Drydyk claims, it would not have been possible to achieve a progressive consensus among a majority of countries on the justifiability of second generation (economic and social) rights and third generation (self-determination and development) rights, following initial consensus on first generation (civil and political) rights. According to transformational strategy, limited and defective conceptions can be transformed only if this dialogic process extends downwards to the grassroots level of each country as well as upwards to the international level and only if dialogue is unimpeded. Thus, Drydyk holds that there must be "substantive participation" at the local, national, and international levels so that voices can participate freely from all corners of the globe.[21] There must be a "worldwide context for moral discussion, a global public sphere of moral deliberation, open to the participation of all."[22]

Thus the dialogic process would require the representation of everyone to some degree—so that all voices are audible to each other—as well as the ability to know what happens in distant parts of the world. In addition, cross-cultural discourse must not be abused, or curtailed, or manipulated in any way that perverts its outcome. For instance, when normative claims are put forward, it must be possible that they be challenged from anywhere on

---

[20]Reasonable exemptions from such justifications sometimes involve the "group rights" of indigenous persons. Such special cases are to be distinguished from those in which claims about the inapplicability of individuals' human rights are used to protect privilege and power, and to maintain patterns of structural oppression and violence.

[21]The term "substantive participation" is from Pierre Sané, "Human Rights: An Agenda for Action," *West Africa*, 39 (December 20, 1993), p. 22, as quoted in Jay Drydyk, "Globalization and Multi-Cultural Knowledge of Human Rights," *Paideia*, Oct. 4, 2002 (Paideia Project On-Line), *http://www.bu.edu/wep/Paper/Huma/HumaDryd.htm*, p. 2.

[22]Drydyk, "Globalization and Human Rights," p. 35.

Earth. In following the theories of German philosopher Jürgen Habermas, Drydyk thus is specifying that a discussion that seeks to reach moral knowledge through deliberation must involve "participatory democracy."[23] All participants must be committed to eliminating coercion and manipulation in the discussion. In other words, all those participating in the discourse must recognize the need for a *moral* discussion, that is, one in which there is a mutual commitment to bring to bear the best resources, and to reach an understanding about the right thing to do.[24] With such commitments, persons will find it irrational not to give each other equal standing and equal consideration within the discussion. As Drydyk says, "If people's common knowledge of care, neglect, and abuse is allowed to prevail in a discussion, the result will be to shape the discussion. Where knowledge of care and neglect prevail, those cultural norms that justify protection against need will also prevail."[25]

Probably the most obvious comment that detractors will make is that the transformational strategy is too idealistic. As the last quotation seems to suggest, is Drydyk assigning too much efficacy to knowledge within a global dialogical process? But, if so, is he just ignoring power politics, or realpolitik, and the ability and willingness of an elite to use force and violence to maintain its privileged position? Critics might contend that even when conceptions of human rights are recognized as defective or incomplete in a society, an oppressive regime or a band of ideologues can put an end to the dialogic process needed for reform. For this reason, a transformational approach seems best suited to states or societies that already are liberalizing and have taken steps to protect rights to participate, through an increased respect for freedoms of speech, press, association, and the rights of political participation that make possible genuine dialogue.

Prospects for the transformational strategy seem dim in very "closed" authoritarian societies such as China, Iran, and Myanmar, or in states with very deep ethnic divisions, such as Sri Lanka and the Congo. In addition, why should we presume that even if a global dialogical process is possible, *knowing* what ought to be done will generate the *will* to change? A critic might wonder whether Drydyk's perspective depends on an overly optimistic view of human nature. Without presuming a Hobbesian view of human life as "nasty, brutish, and short," observers have noted the appalling indifference of humans to the fate of their own kind.[26] Thus, even in

---

[23]Jürgen Habermas elaborated a "discourse theory" of democracy according to which the legitimacy of policy and decision making was to be tested deliberatively by appeal to reasons subject to public discourse among free and equal citizens of a constitutional democracy. See *Between Facts and Norms: Contributions to a Discourse Theory of Law and Democracy,* William Rehg, trans. (Cambridge, MA: MIT, 1996); *Theory of Communicative Action,* Thomas McCarthy, trans. (Boston: Beacon, 1984); and *The Inclusion of the Other: Studies in Political Theory,* Ciaran Cronin and Pablo De Greiff, eds: and trans. (Cambridge, MA: MIT Press, 1998).

[24]Drydyk, "Globalization and Multi-Cultural Knowledge of Human Rights," p. 3

[25]Drydyk, "Globalization and Human Rights," p. 37.

[26]For instance, see Jonathan Glover, *Humanity: A Moral History of the Twentieth Century* (New Haven and London: Yale University Press, 1999), esp. 328–36.

liberal states with participatory politics, there may be insufficient *motivation* for citizens to apply criteria of care, concern, and neglect, and to engage with one another in a dialogic process.

Certainly, these problems demand our attention. It would be a mistake, however, to presume that the transformational strategy or any of the strategies discussed here could be a cure-all or could fit every occasion. Other methods may be justified responses to extremely serious and widespread abuses of human rights perpetrated by authoritarian regimes or by ethnic or nationalist groups against others. For instance, the prevention of genocide and crimes against humanity justifies the use of military force through a United Nations–sanctioned humanitarian intervention. Authoritarian and recalcitrant regimes may need to be resisted by other means such as the publicity and pressure politic methods of human rights IGOs and NGOs.[27] In addition to these *external* measures, increased space for dialogue over rights can be created *internally* by the use of strategies of nonviolent resistance, or activism, first developed by Mohandas Gandhi in South Africa and India, and subsequently used with great success by Martin Luther King, Jr., in America and by many others.[28] Nonviolent resistance is successful for many reasons, but not the least of these is its ability to transform the self-perceptions and worldviews of those willing to resist peacefully, changing them into persons who value dignity and demand their rights. Through processes such as noncooperation and civil disobedience, accompanied by the willingness to accept arrest and punishment, nonviolent resistors are often able to change expectations within a society. For instance, regimes seen as increasingly illegitimate find it harder to justify their rule without entering into negotiations with resisters. Although the subject cannot be pursued fully here, it is hoped that these comments suggest why a transformational strategy might have some success even where indifference, entrenched privilege, or a ruthless regime may seem to make it seem far-fetched.

2. A Strategy of Accommodation

Despite taking a strong universalist position, American political scientist Jack Donnelly argues that universal human rights are not incompatible with *some* relativity of *cultural practice*. Second, Donnelly believes that it is possible to establish guidelines for determining whether individual's rights or group and cultural norms should have priority when conflicts between

---

[27]*Activists Beyond Borders.*
[28]The literature on nonviolent resistance is enormous. For an overview of several major movements, see Peter Ackerman and Jack Du Vall, *A Force More Powerful: A Century of Nonviolent Conflict* (New York: St. Martin's, 2000). For a discussion of the strategies and tactics of nonviolent resistance, see the classic three-volume study by Gene Sharp, *The Politics of Nonviolent Action* (Boston: Porter Sargent, 1973).

them arise. In *Universal Human Rights in Theory and Practice,* Donnelly presents *a strategy of accommodation* for cultural negotiation, although he refers to it as "weak cultural relativism."[29] Despite being presented as a way of negotiating between conflicting norms (universal versus cultural), Donnelly's recommended strategy is best understood as a way of assessing the extent to which a society or cultural group provides the objects or substances ordinarily protected by rights, or of assessing the kinds of correlative duties that correspond to human rights. As we shall see then, what are to be accommodated as a result of negotiations are different ways in which societies or groups may act to fulfill responsibilities to rights-holders, as well as differences in the way that the dignity of persons is respected.

Key to the strategies are distinctions among the *substance* of human rights, *interpretations* of these rights, and the *forms* in which the rights may be implemented.[30] We might think of these terms as identifying successively expanding "circles" in which cultural diversity is allowed increased "play." In this view, we start with a "center" within which rights are so closely tied to *substances,* that is, the objects, capacities, or goods such that life cannot be sufficiently meaningful and dignified to be truly human without the provisions and protections afforded by these rights. These are basic rights of freedom and well-being without which persons cannot be purposive agents. There is very little room, if any, for alternative *interpretations* in this "center."[31] Although Donnelly is never completely clear about how rights are to be described at the "center," he does list the following examples of human rights permitting of very little, if any, interpretation: life, liberty, and security of the person; guarantee of legal personality; and protections against slavery, arbitrary arrest, detention or exile, and inhuman or degrading treatment.[32] In the second, expanding "circle," we find implications of human rights and required behaviors that may be subject to varying interpretations. Here discourse over human rights may involve "essentially contested

---

[29]Jack Donnelly, *Universal Human Rights in Theory and Practice* (Ithaca, NY: Cornell University Press, 1989). Donnelly means that human rights universalism may be consistent with some versions of cultural relativism, *not* ethical relativism. Nevertheless, I prefer to speak of a strategy of accommodation because "weak cultural relativism" suggests misleadingly that universalism is somehow consistent with relativism, whereas, as I argued in Chapter 2, universalism and ethical relativism are inconsistent.

[30]*Ibid.,* p. 110ff.

[31]See Chapter 1 for a discussion of the distinction between rights and their objects, or substances and for Gewirth's account of human rights.

[32]Ibid., pp. 122–3. Donnelly, along with some other theorists such as Henry Shue, presumes that some human rights are more *basic* than others. Hence, in referring to core rights, Donnelly actually intends to demarcate the most basic of human rights. By contrast, although this is not argued for here, I presume the unity and indivisibility of human rights. Donnelly tends to speak of different kinds of human rights in each of the three "circles" and definitely does so in the case of the "center." By contrast, I shall speak of distinctions between different substances of rights and different correlative duties (see Chapter 1) in each of the respective circles. The most influential discussion of basic rights is Henry Shue, *Basic Rights: Subsistence, Affluence, and U.S. Foreign Policy* (Princeton: Princeton University Press, 1980).

concepts" over what is due to rights-holders and what others must do on their behalf.[33] And in this circle, cultural diversity provides defensible mechanisms for selecting among alternative interpretations. For example, what does a right to political participation really entail? Does it require, for example, that there be no qualifications for holding office other than mere citizenship? Does it require direct democracy rather than systems of representation? It is plausible for Donnelly to maintain that practices implementing the right to political participation are subject to interpretation, *but with the proviso, Donnelly notes, that the range of permissible interpretations be limited by the substance of the concept.* For example, the right to political participation makes impermissible any interpretations involving membership confined to a one party system, as well as prohibitive "means tests" for voting (e.g., qualifications systematically excluding some categories of citizens).[34]

Of course, other rights specifications in the inner circle also would limit permissible interpretations of the right to participate. Thus, for instance, Donnelly claims that no acceptable plan for participation could place prohibitions on basic freedoms, including free speech, on the press, or on association. It is easy to consider how hotly contested conceptions of rights in the "interpretation circle" can become. Consider, for instance, that Donnelly accepts as one example of a right that is best viewed as subject to a range of interpretations to be one that many feminists would regard as "central," inasmuch as it implicates security of the person as well as fundamental liberties. The issue concerns marriage and the "right to full consent of intending spouses," a right that Donnelly regards as reflecting "a specific cultural interpretation of marriage that is of relatively recent origin."[35]

Finally, in the third "circle" pertaining to "forms," and farthest removed from the center, we find specifications of rights that are not only highly subject to cultural practice but that may or may not have significance as moral claims for members of a society. Whether or not a substance or an object can be claimed as a human right depends on the presence or absence of a standard threat to dignity in a society, or on the prior existence of institutions and practices within the society that successfully block such threats. In this connection Donnelly notes that in international human rights covenants, a number of listed rights approach specifications "at the level of

---

[33]*Ibid.,* p. 117.

[34]*Ibid.*

[35]*Ibid.,* p. 123. Critics might note, however, that by so reasoning, Donnelly commits the *genetic fallacy,* which as a universalist, he struggles so valiantly to defeat elsewhere in *Universal Human Rights in Theory and Practice.* That is, Donnelly succumbs in this example to the fallacious view that the significance of a practice and, in this case—the right to choose, or be free from choosing—a spouse, is a product of its historical context. But one of the major projects of *Universal Human Rights in Theory and Practice* is to argue that the significance of a practice, i.e., rights practices, are not chained to their historical contexts. Hence, Donnelly is concerned to show in the book that rights theory is not merely Eurocentric cultural imperialism, despite its origins in North Atlantic cultures.

form."[36] Thus, for instance, Article 10(2)(b) of the International Covenant on Civil and Political Rights (ICCPR) requires the segregation in penal institutions of juvenile defendants from adult, potentially dangerous defendants. But Donnelly quickly points out that penitentiary systems are culturally specific institutions. Moreover, in some societies, Donnelly asserts, "the very notion of a juvenile criminal defendant does not exist."[37] This is the case not because youths never do wrong in such societies but because members of the culture have alternative, "corrective," or "reformative" practices and cannot conceive of juveniles as committing crimes, or as being committed to penal institutions.

With respect to varieties of form, Donnelly again insists, as he does with respect to interpretations, that they be limited severely whenever they threaten to encroach on the 'central' *substances* protected by our basic rights. To a large extent, Donnelly sees the distinction of rights into these three "circles" as a result of "disaggregation."[38] Except for specifications of rights at the "center," the broader, or more universal the rights-claim, the greater the need for a process of interpretation. For example, the "right to work" connects to the substance of the right insofar as a government, a majority, or a powerful elite might try unjustly to restrict opportunities, deprive people of a subsistence living, and so forth. But beyond these connections, the "right to work" can be broken out as a variety of different interpretations, ranging, for example, from the "central" right to seek employment, to the peripheral right to have work commensurate with one's abilities.

Donnelly's tripartite division is attractive because it is responsive to much moral complexity surrounding human rights. First, the division is sensitive to the fact that *what counts as behavior in conformity with a right* often does depend on what people claim as their rights, as well as on how well they may be enjoying or receiving the substances or objects of rights through means other than rights practices. In some societies, members are guaranteed the substances that protect them from standard threats to their dignity without the need to invoke all of their human rights; in other societies, claiming one's rights is necessary for receiving comparable protection. There is also a permissible range of ways in which different societies or groups may discharge the duties correlative to rights. In one society a threat to dignity, such as to one's ability to provide for a family, can be met only through the direct provision of employment, whereas in another, correlative obligations for those with a "right to work" may be discharged by ensuring

---

[36]*Ibid.*

[37]*Ibid.*

[38]Donnelly means that a right, e.g., "the right to work," may include various goods that are separable from one another and that persons are not equally entitled to each of these goods. For instance, the "right to work" might be interpreted as the right to seek employment, or it might be interpreted as a right to employment appropriate to one's interests and talents. *Universal Human Rights*, p. 118.

equality of opportunity to education and fair practices in employment. Underlying Donnelly's analysis, I believe, is the notion that all human rights are the same for all humans at the "center", that is, when standard threats to dignity must be blocked but that responsible behaviors to fulfill these rights expand or contract, in permissible ways, as we move outward through the circles of interpretation and form.[39]

Donnelly's perspective is especially helpful in defending the alleged "expansion" of human rights included on various lists promulgated by the international covenants. An example is the right to "rest, leisure and reasonable limitation of working hours and periodic holidays with pay" proclaimed in Article 24 of the UNDHR and subsequently recognized in Article 7(d) of the ICESCR. Critics point out, first, that this right seems hardly as weighty as rights to education and work, let alone freedom of expression and of conscience, and second, that it is meaningless in cultures that are not industrialized and in which the labor of some could not be exploited by others. Consequently, critics argue that regular pay for hours worked and holidays with pay cannot be genuine human rights; rather, these are merely "proviso" rights—that is, recommendations that these goods ought to be supplied.

Donnelly might respond, however, that critics confuse forms and interpretations of these rights with their central core. He can acknowledge that even with the spread of sweatshops and other alienating forms of toil as a consequence of globalization, there are some societies in which the provision of paid holidays is *in fact* unnecessary as a protection against threats to human dignity. A right to periods of rest from labor does not come into play, as it were, where a country has a subsistence economy, or where one's labor cannot be exploited by another, or perhaps where religious commitments prohibit sharp, exploitative practices and cultural arrangements provide safety nets for those in desperate need. Paid holidays are *relative* to industrialization in which labor is easily organized and exploited. Consequently, paid holidays can be conceived as rights only as forms or interpretations of rights closer to the "center." And what would be these basic rights? Although Donnelly does not say so, it appears that they must be such basic, easily recognizable human rights as freedom from slavery (since complete inability to control one's labor is to be bodily enslaved to one who does control it), and to own property, since one must have a share in the value of what one produces through his or her labor, or as John Locke put it, what one "mixes his labor" with. The point, then, of adding the right to rest and leisure as a human right is to "trump" forms of exploitation that, despite appearances (wage labor in a Nike shop does not *look* like slavery), pose standard threats to our dignity.

---

[39]Rather than speaking of human rights as "essentially contested," as Donnelly does (*ibid.*, p. 117), it would be better to speak of contested views over the extent to which rights are or are not respected and protected within respective societies, and disagreement over what must be done to discharge correlative duties.

When are alternative forms or interpretations of human rights justifiable? In response, it must be remembered that the international covenants that comprise the International Bill of Rights and subsequent human rights instruments, such as CEDAW and CRC, do enumerate human rights. Descriptions of human rights in these documents have achieved widespread acceptance in global society. Moreover, the *point* of formulating human rights in these terms was to block certain basic, or standard, violations or threats to human dignity.[40] Thus, Donnelly claims that it is reasonable to place the burden of proof on the social or cultural group seeking to implement a form or interpretation that deviates from the international language of human rights. In particular, Donnelly claims that meeting this burden is equivalent to satisfying one or more of the three following criteria:

1. It must be shown that the anticipated violation is not standard (if it even exists) in that society; that is, it must be shown that claiming the right is gratuitous or that the rights-claim is intended to serve some other purpose, since the right need not be claimed because there is no real invasion that it could be a defense against.
2. The value the right protected is *justifiably* not considered basic in that society by members acquainted with alternative ways and interpretations of life.
3. Some alternative and secure mechanism already existing in the society adequately protects the right.[41]

How helpful are these criteria? Criterion (1) responds to the possibility that certain standard threats may not be present in a society and therefore that some rights need not be claimed in it. Criterion (3) responds to the possibility that some societies may have devised alternative ways (other secure mechanisms) for providing or protecting the substance or object of certain human rights. Therefore, these two criteria help us identify circumstances in which it might be permissible for a social group to depart from international expectations regarding behaviors that appropriately meet human rights standards. Although Donnelly deserves credit for recognizing the importance of these tests, he might have added a criterion to cover cases in which social or cultural groups devise alternate, but equally satisfactory, ways of meeting the duties correlative to human rights.

Criterion (2) is frankly troubling, however. Donnelly expresses confidence that none of criteria (1) through (3) is satisfied by any state, culture, or social group that tries to significantly modify the "core" of human rights that he regards as basic. His list of basic rights includes such human rights as life; liberty; security of the person; guarantees of legal personality; and protections against slavery, arbitrary arrest and detention or exile; and

---

[40]*Ibid.*, p. 121.
[41]*Ibid.*, p. 122.

inhuman or degrading treatment.[42] Infringement of one of these rights can be justified only when conditions of extreme necessity require restrictions in order to protect a fuller measure of the same right held by a larger number of people. But this is just to reiterate the point made in Chapter 2 that for every human right, it must be logically possible that there are circumstances in which it is justifiably derogated. When we consider other human rights that have been thought to offer little room for modification, more serious difficulties arise for Donnelly's position. For instance, many commentators regard such ICCPR rights as freedom of conscience, speech, and religion as subject to little, if any, variation of form or interpretation. But Donnelly disagrees, by saying the following:

> Such civil rights as freedom of conscience, speech, and association may be a bit more relative. Because they assume the existence and positive evaluation of relatively autonomous individuals, they may be of questionable applicability in strong, thriving traditional communities. In such communities, however, they would rarely be at issue. If traditional practices truly are based on and protect culturally accepted conceptions of human dignity, then members of such a community simply will not have the basic desire or need to claim such civil rights.[43]

There are two major difficulties with the view expressed in this passage. One is that the perceived "desire or need" to claim rights, as well as perceptions of standard threats, is based on general consensus within the society, rather than on conceptions of standard threats or of human dignity that are cross-cultural in an important sense. But the point of a strategy for cross-cultural negotiation is that a group's suspension of protections afforded by a right should be defensible from the *external* perspective shared by persons outside the group as well as internally among group members. For instance, in many Southern communities in the United States before the civil rights movement, many persons, including those of European American and those of African American ancestry, did not desire or feel a need to overturn legally discriminatory practices. But this was far from evidence that human dignity was protected by Jim Crow laws. Quite the contrary: From an external perspective, the absence of a desire or perceived need to claim rights was itself an attitude that needed to be challenged, and it is one function of cultural negotiation to provide strategies for mounting such challenges.

A second difficulty can be seen when it is asked, Who is to be privileged to decide the issue and to determine whether criterion (2) has been met? Those who may best know of "alternative ways and interpretations of life" may be a governing and professional elite educated in the U.S. or in

---

[42]*Ibid.* It must be reiterated that Donnelly's approach emphasizes a sharp or hard distinction between basic human rights and less basic rights. In employing Donnelly's position for purposes of cultural negotiation, I do not pursue a similar distinction.

[43]*Ibid.*, p. 123.

major Western European cities and who benefit from their positions of social and political privilege.[44] Asking them to serve as spokespersons for the
value of compatriots' civil and political rights might involve conflicts of interest. Since a government or dominant class or majority disinterested in or
hostile to human rights cannot speak for the dispossessed and downtrodden, who should? We can conceive of IGOs, such as the UN, or NGOs taking over this function, but they will be effective only if they are allowed
access to study the situation and to investigate complaints. And such access
already implies the possible need for external coercion and, therefore, possible intrusion on the norms and practices of a refractory society. As we can
see, each of these ways of attempting to determine whether it is justifiable to
ignore the value protected by the right involves the potential for conflict.
But strategies for cultural negotiation are intended to avoid precisely this
kind of conflict; thus, the strategy of accommodation *defaults* at this point.

Furthermore, as we saw in Chapter 1, a person can waive a right or
refuse to claim it, but it does not follow that the right in question (e.g., for
shelter) is simply nonexistent (even if no one in the society claims it).[45] Presumably, then, Donnelly would concede that as soon as some individuals in
a society assert their human rights, the society would be required to recognize and protect them. Thus, we can easily imagine resulting conflicts between cultural traditionalists and individualistic, rights-modernists over
practices such as child betrothal, widow inheritance, or female circumcision,
which are widely accepted in parts of Africa and Asia but which are frequently cited as violating conceptions of human rights imbedded in international rights covenants. Such controversies are marked by sharply divergent
views; on the one side, some communal worldviews hold that such practices are permissible because they are (in Donnelly's terminology) matters of
cultural interpretation or form; on the other side, however, many individuals from a wide range of social and cultural groups hold personal worldviews that condemn such practices. The strategy of accommodation does
not offer a clear justification of one position or the other; or at least rights
theorists seem intensely uncomfortable with arguments purporting to justify these cultural practices. Perhaps this is the reason why Donnelly en-
dorses political scientist Rhoda Howard's recommendation that individuals
should be allowed to opt out of a traditional practice.[46] Rather than concede
to liberal feminist views in the case of child betrothal, for instance, and to
ban it outright, Howard and Donnelly advocate a "guaranteed right" of

---

[44]It is equally likely, of course, that an elite or self-professed leaders may be traditionalists who claim to represent the "true" values of the social group.

[45]Donnelly certainly did not intend to say anything inconsistent with the logic of rights,
and he hurriedly adds that it is hard for him to imagine a defensible "modern" conception of
human dignity that did not include at least most of these civil rights. *Ibid.*, p. 123.

[46]*Ibid.*, p. 124.

women and female children to opt out of such practices.[47] This solution, Donnelly believes, would allow an individual likely to be affected "to choose his or her culture, or the terms on which he or she will participate in the traditional culture."[48]

But this proposed solution involves insurmountable impracticalities, if not logical inconsistency. What can we do for people (e.g., oppressed women in less developed countries) who lack knowledge of what they would choose as a better way of life if only they knew about it? What can we do for persons (e.g., female children) who lack the capacity or opportunity for asserting their desires to opt out? What is to be done if the only effective way to opt out involves emigration, when foreign countries refuse to accept new immigrants? Furthermore, to speak of *guaranteeing a right to opt out* seems inconsistent with the notion of an accommodation between traditionalists and rights claimants. It suggests first that the disputed practice (e.g., child betrothal) is constrained by the "core" of human rights after all, and that traditionalists must respect the freedom of individual members to emigrate, leave, refuse to obey the law or to go along (through passive resistance), or otherwise opt out in some other meaningful way. Second, it suggests that others—presumably the vindicators of norms upholding refusals to participate in these cultural practices, whether within the culture or elsewhere in global society—need to be prepared to use coercion to implement persons' decisions to opt out, because otherwise such a right cannot be guaranteed.

A distinction Donnelly made earlier in *Universal Human Rights in Theory and Practice* may offer a way of working toward a solution to these difficulties. This is a distinction between *internal* and *external* judgments.[49] The distinction will help us appreciate the possibility of more refined criteria that Donnelly develops in a later chapter (Chapter 6) and thereby strengthen the strategy of accommodation. Basically, in forming an *internal judgment*, one asks only whether a practice is defensible within the fundamental value framework of a particular society. In using an *external judgment*, in contrast, one employs the perspective of an impartial observer who is aware both of the cultural sensitivity of the issue for a society and of the broader (or deeper) ethical frameworks and worldviews supporting rights.

Thus, rather than trying to adjudicate between conflicting parties—say, a majority versus religious dissenters—focus is shifted to efforts to adjudicate between the internal and external judgments of a practice. To a large extent, this treatment involves a dialogic process similar in important respects to the dialogic process in the strategy of transformation (Section 1) and also

---

[47]Rhoda Howard, "Evaluating Human Rights in English-Speaking Sub-Saharan Africa," in *Human Rights and Development in Africa*, Claude E. Welch and Ronald I. Meltzer, eds. (Albany, NY: State University of New York, 1984), pp. 66–8.

[48]*Ibid.*, p. 124.

[49]*Ibid.*, p. 114.

in the strategy of worldview integration (Section 4). The importance of this shift is demonstrated well in Donnelly's discussion of discrimination in India of orthodox, higher caste Hindus against *Chandals*, or "untouchables." As Donnelly indicates, an informed "external judgment" will comprehend how patterns of life to which "untouchables" are subjected involve very serious violations of human rights. But an informed "external judgment" must also respect the "internal" significance of the caste system as an important, perhaps indispensable, aspect of the orthodox Hindu ontology as an understanding of how particular selves are manifest in larger reality.

Donnelly feels confident that the external judgment will result in a condemnation of untouchability.[50] But what warrants the confidence that Chandals and others can justifiably condemn discriminatory orthodox Hindu practices, especially when they seem so deeply ingrained and command such strong allegiance among higher caste Hindus? Here Donnelly suggests a number of tests that can be extended, I believe, into four criteria, which if satisfied, justify insisting that the external judgment be accepted. The criteria are as follows:

1. When the dangers of imposing one-sided moral/cultural judgments are reduced by strong cross-cultural international consensus, including the consensus of many non–North Atlantic cultures, then the external judgment is correspondingly justified.

2. When the internal judgment supports practices that external observers regard, with near unanimity, as very serious rights violations, then the external judgment is correspondingly justified.

3. When the internal judgment supports an entire system—in this case, the caste system—that violates virtually all internationally recognized human rights, and under all plausible interpretations of those rights, then again, the external judgment is correspondingly justified.

4. When the external judgment is widely shared among those subjected to discrimination and/or among large and significant constituencies (e.g., successive Indian national governments) that also seek to preserve the overall cultural identity of the Hindu Indians, then again, the external judgment is correspondingly justified.[51]

The first test increases the impartiality of the external judgment. This test, along with the second, also addresses the extent of agreement among those sharing the external judgment, whereas the second test also concerns agreement on the seriousness of the rights violation. The third test is concerned with the extent to which a specific practice fits into and reinforces a systematic pattern of discrimination or rights violations. The fourth test looks to

---

[50]*Ibid.*, p. 123.
[51]These four tests represent my extension and enumeration of points made by Donnelly, *Universal Human Rights*, pp. 136–7.

the convergence between internal and external judgments, especially when agreement involves those subjected to the rights violation and/or constituencies who agree that the external judgment is not inconsistent with the communal worldview of the cultural group. When there is strong disagreement over what duties and actions are required by human rights, or whether a state or members of a group must protect interests as "matters of rights," these four tests will go a long way to determining whether the "external" view—that is, the view of rights advocates—or the "internal" view—the view of objectors or detractors—should prevail.

Often talk about different *conceptions* of human rights leads to the concern that the "incommensurability thesis" might be true after all. This is the view that different social or cultural groups really do operate with different, incommensurable concepts of human rights (Chapter 2). But conceding Drydyk's view that all social groups' conceptions of human rights are limited or defective to some degree is not an admission that different conceptions are incommensurable. This is a concession, instead, that contributions to the formation of a genuinely "shared communal worldview," that is, a global understanding of human rights, must come from every corner of the world.[52] The strategy of accommodation greatly facilitates this process by enabling us to see that differences of conception often turn on highly contingent and changeable differences in *practices* related to rights. In other words, discourse about different conceptions often concerns the ways that the objects of right are protected, the relative presence or absence of standard threats, or different ways of fulfilling correlative duties. And it is through exploring such differences that individuals can work collectively to a globally shared communal worldview. Indeed, because the strategy distinguishes between practices or behaviors at the core of human rights, in contrast to those that involve permissible cultural deviations of interpretation and form, it demonstrates that different social and cultural groups can achieve unanimity on human rights without a forced or an unhappy consensus on the ways in which peoples must live and behave.

At the same time, a strategy of accommodation needs to be complemented by the other strategies discussed in this chapter, just as the others need this one. Controversies over such painful issues as child betrothal, widow inheritance, and female genital mutilation cry out for dialogue, even when reasoned arguments can show that on the basis of the criteria presented earlier, they should be condemned. It is difficult for those who are oppressed to perceive their condition when they know of no other, and it may be more difficult for oppressors to know how cruel they are unless they confront firsthand the suffering of their victims. It is therefore important

---

[52]The notion of a shared community worldview is taken from Boylan, *Basic Ethics,* pp. 154–6. Given that the Personal Worldview Imperative bids each of us to create a single, coherent worldview, when we engage in a dialogical process, we are then enjoined "to integrate various disparate worldviews into a single integrated vision." *Ibid.,* p. 155.

that members of every social and cultural group appreciate, as Drydyk urges, the ways in which their own conceptions of rights might be defective and limited. It is desirable, insofar as possible, that all members of the group are able to engage in a dialogic process with each other, as well as with those outside the group. And when necessary, there should be "internal validation" of human rights conceptions as explained in the next section. Finally, the reevaluation and possible revision of our conceptions of human rights should involve deep reflection about our personal worldviews and efforts to bring the communal worldview that we share with others into harmony with our personal worldviews. These efforts are discussed more fully in Section 4 of this chapter.

3. INTERNAL VALIDATION AS A STRATEGY

The strategy of cultural negotiation that I call *internal validation* shares with the strategy of transformation the view that, in order to be viable, conceptions of human rights must emerge from within particular cultures. But once firmly rooted in a culture and accepted as legitimate by members of the culture, these conceptions can be shaped and reshaped until a global "overlapping consensus" has been achieved among numerous conceptions, each anchored in its own society. The strategy of internal validation to be discussed here is developed primarily from the work of the Sudanese international lawyer Abdullahi Ahmed An-Na'im and Malaysian anthropologist and feminist Norani Othman. And as these authors are concerned with the advance of human rights norms in Islamist states, the discussion here also will focus on Muslim societies.

Along with Drydyk, An-Na'im foresees convergence, or an "overlapping consensus," among major cultural traditions of the world to support universal norms.[53] But this process must be complemented by "cultural mediation" that grounds discourse in the conceptual framework of a particular society and through which human rights receive "internal validation" within each cultural tradition.[54] The first element is established through "cross-cultural dialogue," the latter via "internal discourse." He stresses the importance of assuring that human rights standards are seen as legitimate within each culture in which they will be implemented. Norani Othman shares An-Na'im's view that discourse about human rights in Muslim

---

[53]See An-Na'im, "State Responsibility under International Human Rights Law to Change Religious and Customary Law," in *International Human Rights in Context*, p. 426.

[54]Abdullahi Ahmed An-Na'im, "Cultural Mediation of Human Rights: The Al-Arqam Case in Malaysian," in *The East Asian Challenge for Human Rights*, Joanne R. Bauer and Daniel A. Bell, eds. (Cambridge, UK: Cambridge University Press, 1999), pp. 147–68.

societies must be grounded in non-Western terms.[55] She states that "universality needs to be negotiated within the internal discourse of contemporary Muslim societies."[56] The key in Islamic traditions is said to be "cultural legitimacy." Human rights must not be perceived as alien or at variance with values and institutions of the people.[57]

An-Na'im notes that for most Muslim countries, the body of law known as *Shari'a* was never displaced in personal or private law, although constitutional, criminal, and other public law matters came increasingly to be based on secular, mostly Western legal concepts and institutions. In recent decades, however, there has been an increased struggle to Islamitize public law by reestablishing *shari'a* in areas where it had been absent.[58] *Shari'a* is a vast body of religious and customary law.[59] The validity of this body of religious law is defended as divinely sanctioned, whereas long practice is assumed to have proved the utility of customary laws. Moreover, in Islamic societies, common perceptions of the authority of religious and customary laws are founded on a complex web of economic, social, and political factors; they tend to reflect existing power relations in the community as well as processes of individual socialization and communal identification.

Despite the very strong role of *shari'a* in Muslim societies, An-Na'im believes it possible to distinguish between the *content* of law, which varies as it includes greater or less respect for and protection of human rights, and common perceptions of the *authority* of law. For An-Na'im the focus should be on changing the content of religious and customary law without challenging the perception of its legitimacy. The objective is to bring religious and customary laws into conformity with human rights instruments, not to

---

[55]Norani Othman, "Grounding Human Rights Arguments in Non-Western Culture: Shari'a and the Citizenship Rights of Women in a Modern Islamic State," in *The East Asian Challenge for Human Rights*, pp. 169–92.

[56]*Ibid.*, p. 170.

[57]An-Na'im, "Human Rights in the Muslim World," in *International Human Rights in Context*, pp. 389–97. In arguing that universal human rights norms must be justified from *within* Islamic tradition, An-Na'im offers a strategy for cultural negotiation that should be amenable to at least some Islamic fundamentalists who are thought to be most opposed to "Western" human rights conceptions. Abu Al'a al-Maududi and Sayyid Qutb of Egypt, who have been enormously influential in shaping fundamentalist Islamic movements, do not reject the concept of human rights, although they vehemently reject the idea of Western human rights. For Abu Al'a al-Maududi, Islamic human rights are given by God and thus have genuine moral sanctions behind them. See Farhat Haq, "Jihad Over Human Rights, Human Rights as Jihad: Clash of Universals," in *Negotiating Culture and Human Rights*, Lynda S. Bell, Andrew J. Nathan, and Ilan Peleg, eds. (New York: Columbia University Press, 2001), pp. 242–57.

[58]*Ibid.*, p. 395.

[59]*Shari'a* consists of three parts: the Qur'an and the *hadith*, or sayings of the Prophet came first. Sunna, or "the way," is Mohammad's and his followers' elaboration of the Qur'an. It took 200 years to collect and record, and some parts are still highly controversial. *Shari'a* developed third, in the next 100 years. It is not a formal code but is a vast body of jurists' views on the Qur'an, Sunna, and legal implications. Although *shari'a* is treated as a single logical whole, it contains much diversity of opinion. See An-Na'im, "Human Rights in the Muslim World," p. 391.

extinguish religious and customary laws themselves or to transform their jurisprudential character.[60] There is room for legitimate disagreement over the precise nature of *shari'a* dictates in the modern context.[61] An-Na'im proclaims, "I believe that a modern version of Islamic law can and should be developed. Such a modern '*shari'a*' could be . . . entirely consistent with current standards of human rights."[62]

An-Na'im proposes a reform methodology based on the work of Sudanese reformer Ustadh Mahmoud Mohamed Taha, according to whom *shari'a* reflects a historically conditioned interpretation of Islamic scriptures. Mohamed Taha stressed that the founding jurists had to understand religious sources in accordance with their own social, economic, and political circumstances. For instance, in their own eighth- and ninth-century environment, equality between the sexes was inconceivable. They saw the relevant texts of the Qur'an and Sunna as confirming the realities of the day—that is, existing social attitudes and institutions.[63] The jurists also "enacted" certain emphasized texts into *shari'a* while de-emphasizing others in interpreting them in ways consistent with what they believed to be the intent and purposes of the sources.[64] But, An-Na'im notes, texts held to be relevant can be emphasized and others set aside, while other texts can be appropriately reinterpreted.[65] "Working with the same primary sources, modern Muslim jurists might shift the emphasis from one class of texts to the other, and interpret the previously enacted texts in ways consistent with a new understanding of what is believed to be intent and purpose of the sources." In addition, muslim jurists could emphasize passages in the Qur'an presently overlooked or de-emphasized by fundamentalists.[66] New understandings would be informed by contemporary social, economic, and political circumstances. Othman agrees that a method of critical reasoning, known in Islamic traditions as *ijitihad*, should be applied in reexamining the Hadith and Sunna. This process would afford jurisprudence with a more historically sensitive interpretation of central texts while emphasizing more permanent and emancipatory aspects of the Qur'an.[67]

---

[60]"State Responsibility under International Human Rights Law to Change Religious and Customary Law," p. 426.

[61]"Human Rights in the Muslim World," p. 390.

[62]*Ibid.*, p. 392.

[63]*Ibid.*, p. 395. See Ustadh Mahmoud Mohamed Taha, *The Second Message of Islam*, translated and introduced by Abdullahi Ahmed An-Na'im, (Syracuse, NY: Syracuse University Press, 1987).

[64]"Human Rights in the Muslim World," p. 395.

[65]A relevant comparison can be found in the decision of societies strongly influenced by Judaism and Christianity to set aside the Old Testament charge in Leviticus that the death penalty be meted out for bestiality.

[66]For instance, the view that apostasy is a crime warranting the death penalty should be set aside given the Qur'anic verses recognizing the legitimate multiplicity of religious convictions. This is part of the argument made by Khaled Abou El Fadl, *The Place of Tolerance in Islam*, Joshua Cohen and Ian Lague, eds. (Boston: Beacon Press, 2002).

[67]"Grounding Human Rights Arguments in Non-Western Culture," p. 170ff.

In "Human Rights in the Muslim World," An-Na'im discusses three examples of Islamic conflicts with international human rights standards: the law of apostasy, the status and rights of non-Muslims, and the status and rights of women. An-Na'im believes that each of these conflicts can be resolved in ways that bring religious and customary laws into conformity with human rights standards. It is first necessary to briefly describe each conflict before considering An-Na'im's recommendations for a resolution.

Apostasy pertains to Muslims who are held to have repudiated their faith, either directly or indirectly. Apostasy is a capital offense punishable by death. It may be inferred by a court from a person's views or actions deemed by the court to contravene the basic tenets of Islam, regardless of the accused person's personal belief that he or she is a Muslim.[68] For instance, although it was a work of fiction, Salman Rushdie's *Satanic Verses* made irreverent references to the Prophet, his wives, and leading companions. The novel was widely banned by Muslim governments; and although Rushdie is a British national of Muslim background, because the late Imam Khomeini of Iran sentenced Rushdie to death in absentia without charge or trial, he was forced into years of hiding.[69] The law of apostasy is a fundamental violation of freedom of religion and conscience, and as the Rushdie case shows, often of freedom of expression and other civil and political rights.

In many Muslim states, persons are divided into three groups: Muslims; *ahl al-kitab* (non-Muslims but believers in a holy book, especially Christians and Jews); and unbelievers. Muslims are the only full citizens of an Islamic state. Persons classified as *ahl al-kitab* have secondary status as *dhimma* in virtue of a special compact with the Muslim state maintained through *jizya*, or poll tax. *Dhimmis* are not entitled to equality with Muslims.

Regarding the status and rights of women in Muslim states, according to the standard, "traditional" position, the Qur'an at 4:34 establishes *Qawamu* or male guardianship and authority over women. Among many other things, women are disqualified from holding general public office, which would involve exercise of authority over men. According to *shari'a*, provisions of *al-hijab*, or practices known also as "the veil," are based on interpretation of Verses 24:31, 33:33, 33:53, and 33:59 of the Qur'an. Women are supposed to stay at home and not leave it except when required by urgent necessity. They are not supposed to participate in public life, because they must not mix with men, even in public places.[70] And when they are outside the home, women must cover the body and face. Men may marry up to four wives, and often men have almost complete control over their wives, including beating them. Women have little recourse against domestic violence; they may not obtain divorces except by juridical order on very specific and

---

[68]"Human Rights in the Muslim World," p. 392.
[69]*Ibid.* Ian Lague eds. (Boston: Beacon Press, 2002).
[70]*Ibid.,* p. 394.

limited grounds. By contrast, a husband may divorce a wife at will. In matters of inheritance, women are entitled to only half the share of men.[71] *Shari'a* holds women to be incompetent witnesses in serious criminal cases, regardless of their individual character and knowledge of the facts. In civil cases, in which a woman's testimony is admitted, it takes two women to make a single witness. *Diya*, monetary compensation to be paid to victims of violent crimes or survivors, is less for female victims than for male victims.[72]

An-Na'im stresses that the Qur'an and other Islamic sources do support fundamental principles of equal worth and dignity regardless of gender, religion, or race. Numerous verses of the Qur'an speak of honor and dignity for "humankind" and "children of Adam" without distinction as to race, color, or gender. For instance, numerous verses of the Qur'an provide for freedom of choice and noncompulsion in religious belief and conscience. Verse 2:256 of the Qur'an proclaims, "Let there be no compulsion in religion: Truth stands out clear from error. . ." At Verse 18:29, God instructs the Prophet, "Say, the Truth is from your Lord. Let him who will believe, and let him who will reject [it]." The problem is that these verses have either been de-emphasized by traditionalists as having been "overruled" by other verses that were understood to legitimate coercion or been "interpreted" by traditionalists in ways that permit such coercion. For instance, Verse 9:29 of the Qur'an was taken as the foundation of the whole system of *dhimma* and discrimination against non-Muslims. However, by relying on verses that extol freedom of religion, one can argue now that the *dhimma* system should no longer be part of Islamic law and that complete equality should be assured.[73]

An-Na'im adds, "we can provide Islamic legitimacy for the full range of human rights for women."[74] Gender equality would qualify for Islamic legitimacy if it is based on specific texts in opposing the application of other texts, and can be shown to be in accordance with the Qur'an and *Sunna* as a whole."[75] For instance, the significance of Verse 4:34 should fade, since *qawama* is a consequence of considerations that are today irrelevant; for instance, where the rule of law prevails, physical strength and military prowess are not necessary to provide protection. Thus, Muslim advocates for universal human rights must claim the "Islamic platform" and not concede it to the traditionalists and fundamentalists in their societies. Moreover, insofar as religious and customary laws are deeply intertwined in complex ways with economic, political, and social factors, popular beliefs about the validity of reinterpretation of these passages will coincide with in-

---

[71]*Ibid.*
[72]*Ibid.*
[73]*Ibid.*, p. 397.
[74]*Ibid.*, p. 396.
[75]*Ibid.*

creased awareness of the competence of women to participate in the economy.[76] An effort to discredit a repressive practice, such as land tenure or inheritance, must seek to challenge and discredit whatever economical, sociological, or other rationale that it is perceived by the public to have. But this task must be done without challenging the more fundamental notion that land tenure and inheritance practices are justified by the Islamic, scriptural social order.

Othman agrees with An-Na'im not only on the need to revise misinterpreted verses of the Qur'an and other scriptures but also on the need for consistency between spiritual equality and full equality before the law. She asks, "Because the equal status of women and men in spiritual matters is not only recognized but insisted upon in the Qur'an, can the Islamic insistence upon equal rights and obligations of women and men be any less in daily matters?"[77] Practices such as spousal abuse and polygamy that are currently allowed or argued as desirable by traditionalists would undermine the principle of equality deeply embedded in the Qur'an.[78]

Othman also shares An-Na'im's view that insofar as religious perspectives are so completely intertwined in Muslim societies with economic, political, and social practices, any changes in popular belief must accompany efforts to justify human rights norms from within Islamic religious traditions. Othman regards it as a failing of many Islamic societies that there is insufficient recognition of the "common human ontology" of men and women. In addition (and as Drydyk would argue), there must be genuine discourse between men and women. Thus, to some extent, the problem is not with Islam per se but with the absence of appropriate experiences in relatively closed societies. For instance, Othman believes that there is a failure of moral imagination regarding women's citizenship rights. Islamic ideologues do not recognize the repression caused by their policies on gender because their own experiences with modern citizenship are so limited, and images of women as equals at work or in politics are "beyond the reach of the ideologue's socio-legal consciousness."[79]

What I am here calling the strategy of internal validation is not without its detractors. Among those doubting its efficacy is Fouad Zakaria. In "Human Rights in the Arab World," Zakaria agrees with An-Na'im and Othman that Islamic human rights conceptions have a static character because

---

[76]"State Responsibility under International Human Rights Law to Change Religious and Customary Law," p. 427.

[77]"Grounding Human Rights Arguments in Non-Western Culture," p. 182.

[78]Although Othman advocates an aggressive policy of critical reflection and contextualizing historical interpretations inconsistent with human rights norms, she differs from An-Na'im in relying on secular law in areas that lie, or should lie, outside *shari'a*. Thus, in view of the inadequacy of *shari'a* to provide for legislation protecting women from domestic abuse in Malaysia, Othman advocates appealing to the national penal code. *Ibid.*, p. 187.

[79]*Ibid.*, p. 175.

of the limited experiences within Islamic cultures.[80] Muslim societies need to be tolerant of a wider range of experience; only the emerging of social, economic, and political realities will make some rights conceivable. But Zakaria is extremely skeptical of the advisability of incorporating broader conceptions of human rights within religious and customary law. There are two major concerns, he believes; first, there is the danger that "the generality of religious text makes it easy to derive all shades of meaning from it."[81] Secondly, Zakaria is concerned that because religious-based interpretations of human rights would be grounded in a divine text that is sacred, permanent and unchanging, and eternal, certain human rights conceptions might become "frozen" and thereby lose their dynamism and historical development.[82] It appears, then, that Zakaria's perspective is closer to those who believe that there needs to be a larger scope for the secular within Islamic societies. Some who take an even more extreme version of this position argue that real reform is possible only with the coming of genuine rule of law and democratic process. In fact, this is the view of Thomas Franck, who claims that the development of universal human rights "is the consequence of modernizing forces that are not culturally specific."[83] Rather, they occurred

> not by inherent cultural factors but by changes occurring, at different rates, everywhere: universal education, industrialization, urbanization, the rise of the middle class, advances in transportation and communications, and the spread of new information technology. These changes were driven by scientific developments capable of affecting equally any society. It is these trends, and not some historical or social determinant, that—almost as a by-product—generated the move to global human rights.[84]

In her essay "Jihad over Human Rights," political scientist Farhart Haq offers both reasons for being pessimistic about the success of internal validation and reasons for optimism. Haq is most concerned about the prospects for gender equality. In her view, there are three major obstacles to genuine dialogue. First, the role and status of Muslim women has become a charged symbol in "cultural wars." In response to charges of "oppression," a great deal of literature is produced by Muslim men and women to demonstrate the "honor" and "respect" accorded to women in Islam.[85]

---

[80]Fouad Zakaria, "Human Rights in the Arab World: The Islamic Context," in *Philosophical Foundations of Human Rights,* United Nations Publications (Paris: UNESCO, 1986).
[81]*Ibid.,* p. 228.
[82]*Ibid.,* p. 237.
[83]Thomas M. Franck, "Are Human Rights Universal?" *Foreign Affairs,* Vol. 80, No. 1 (January/February 2001), p. 202.
[84]*Ibid.*
[85]Farhart Haq, "Jihad over Human Rights," p. 251. One Muslim feminist cited in particular is Fatima Mernissi, *Beyond the Veil* (New York: John Wiley, 1975).

The second obstacle is that legal reforms in Muslim societies cannot follow the Western pattern. For Western feminists, a very serious obstacle to gender equality is the distinction between public and private spheres. Consequently, feminists prompted the state to intervene in the private sphere to expand protection of women, while abolishing restrictions on the participation of women in the public sphere on an equal footing with men. But because governments of most Muslim nation-states are authoritarian rather than liberal democracies, this pattern cannot be replicated for the Muslim world. Furthermore, because much of the fundamentalist reform movement in Islam is directed at efforts to block the power of secular governments, Haq claims that Muslim feminists who identify cultural practices as the sites of oppression must avoid calling on the intrusive approaches of unrepresentative and undemocratic governments

The third obstacle to gender equality in Islam is the deep anxieties engendered by perceived challenges to Muslim fundamentalists' conception of the family. Haq notes that for Maududi, a widely influential fundamentalist, the proper sexual division of labor was foundational, as he indicates in his book *Purdah and the Status of Women in Islam* that has been widely translated and disseminated throughout the Muslim world.[86] The family is the primary unit for ritual observance, as well as an influential site of religious and secular education and the transmission of religion and worldly knowledge from one generation to the next. It serves, as well, as the locus for developing notions of trust, authority, and responsibility. In effect, the family and its primary expression in domestic space, the household, is frequently taken as "a microcosm of the desired moral order."[87] Consequently, the "desired moral order" represented by the family in the Muslim world is such that for Muslim fundamentalists, "the adoption of the Western model of the family is to commit cultural suicide."[88]

Yet, despite pessimism about advances towards gender equality, at least for the near future, Haq says much that suggests a possible convergence between the concerns of fundamentalists and an enlarged human rights regime. Islamic fundamentalism is a modern phenomenon, arising out of a pervasive need to think about what it means to be a Muslim, given modern challenges to collective identity. Literature on Islamic human rights is not principally produced by traditional scholars of Islam (the *ulama*) but rather by lay intellectuals described as "fundamentalists," who desire to turn Islam into a complete ideological system.[89] The efforts of the fundamentalists are to use human rights to preserve an Islamic sense of identity

---

[86]*Ibid.*, p. 253. See Abu Al'a Maududi, *Purdah and the Status of Women in Islam* (Lahore: Islamic Publications, 1993).

[87]Farhart Haq quoting Dale F. Eickleman and James Piscatori, *Muslim Politics* (Princeton: Princeton University Press, 1996), p. 83.

[88]"Jihad Over Human Rights," p. 254.

[89]*Ibid.*, p. 245.

and superiority. For Maududi and Islamic fundamentalists, a secular modern state is the greatest threat to the existence of human rights.[90] They therefore share with human rights advocates from the West a view of human rights that sees them as protections against otherwise overweening state power. Ironically, however, fundamentalists now associate Western human rights conceptions with the secularism they oppose. Consequently, they believe that reversion to earlier Islamic principles best protects fundamental rights against political power. Nevertheless, by attempting to craft an Islamic framework for human rights, fundamentalists are both affirming human rights discourse and challenging its Western "accent." Thus, in Haq's view, fundamentalist articulations of Islamic conceptions of human rights should neither be dismissed outright nor embraced as authentic. Like An-Na'im and Othman, Haq emphasizes the flexibility of Islamic tradition; she claims, "the plurality and ambiguity of Islamic values and symbols allow for a link with the past and room for change."[91]

Writing about feminism in Iran following the 1979 revolution, Afasaneh Najmabadi reports on some success among feminists who have adopted a process comparable to *ijitihad* and similar to internal validation.[92] According to Najmabadi, in Iran "West and East, modernism and Islam, feminism and cultural authenticity, have been constructed as exclusionary categories, forcing Iranian women to choose between claims to a cultural self and a feminist self."[93] As a result of these extreme dichotomies, women were led to a "search for a more culturally authentic genealogy of women's rights."[94] This revived and "culturally authenticated feminism" did not presume the opposition between feminism (supported by the authoritarian state) and cultural traditionalism, as Farhat Haq fears. Rather, the new feminism deconstructs the traditionalists' notion of womanhood from the "inside," that is, by rejecting misogynistic exegetical interpretations in *shari'a*. In women's journals such as *Zanan,* these emerging voices reinterpret Islamic sources; for example, an examination of root words shows that what may be interpreted in one context to mean "guardianship over" can be understood as "in support of" in another context. In effect, these feminists are trying to "expand the domain of re-interpretation to new linguistic constructions of the Arabic language" by using a women-centered rather than male/clergy-centered approach.[95] They thus agree with Othman, An-Na'im, and even Farhat Haq in concluding that there are no natural reasons that

---

[90]*Ibid.,* pp. 247–8.

[91]*Ibid.,* p. 251.

[92]Afsaneh Najmabadi, "Feminism in the Islamic Republic of Iran: 'Years of Hardship, Years of Growth,' " in *Islam, Gender, and Social Change,* Yvonne Y. Haddad and John L. Esposito, eds. (New York: Oxford University Press, 1988), pp. 59–84.

[93]*Ibid.,* p. 75.

[94]*Ibid.*

[95]*Ibid.,* p. 66.

justify the exclusion of women from all aspects of political and social life.[96] As the Qur'an reports, "I waste not the labor of any that labors among you, be you male or female—the one of you is as the other."[97]

Perhaps the sharpest criticism of internal validation is implied by Ann Elizabeth Mayer's conclusions in *Islam and Human Rights*.[98] Mayer casts doubt on any strategy that concedes a special status to a culture and that therefore recommends the need for a process of internal validation. In her view, international human rights standards can apply to Islamic societies in the same way as they do, or should, in other societies. Muslim countries have very uneven records of ratifying major human rights conventions. But Mayer claims that the very unevenness and dissimilarities in the patterns of ratification and nonratification indicate that, from the governmental perspective, there is no single, definitive interpretation of Islamic rights principles standing in the way of accepting international human rights conventions.[99] In addition, Mayer examines a selection of sources and contexts for Islamic human rights, including the Cairo Declaration on Human Rights, the Universal Islamic Declaration of Human Rights, the Saudi Basic Law, Iran's 1979 Constitution, and Maududi's *Human Rights in Islam*. On the basis of this review, Mayer concludes that Islamic law is fundamentally discriminatory. In contrast to protecting human rights, Islamic doctrines take away rights in a number of areas, including women's rights. Of most importance, however, Mayer claims that there is nothing distinctively *Islamic* about the biased and self-interested appraisals of women's characteristics offered by Islamic law. Indeed, for Mayer, the "most serious and pervasive human rights problems afflicting the Middle East are . . . policies and laws that are designed by elites for implementation by modern state systems at the expense of the rights and freedoms of the individual."[100] This perception explains, in Mayer's view, why Muslim states that have been slow to implement human rights standards have been disingenuous and hypocritical (although she does not use this harsh description).[101]

---

[96]*Ibid.*, p. 77.

[97]Najmabadi, p. 73, quoting the Qur'an, Sutra 3:194.

[98]Ann Elizabeth Mayer, *Islam and Human Rights: Tradition and Politics* (Boulder, CO: Westview, 1995).

[99]*Ibid.*, p. 11.

[100]*Ibid.*, p. 69.

[101]In support of this claim, Mayer notes first, "regimes pursuing Islamization have reacted defensively and angrily when accused of violating human rights. This suggests that, by and large, despite their assertions that Islamic law justifies breaching human rights, states regard international human rights as normative and fear criticism for violating them." *Ibid.*, p. 29. Second, Mayer says that the most contentious points of disagreement with international human rights law are intentionally obscured or not addressed at all. For instance, English translations of international human rights documents are misleading, since they are more in line with UN standards, whereas their "equivalent" Arabic translations are not. Third, one of the most important ways in which Islamic human rights differ from those in international law is that Islamic qualifications on rights have been deliberately left so vague that that they allow states vast discretion in circumscribing rights," *Ibid.*, p. 66.

If Mayer's critical review is correct, then, at most it shows that responsible Muslims fail to meet their moral obligations when human rights norms are not implemented and that Muslim governments and societies do not, morally speaking, merit special treatment. But even if we were to agree with Mayer, there still remains a serious pragmatic problem: how to facilitate change in the direction of greater respect for human rights. Nothing that Mayer or other critics have said suggests that the strategy of internal validation fails this pragmatic test. On the contrary, the evidence cited by the authors reviewed here suggests that the strategy is having some success, and we have now considered persuasive reasons for believing that internal validation is the best strategy for many Islamic societies. It ought to be a matter of concern, of course, that not all social or cultural groups with poor human rights records do have adequate internal, cultural resources to serve as the basis for the internal validation of human rights. It has been claimed for some non-Muslim Asian cultures that they do have rich resources or meaningful equivalents in other conceptions of "vital human interests."[102] On the other hand, some authors have denied this claim.[103] But, in addition to a recommendation or a prescription about how to proceed, the claim has empirical content. It may turn out that some cultures do have these resources, whereas others simply do not, although it is more likely that this is not an all-or-nothing proposition; rather, groups will differ greatly in the extent to which they have resources for the internal validation of human rights. This possibility just goes to show, however, that although the strategy of internal validation may be extremely valuable in social and cultural groups where it can be applied, it needs to be supplemented by other strategies, especially where internal validation is less likely to make progress. But as noted earlier, each of our strategies for cultural negotiations is wholly compatible with the others.

4. THE STRATEGY OF WORLDVIEW INTEGRATION

The final strategy to be considered is adapted from the work on worldviews of American Philosopher Michael Boylan.[104] In order to comprehend *worldview integration* as a strategy, it is necessary first to understand what is

---

[102]Among those supporting this view are Joseph Chan, "A Confucian Perspective on Human Rights for Contemporary China," in *The East Asian Challenge for Human Rights*, Joanne R. Bauer and Daniel A. Bell, eds. (New York: Cambridge University Press, 1999), pp. 212–37; Edward Friedman, "Asia as a Fount of Universal Human Rights," in *Debating Human Rights*, Peter Van Ness, ed. (London: Routledge, 1999), pp. 56–79; and Aung San Suu Kyi, *Freedom From Fear* (New York: Penguin, 1991), pp. 173ff.

[103]See, for example, Roger Ames, "Rites and Rights: The Confucian Alternative," in *Human Rights and the World Religions*, Leroy Rouner, ed. (Notre Dame, IN: University of Notre Dame Press, 1988); Steven J. Hood, "Rights-Hunting in Non-Western Traditions," in *Negotiating Culture and Human Rights*, pp. 96–122.

[104]Michael Boylan, *Basic Ethics* (Upper Saddle River, NJ: Prentice Hall, 2003).

meant by "worldview" and how individuals may revise their personal worldviews. Boylan defines a worldview as "the acceptance of a network of beliefs that together express values concerning the critical concerns of life: ethics, politics, religion, aesthetics, and so forth."[105] Because humans are purposive beings who must act, and who act, when rational, on the basis of judgments about the way that actions advance their values, all persons have a worldview, or a "worldview web of beliefs." Worldviews may be very fragmentary or inchoate, however, and individuals may fail even to reflect about their choices, and hence, about relations between different beliefs and values in their worldviews. It is common for people to have inconsistent elements in their worldviews or even to slip between different and incompatible worldviews depending on their roles, or functions, without attempting to reconcile these contradictions. This tendency explains why a brutal dictator who orders a massacre for "reasons of state" nevertheless perceives himself or herself as a sensitive, humane person when he or she retreats to the private precincts of the palace to read poetry and listen to refined music.

Boylan points out, however, that living with inconsistent or conflicting worldviews, or "living the unexamined life," as Socrates had called it, is inconsistent with three of the strongest impulses directing human life: rationality, autonomy, and the search for integrity and wholeness (characterized by Boylan as a holistic self-conception). Thus, one must avoid acting in a fragmentary and self-defeating manner, that is, irrationally. One must avoid making one's actions dependent on external circumstances, thus rendering one nonfree and not responsible. In addition, one must seek a holistic self-conception, otherwise one risks guilt, shame, or the stress of feeling torn in different directions. Fortunately, as Boylan notes, it is possible not only to reason critically about one's worldview and life plan in a holistic manner but also to apply evaluative criteria to worldviews, despite the fact that they are subjective in nature.[106]

Boylan says that the criteria for evaluating our personal worldviews "are formal and logical principles that are virtually devoid of empirical content."[107] It is important to emphasize the formal and logical, or in one word, *procedural*, character of the criteria. It cannot be complained by spokespersons for a social or cultural group that these criteria import value-laden content from external sources. Actual *content*—that is, the beliefs, values, and practices to which a person commits himself or herself—come from elsewhere. Thus, in cases calling for cultural negotiation, the internal traditions, practices, beliefs, and values that often seem to be at odds with twentieth- and twenty-first century human rights norms supply the primary content. Therefore, for the purposes of cross-cultural negotiation, Boylan's criteria

---

[105]*Ibid.*, p. 24.
[106]*Ibid.*, pp. 25–6.
[107]*Ibid.*, p. 27.

for worldview evaluation can be regarded as culturally neutral in an important sense.[108]

Not only is it possible to apply evaluative criteria to our personal worldview, but also we morally *ought* to do so, Boylan argues. Although this argument will not be rehearsed here, suffice it to say that it is based on the same considerations concerning our full development as humans expressing our natures. Briefly, the moral force behind worldview self-examination is the necessity to live with rational consistency, genuine responsibility for our actions, and integrity, or to suffer the psychological (and probable) social consequences. Given that the three criteria are moral, they can be stated, respectively, as the *duty to develop and to act out our worldview,* the *duty to develop a single worldview that is both comprehensive and internally consistent,* and the *duty to create a worldview that is good.* The three criteria can be put together to form the Personal Worldview Imperative (PWI): "All people must develop a single, comprehensive and internally coherent worldview that is good and that we strive to act out in our daily lives."[109]

The duty to *develop and act out our worldviews* means that we are expected to choose and to fashion a point of view for our lives. This developing view should both influence and reflect our day-to-day consciousness as well as our choices.[110] To act unreflectively on the basis of others' beliefs, attitudes, and commands, Boylan avers, is tantamount to abandoning a crucial element of our humanity. "If freedom and autonomy are part of the human condition and if we are content only if we act out our human nature, we must seek to exercise freedom by choosing and fashioning a worldview."[111]

---

[108]It might be objected that these procedural criteria are still value-laden, since they privilege rationality, individual autonomy, and personal holism, and that Western-style rationality and autonomy may not be valued in a non-Western and traditional society. This objection is misdirected, however, insofar as it conceives of worldview integration as a strategy dependent on narrow, culturally specific (e.g., Enlightenment-inspired) conceptions of rationality and autonomy as these have played out in liberal democracies and welfare economics. Boylan's procedural criteria do not depend on such cultural-specific conceptions, however. Rationality refers to the interest of persons in avoiding self-defeating actions and in opportunities to understand that their actions are purposive or meaningful rather than futile. The interest in autonomy presupposes only the natural inclination to be the willed author of one's own actions, whatever the source of the principles upon which one acts, and to act as a consequence of one's own volition rather than overt or covert coercion. Application of these criteria does not generate a bias in favor of modern, individualistic, materialistic, and secular societies. There is no inconsistency, then, in supposing that persons might rationally, autonomously, and holistically choose to retain a traditional, religious society that rejects the major features of modern democratic and capitalistic organization.

[109]*Basic Ethics,* p. 27. Stated in this way, the PWI seems to require a single universal worldview, but it is clear from the context that Boylan means the PWI to be an imperative *for each and every* individual agent. It is possible, however, for agents to develop a "shared community worldview" (see *ibid.,* pp. 155–6), and, as we shall see, a shared community worldview may be needed to reach consensus on human rights.

[110]*Ibid.,* p. 27.

[111]*Ibid.*

The duty to *develop a single worldview* that is both comprehensive and internally consistent follows from the requirements for reasonably coherent, self-directed activity. As rational agents, we should want to reform a worldview that leads to contradictory courses of action, for instance, or that leaves one hopelessly torn and indecisive when a choice must be made. Likewise, a worldview that cannot become increasingly comprehensive with greater knowledge and experience is not one on which we can depend to help us grow and develop in life.

The duty to *create a worldview that is good* requires that we subject to ethical reflection the worldview that we fashion and develop. Our worldview must be constrained by fundamental principles that are widely recognized and accepted as ethical.[112] One ought not create a worldview that is self-destructive, for instance, but neither should one accept as his or her worldview one flagrantly espousing racism or sanctioning the exploitation of others. The same must be said for a worldview that depends on principles for treating some persons (e.g., ethnic minorities) in ways that one would not accept for oneself. In the context of the controversy over human rights, this duty cannot be seen as requiring that to be *good,* a worldview must endorse human rights norms as fundamental. To insist on this would bias the debate against those who deny that human rights norms are fundamental and would thereby surrender the neutrality of this criterion for worldviews. Nevertheless, it can be said that there are some specific action patterns and attitudes specified by this third duty. These require being open-minded about arguments over human rights, being sensitive to the ways that one's worldview might be prejudicial to the interests of others, and being prepared to revise one's worldview in accordance with honest judgments about the strengths and weakness of these arguments.

Personal worldviews are subjectively centered because they refer to ways in which individuals view the important features of their world of experience. Quite often, however, personal worldviews overlap or coalesce, giving rise to a *shared community worldview* that expresses a comprehensive vision that defines the group (from both inside and outside).[113] The PWI requires that individuals test the shared community worldview rather than passively accept it. The PWI enjoins us to integrate disparate elements into a single integrated vision.[114] In the same measure, the PWI requires that we seek possible integration when our personal or shared worldview encounters a worldview that seems incompatible with it. Thus, a cultural traditionalist must consider whether human rights norms, though they seem to be part of a different worldview, can be integrated with cultural values that are

---

[112]Boylan acknowledges the diversity of ethical systems and positions from which one might derive fundamental principles.

[113]*Ibid.,* p. 154.

[114]*Ibid.,* p. 155.

critical, from the perspective of his or her personal or shared worldview. The *strategy of worldview integration* thus depends on the personal responsibility to engage honestly in critical reflection, as directed by the PWI, but it also consists of procedural steps that can be referred to as *dialectical interaction.*[115]

Consider a situation in which the worldview of human rights activists seems to have collided with the worldview of traditionalists. If the strategy of worldview integration and the four steps that it prescribes are followed, then the conflict can be constructive. In fact, features of the novel view (the human rights stance) and the old worldview can be discarded or softened, thus generating a new amalgam that can be claimed by all as the revised and shared community worldview. The steps to be followed are the following:[116]

1. Honest critical reflection about one's own worldview. We should examine the internal consistency, coherence, and comprehensiveness of our own worldview. In doing so, we should identify those beliefs we regard as *primary,* that is, as least subject to possible revision; and we should give special attention to how well our background theories or underlying beliefs and assumptions (political, ethical, metaphysical, etc.) justify our primary beliefs and values. In making this review, we should consider whether we are depending on any personal preferences or biases that have gone undetected or that will not stand up under examination.

2. Encounter with the new or opposing worldview. At this stage a good-faith effort is made to understand the new or opposing worldview, and not just from an *external* point of view, that is, in terms of how it differs from one's own, how one reacts to it emotionally, and so on, but also from an *internal* point of view, so far as this is possible. In adopting an internal point of view, one ought to imagine oneself in the position of the other person or community and to see the world through the lens of the other's interests and concerns.[117]

3. Comparison between worldviews. Initially at this stage, persons on both sides compare their own worldview with the one they have attempted to understand, or alternatively the same person or persons entertain each of the different worldviews. Assuming that the first two stages have been completed in good faith, a thorough comparison at stage three will lead to one of the following three outcomes:

   a. Coincidence and amplification. It may turn out that what appeared to be significant differences were only superficial or rhetorical, and the two coincide on most important points. By adapting the new worldview to our

---

[115]*Ibid.,* p. 174.

[116]This is a very general adaptation from Boylan, *Basic Ethics,* pp. 174–7 and 188–90. Boylan describes these steps as a process by which we attempt to make new theories consonant with our personal worldviews.

[117]Adoption of an internal point of view also can be understood as empathy, or taking the role of the other. Empathy is an important feature of conflict resolution. See, for example, Louis Kriesberg, *Constructive Conflicts: From Escalation to Resolution* (Lanham, MD: Rowman & Littlefield, 2003), pp. 193–4.

own in such cases, we enhance and extend the logical structure and comprehensiveness of our worldview, without distortion of the original, primary principles of our worldview.

b. <u>Dissonance and rejection.</u> After careful consideration of worldviews, from the internal as well as external viewpoints, the two worldviews may remain far apart, and one will be rejected in favor of the other.

c. <u>Worldview overlap and modification.</u> Although worldviews may be far from identical, there will be enough consonance, or overlap, around key principles and values that we will be compelled—insofar as we are true to the PWI—to undertake a more complicated process known as a *dialectical interaction.*[118] The point of dialectical interaction is to remove anomalies and to examine whether features that are still keeping worldviews apart can be overcome. In dialectical interaction, one goes back and forth between each of the worldviews, viewing each "mediately," that is, from the perspective of the other. The point is to take (insofar as possible) the perspective of each and to seek modifications of each worldview in the interests of a new, coherent whole. The process continues until equilibrium is achieved, that is, until one no longer feels and perceives between two or more "competing" worldviews in tension. The result will be a transformation in which the former worldviews are superseded by a fusion that coherently combines the best features of each.[119]

Some comments are in order. First, there is no guarantee that one who entertains contrasting worldviews, even from the internal perspective, will succeed in completing the process of worldview overlap and modification at stage three. The PWI concerns process, but it does not guarantee outcomes. Consequently, the result may be dissonance and rejection. Boylan requires only that each of us *do our best* to create a comprehensive, internally coherent worldview that is good and that we strive to act out in daily life. And the ultimate authority is always the subject (the "me").[120] At the same time, however, the PWI requires a commitment to rationality and truth. If we adopt the PWI, then we cannot opt to live with a worldview that is incoherent from the perspective of another worldview or that is in conflict with values that others regard as paramount, without reexamining our own worldview. Likewise, persons who decide to reject a worldview they regard as "alien" bear the burden of justifying their decision to do so. The PWI requires a willingness to consider revision of one's own worldview when moral conflicts arise. Only worldviews that satisfy conditions of rationality can be regarded as good, that is, as morally satisfactory.

---

[118] *Basic Ethics*, p. 174.

[119] As Boylan notes, the German philosopher Hegel believed that a new position, the *synthesis*, arose out of two conflicting opposites, the *thesis* and the *antithesis*. For our purposes, the best-detailed analogue for dialectical interaction is to be found in Mohandas K. Gandhi's thought. See *supra* Note 3.

[120] *Basic Ethics*, p. 196.

In concluding this overview, we note—as we did with other strategies—major criticisms made by detractors. Boylan himself responds briefly to a number of criticisms of his application of the PWI in ethics.[121] We will be concerned with only two objections and only as they apply specifically to the strategy of worldview integration as adapted here.

The first objection relates to the sincerity of belief in a mistaken worldview. A detractor could maintain that an immoral worldview could nevertheless be sincerely held and coherent. For instance, it might be charged that paternalists can consistently believe that men are intellectually superior to women, or pastoral traditionalists can consistently believe that girls must be ritually "purified" by genital cutting. Hence, the detractor maintains, dialectical encounters with alternative worldviews will not motivate people who share such beliefs to change them.

It must be admitted that it is an *empirical question* whether or not persons embracing a particular worldview will revise it when they are confronted with information that does not fit into it. As noted in the next section, people may cling tenaciously to beliefs that they know, or should know, to be false or inconsistent with other things that they believe. The question to be addressed here, however, is different. Is there any *justification* for a worldview when its consistency must be "purchased" at the price of comprehension, for instance, if belief in the inferiority of women is maintained by a steadfast refusal to test, through experience, the capacity of women to benefit from education? In addition, can an immoral worldview really be consistent? In other words, can a worldview be consistent, comprehensive, *and* immoral when its adherents are fully open and attentive to what Drydyk calls "knowledge of care, neglect, and abuse"? As noted before, the PWI requires that one's worldview be internally consistent and comprehensive and that one strive to make it morally good.

A detractor may object, secondly, that the strategy of worldview integration presupposes values that may be rejected or esteemed much less highly within some social or cultural groups. Boylan would not deny that adopting the PWI requires accepting the challenge of freedom and autonomy as well as the critical use of our rational capacities.[122] Worldview integration thus privileges the values of rationality, freedom, and autonomy. But, the detractor asks, why would traditionalists or those with fundamentally different ideals commit to these values? Why would they agree to accept these particular (liberal and Western) values as the terms of debate, that is, as underlying the dialectical process?

Again, it must be conceded that *in fact*, traditionalists or others might reject the strategy of worldview integration if they see it as being tainted by

---

[121]*Ibid.*, pp. 196–200.
[122]Boylan says of people who do not accept this challenge that they "fail to realize the fullness of their humanity," *Ibid.*, p. 199.

values alien to their own. The key issue, however, is whether denial of the *minimal* rationality and autonomy that the strategy needs can be consistent with an effort to justify refusal to engage in worldview integration. Against the detractor it can be asked, What are the grounds for refusing to participate in the dialectical process? It might be said that the strategy can't work, but we can't get this verdict without a fair trial. And any other response would seem to be based on *nonrational* grounds, that is, at worst on naked power or coercion, and at best on traditional beliefs or values that cannot be subject to critical reflection (because to critically reflect about them *is* to employ this strategy or one of the others). In other words, any justifiable position is one that both commends itself to our reason and is responsive to the universal desire to be free from the yoke of oppression.

5. SUMMING UP AND LOOKING FORWARD

It should not surprise us that the four strategies for cultural negotiation explored in this chapter share much in common. Indeed, all share three critical features.[123] As noted at the outset, each strategy aims to extend respect for human rights through a process of dialectical interaction. *Thus one feature common to all strategies is an emphasis on dialectics understood as the emergence of a new position satisfactory to the different sides in a dispute.* Dialectical interaction is most explicitly part of the process in the fourth strategy considered, worldview integration, but it is also a critical feature of the other three. *A second key element of each strategy is a dialogic process.*

The transformational strategy is, like worldview integration, based on the underlying belief that resistance to human rights norms flows from worldviews whose limitations or defects become much more difficult to sustain when narrow, limiting, incoherent, and immoral features of these worldviews are opened for critical reflection and challenged by alternative beliefs. The transformational strategy does conceive of the new synthesis, or amalgam, as arising out of a broad participatory process of discourse. Broad participatory discourse is intended to overcome defective and limited conceptions of human rights. Thus this dialogical process could be understood, from the perspective of worldview integration, as an effort to obtain a shared, common worldview. By contrast, worldview integration leads to a new, synthetic shared worldview through dialectical interaction

---

[123]The decision about which strategy to employ will depend on *contingent* features of the case, that is, the nature of the conflict and the most advisable way of addressing it. Three of the strategies are logically consistent and might be used successively or in tandem. Only the strategy of internal validation is restrictive in its use and thus is not consistent with the others. Although a situation best addressed by this strategy might yield, at a later point, to cross-cultural negotiation of another kind.

between personal worldviews or between the shared worldviews of particular groups.

Dialectical interaction is apparent at two levels in the strategy of accommodation. On one level we consider how different claims about the core, interpretations and forms of human rights express or capture the beliefs and intuitions of different persons or groups. Because of likely and serious disagreement over what belongs in each of these categories, there is need—on a second level—for dialectic interaction leading to an understanding of when differences of interpretation are permissible. For this strategy, therefore, the new synthetic position represents a set of criteria in deciding difficult cases acceptable to all sides, if not also agreement on core rights in contrast to variations of interpretation or form.

The dialogic process is present, as well, in the strategies of accommodation and internal validation. The strategy of accommodation recommends that, beyond a certain core of meaning and application, it is permissible to subject human rights to various differences of interpretation and form. As we have seen, however, questions arise about the moral justifiability of certain variations (as in the case of caste in India). These questions must be settled, as we have also seen, by a dialogical process involving persons who have an external point of view as well as those with an internal viewpoint.

The strategy of internal validation also aims at achieving a new, synthetic position through a dialogic process, but one taking place among those who can be understood as sharing common commitments and loyalties (e.g., Muslims who regard the same texts as authoritative), even if other differences are too great to think of them as sharing a common worldview. The strategy recognizes, however, that it is not possible for human rights norms, or for certain interpretations of these norms, to be validated within a social or cultural group unless a process of discourse succeeds in persuading all sides to reevaluate social values. Through this dialogical process, members of the group also would reconsider the moral claims that can be made by all members (e.g., including women or apostates) as well as what should count as proper responses to these claims.

The third critical feature common to all four strategies is <u>critical reflection.</u> Reliance on rationality is so pervasive in each strategy that it is not necessary in this conclusion to say much more about its presence. It should be emphasized, however, that the rationality embedded in each strategy ensures its impartiality. In other words, each strategy is impartial since what each recommends is defensible solely because of its reasonableness. Some critics note that although human rights are universal, the West dominates discourse and, consequently, that there is little room to think that something outside of non-Western discourse can be universally valid.[124] This is a

---

[124]See, for example, Onuma Yasuaki, "Toward an Intercivilizational Approach to Human Rights," in *The East Asian Challenge for Human Rights,* pp. 103–23.

concern that might be directed at the discussion of this chapter. But the remedy is at hand. Since our strategies for cross-cultural negotiation are neutral, "practitioners" from other cultures should be able to advance these strategies with equal results and in terms of their own discourses, so long as their objective is a fair and an even-handed engagement with the perspectives, or worldviews, of others including Westerners.

In conclusion, it is important to remember the focus of this chapter. It might be objected that, despite the best possible methods for cross-cultural negotiation, people will lack sufficient motivation to employ these strategies. This is an open possibility. The direction of thought emphasized throughout this chapter has been on consistency between what we believe and how we act; that is, when we come to believe fully in certain principles, for example, the complete equality of all humans, we act to uphold this principle in any situation threatening our commitment to it.

There are many circumstances in which the connection between *belief* and *motivation* can be overcome, however. Not the least of these have to do with self-advantage and indifference. Perhaps there is a more pervasive gap between belief and motivation. American philosopher Thomas Wren refers to the difference between two kinds of moral judgments: "deontic judgments" and "responsibility judgments."[125] Whereas the former are judgments about the rightness of actions as such, the latter refer to judgments about one's responsibility to act, that is, whether or not it is incumbent upon one to act on one's beliefs.

It is important to explore how a person's responsibility judgments might alter based on changes in his or her self-identity, including perceptions of how others see him or her, as well as how the individual is affected by life experiences. Such an investigation would take us well beyond the scope of this chapter, however. Our concern is not with the psychological basis for moral motivation, but rather with justifiable procedures for addressing conflicting answers to questions such as the following: Do human rights norms apply in this situation, and if so, how? My concern in discussing strategies for cross-cultural negotiation was to show that parties with opposing viewpoints could achieve reasonable, justifiable answers. This task has now been completed. Moreover, given the implausibility of particularism, as demonstrated in Chapter 2, and the demonstration in Chapter 1 that human rights are fundamental moral goods, a strong *prima facie* case has been made against any state, social, or cultural group not willing to engage in cross-cultural negotiation.

---

[125]Thomas E. Wren, *Caring About Morality: Philosophical Perspectives in Moral Psychology* (Cambridge, MA: MIT Press, 1991), pp. 111–4ff. Wren bases this distinction on the research of Lawrence Kohlberg. See, for example, Lawrence Kohlberg, *Essays on Moral Development, Vol. 2, The Psychology of Moral Development* (New York: Harper & Row, 1969/1984).

appendix a

The International Human Rights Regime

Mention is made in the text of the international human rights movement as a "regime." This designation is intended to indicate that the international human rights movement is a complex system consisting of a number of functionally distinct but highly interrelated parts. These parts can be identified as (1) the conceptualization of the regime; (2) definitions of human rights and creation of compulsory international norms; (3) monitoring and implementation; (4) instruments and organizations that are regional in scope; and (5) international citizens' advocacy groups.

1. CONCEPTUALIZATION OF THE PROGRAM

a. Charter of the United Nations

The Charter of the United Nations was adopted in 1945 as a means of avoiding wars between states and preventing future crimes against humanity such as those committed by Fascism during World War II. Key to attaining these objectives, as recognized in the Charter's Preamble, would be respect for human rights. Human rights are an important guiding thread throughout the fabric of the Charter.

Article 1, para. 3, of the Charter charges that the UN shall "achieve international cooperation in promoting and encouraging respect for human rights and for fundamental freedoms for all without distinction as to race, sex, language, or religion." Other prominent provisions charge the General Assembly (Art. 13, para. 1) and the Economic and Security Council (ECOSOC) (Art. 55 c.) with promoting respect for human rights and give a similar mandate to the Trusteeship System (Art. 76 c.). The Charter foresaw that the universal observance and protection of human rights could not be "matters which are essentially within the domestic jurisdiction of any state" (Art. 2, para. 7). Thus, the initial vision was to empower organs of the UN to discuss violations of human rights.

As signatories to the Charter, all member states, or states parties, legally bound themselves to strive toward the full realization of all human rights and fundamental freedoms. Moreover, actual human rights violations were to be dealt with after the creation of the necessary instruments.

b. Universal Declaration of Human Rights

The San Francisco Conference in 1945 decided not to include an international bill of human rights in the charter itself. However, it did demand in Article 68 the establishment of a commission for the promotion of human rights that had as its first task the drafting of this code.

The UN General Assembly adopted the Universal Declaration of Human Rights on December 10, 1948. The Declaration demands of member states a "common standard of achievement for all peoples and all nations" and is formulated in general terms. Fundamental freedom rights (Arts. 3–19) and political rights (Arts. 20–21) are articulated, as well as economic, social, and cultural rights (Arts. 22–28) without any ranking among them.

The Universal Declaration constituted a preliminary, rather than comprehensive, attempt at defining human rights. In addition, when adopted it was understood as reflecting member states' aspirations and therefore was not binding. It took almost twenty years to draft the two international covenants, the International Covenant on Civil and Political Rights (ICCPR) and the International Covenant on Economic, Social and Cultural Rights (ICESCR). In 1966, the General Assembly adopted the ICCPR and the ICESCR, and both entered into force in 1976. Together with the Universal Declaration, these two covenants comprise the International Bill of Rights (IBR). The basic rights laid down by the Universal Declaration and the International Bill of Rights have given rise to over ninety international treaties, declarations, or other instruments within the UN system.

2. DEFINITIONS OF HUMAN RIGHTS AND CREATION OF COMPULSORY NORMS

a. International Bill of Human Rights

The ICCPR and ICESCR are among the two most important international covenants, or treaties, defining human rights. These covenants are reviewed later as well as three other covenants (in historical order). In addition to defining human rights, covenants often establish organs for their implementation, as well as specifying conditions for ratification and becoming international law.

b. Convention on the Prevention and Punishment of the Crime of Genocide

Among the first international conventions adopted as international law in 1948 were the two Geneva Conventions. The first Geneva Convention (officially the UN Convention on the Condition of the Wounded and Sick in Armed Forces) focuses on the rights of individuals, combatants, and noncombatants during war, including enemy captives and prisoners of war.

The Convention on Genocide, or second Geneva Convention, defines genocide as acts committed with the intent to destroy, in whole or in part, a national, ethnic, racial, or religious group. It declares genocide a crime under international law whether committed during war or peacetime, and binds all states parties to the Convention to take measures to prevent and punish any acts of genocide committed within their jurisdiction.

The Convention further bans killing of members of any racial, ethnic, national, or religious group because of their membership in that group, causing serious bodily or mental harm to members of the group, inflicting on members of the group conditions of life intending to destroy them, imposing measures intended to prevent births within the group, and taking the children of group members away from them and placing them with members of another group.

The convention makes illegal any attempts to commit genocide, complicity in its commission, and conspiracy or incitement to commit genocide, as well as genocide itself. Individuals are to be held responsible for these acts whether they were acting in their official capacities or as private individuals. States parties are bound to enact appropriate legislation to make acts specified in Article 3 illegal under their national law and to provide appropriate penalties for violators.

Moreover, national tribunals in territories where the acts were committed are authorized to try persons suspected of acts of genocide, as well as properly constituted international tribunals whose jurisdiction is recognized by the state or states involved. For purposes of extradition, an allegation of genocide is not to be considered a political crime, and states are bound to extradite suspects in accordance with national laws and treaties. Any state party to the Convention may also call upon the United Nations to act to prevent or punish acts of genocide.

The remainder of the Convention specifies procedures for resolving disputes over whether specific acts constitute genocide, and provides procedures for ratification of the Convention.

c. International Covenant on Civil and Political Rights (ICCPR)

The ICCPR entered into force in 1976. (It was ratified, with reservations, by the United States in 1992.) The 53 articles of the ICCPR detail the basic civil and political rights of individual persons, as well as certain duties of both persons and states.

Among the rights of individual persons are the following:

- The right to life
- The right to liberty and freedom of movement
- Freedom of thought, conscience, and religion
- Freedom of opinion and expression
- Freedom of assembly and association
- The right to be recognized as a person before the law
- The right to equality before the law
- The right to presumption of innocence until proven guilty
- The right to appeal a conviction
- The right to legal recourse when one's rights have been violated, even if the violator was acting in an official capacity
- The right of the convicted to appeal for commutation to a lesser penalty
- The right to privacy and the protection of privacy by law
- The right to choose whom to marry and to found a family

The ICCPR provides that members of ethnic, religious, or linguistic minorities of states members shall have rights to enjoy their own cultures, to practice their religions, and to use their languages. The text provides for rights of children to have a name, acquire a nationality, and to be protected against discrimination on the basis of race or gender. The ICCPR also requires that the duties and obligations of marriage and family be shared equally between partners.

As to duties of states, the ICCPR specifies the following:

- Forbids torture and inhumane or degrading treatment
- Forbids slavery or involuntary servitude

- Forbids arbitrary arrest and detention
- Forbids propaganda advocating either war or hatred based on race, religion, national origin, or language
- Prohibits discrimination based on race, sex, color, national origin, or language
- Prohibits debtors' prisons
- Restricts the death penalty to the most serious of crimes
- Forbids the death penalty entirely for persons under 18 years of age

In addition, the ICCPR permits governments to temporarily suspend some of these rights but only in cases of extreme emergency, and it lists those rights that cannot be suspended for any reason. It also establishes the UN Commission on Human Rights.

d. International Covenant on Economic, Social, and Cultural Rights (ICESCR)

The ICESCR entered into force in 1976. (Although it has 136 states parties, the United States has not ratified it.) The 31 articles of the ICESCR set forth the basic economic, social, and cultural rights of individual persons and peoples, as well as certain duties of both.

Specified rights of individual persons include the following:

- The right to work, including the opportunity to gain one's living through work freely chosen
- The right to wages sufficient to support a minimum standard of living
- The right to equal pay for equal work
- The right to safe and healthy working conditions
- The right to equal opportunity for advancement in employment
- The right to rest, leisure, and a reasonable limitation of working hours
- The right to form trade unions and to join the trade union of one's choice
- The right to strike
- The right to social security, including social insurance
- The right to maternity leave with pay or other social security benefits
- The rights of children and young persons to be protected from economic and social exploitation
- The right of everyone to an adequate standard of living, including adequate food, clothing, and housing
- The right to the enjoyment of the highest attainable standard of physical and mental health
- The right to free primary education and to accessible education at all levels
- The right of parents to send their children to parochial schools
- The right to take part in cultural life

- The right to benefit from scientific, literary or artistic production through copyright, patent, or trademark protection.

The ICESCR recognizes two fundamental rights of peoples as follows:

- The right to self-determination
- The right of a people to own, trade, and dispose of their property freely, and not to be deprived of their own means of subsistence

Many articles of the covenant address the duties of states, both singly and in cooperation, to fulfill individual rights. Most notably, the ICESCR requires that states parties cooperate "to ensure an equitable distribution of world food supplies in relation to need." In addition, while recognizing the difficulties of lesser-developed states in fulfilling some individual rights (e.g., free compulsory elementary education), the ISCESCR requires states to take steps toward their implementation. (See 3a later.)

e. Convention Against Torture and Other Cruel, Inhuman, or Degrading Treatment or Punishment (CAT)

The CAT entered into force in 1987. (The United States joined 101 other states parties in ratifying the convention in 1994, although with reservations.)

The CAT defines torture, bans torture under all circumstances, and requires states to take effective legal and other measures to prevent torture. It declares that no state of emergency, other external threats, or orders from a superior officer or authority may be invoked to justify torture. It also forbids activities that do not rise to the level of torture but that constitute cruel, inhumane, or degrading treatment.

States are required by the CAT to make torture illegal and to provide punishment for those who commit it. The CAT requires states to assert jurisdiction when torture is committed within its borders or under its control, to investigate reports of torture and to prosecute alleged torturers, or to extradite suspects to face trial before another competent court. It also requires states to cooperate with any civil proceedings against accused torturers.

The Convention obliges each state to provide training to law enforcement and military personnel on torture prevention, to review its interrogation methods on a regular basis, and to promptly investigate any allegations that its officials have committed torture.

States must ensure that individuals who allege that someone has committed torture against them are permitted to make an official complaint and to have it investigated, and if complaints are proven, to compensate victims, including full medical treatment and payments to survivors if the victim has died as a result of the torture. Also, it forbids states to admit into evidence during a trial any confession or statement made during or as a result of torture.

The CAT forbids the return of any refugee to his or her country if there is reason to believe that the refugee will be tortured, and it requires the country of asylum to consider the human rights record of the refugee's native country in making this decision.

The second part of the CAT establishes the Committee Against Torture and establishes rules for its membership and activities.

f. Convention on the Rights of the Child (CRC)

The CRC entered into force in 1992. (Every state by 1992, a total of 191, except the United States and Somalia, had ratified the convention.) Article 3 imposes a central duty: "In all actions concerning children, whether undertaken by public or private social welfare institutions, courts of law, administrative authorities or legislative bodies, the best interests of the child shall be a primary consideration."

The CRC recognizes that children are independent beings entitled to freedom of thought and speech, and that they should have an opportunity to be heard regarding any decisions materially affecting their welfare and "given due weight in accordance with age and maturity." States must take effective steps to protect children from economic or sexual exploitation and to abolish "traditional practices prejudicial to the health of children." The Convention requires that states respect the family as the most desirable environment for a child's upbringing and asserts that the child should have "the right to know and be cared for by his or her parents." Article 23 endows physically or mentally disabled children with a special right to claim such assistance from the state as may be necessary to develop into full and useful members of society. States are prohibited from executing children or jailing them for life, or from imprisoning them with adult offenders. States must also establish a minimal age for criminal liability.

3. MONITORING AND IMPLEMENTATION

The monitoring, implementation, and enforcement of human rights instruments is an enormous topic. Here only a brief overview is offered of some of the major aspects of this subject and under the following headings: (a) implementation provisions of treaties and covenants, (b) influences on national law, (c) role of the Commission on Human Rights, (d) Office of the High Commissioner for Human Rights, (e) peacekeeping and humanitarian intervention, and (f) tribunals.

a. Implementation Provisions of Treaties and Covenants

Most of the international treaties and covenants contain articles specifying methods for oversight and implementation. For instance, the ICESCR requires states to adopt detailed plans for the progressive implementation of these protections. Each state party is required to submit annual reports on providing for these rights to the Secretary General, who is to transmit them to the Economic and Social Council. The ECOSOC, in turn, may make recommendations to the General Assembly and may seek from subsidiary organs and specialized agencies of the UN advice regarding measures conducive to the progressive implementation of the covenant.

The Convention on the Elimination of All Forms of Discrimination Against Women (CEDAW), entering force in 1979 (but not ratified by the United States), provides instructions of three types. It specifies what states must do to implement specific articles; second, it details how a commission overseeing the convention is to be constituted and to operate; and third, it specifies how state parties must report to demonstrate their implementation of the convention.

In some cases, the UN has created instruments, known as Option Protocols, after a convention has entered into effect, but with the intent to remedy oversights. One Optional Protocol to the ICCPR enables private parties claiming to be victims of a violation of their civil or political rights to file individual complaints, although this protocol formalized a practice already begun by the UN Commission on Human Rights. (There are two Optional Protocols to the ICCPR, but the second concerns a substantive issue as it aims at the abolition of the death penalty.)

b. Influences on National Law

Many countries have incorporated provisions from the basic UN instruments directly into their national law. The constitutions of many states organized in the postcolonial and post–Cold War eras in Africa, Asia, and Eastern Europe contain language taken from the International Bill of Rights (IBR). But even the well-established democracies of Australia, Canada, and New Zealand enacted new legislation for their immigration policies and toward indigenous peoples, publicly declaring their intention to conform more closely to the standards of the Universal Declaration. In addition, the laws of nations have been reformed by judicial decisions. This outcome is especially true for the 41 European states bound by the decisions of the European Court (see item 4 later); however, judges of appellate courts in postcolonial states (e.g., Kenya) also have decided cases by relying on human rights instruments as authoritative international law.

c. Role of the UN Commission on Human Rights

Although committees of experts (nominated by states parties but act-ing on their own recognizance and not as representatives of their states) oversee the major instruments, the Commission on Human Rights (CHR) came into existence in 1976 when the ICCPR entered into force. Its primary purpose was to examine reports from states parties and from committees of experts and working groups concerning rights violations. These were dis-cussed with representatives of governments, often at the ministerial level. At a later point, special rapporteurs were appointed to investigate the facts in specific countries or territories and to report back to the CHR and to the General Assembly.

The most important development, however, was the HRC's increased ability to respond to grievances submitted by individuals against their own governments. Able at the outset only to consider complaints brought by representatives of states parties or UN committees, the CHR nevertheless had been deluged with "communications" from individuals or NGOs acting on their behalf, numbering eventually into the hundreds of thousands. In 1970, ECOSOC resolution 1503 first opened the door by enabling the HRC to consider petitions from individuals. The following year this authority was broadened so that the CHR could consider complaints from individuals against states parties where there were "reasonable grounds to believe that they reveal a consistent pattern of gross and reliably attested violations of human rights and fundamental freedoms." In the 1990s, an average of 100,000 such appeals were processed annually, and to date, the CHR has considered complaints against more than 70 different countries ranging from Afghanistan and Argentina through the alphabet to Uganda, the United States, Vietnam, and Zaire.

Although the CHR's studies of systematic human rights violations are confidential, it can send communications to the Secretary General recom-mending formal charges against a state. The accused government must then face a highly elaborate and embarrassing process before the representatives of other governments who, in turn, determine whether the specific situation requires further study or "investigation" (i.e., some appropriate action).

d. Office of the High Commissioner for Human Rights

In 1993, the UN created the Office of the High Commissioner for Human Rights, which is based in Geneva, and appointed the first High Commissioner. The appointment by the Secretary General of persons of in-ternational distinction and expertise as High Commissioners gives to the human rights "division" of the UN ambassadorial, or ministerial, status. It enables the High Commissioner to engage in dialogue with world leaders, as well as to oversee all operations of the UN relating to human rights. Consequently, this office coordinates the many committees and activities directed at human rights promotion and protection; and the office also strengthens and streamlines bureaucratic machinery. In addition, this office has put an increased emphasis on providing advisory services and technical and financial assistance to states requesting them. It also coordinates education and public information programs in the field of human rights.

e. Peacekeeping and Humanitarian Intervention

The UN has the authority, subject to determination of last resort and Security Council approval, to request armed forces from member countries to intervene in cases involving genocide and crimes against humanity. In addition, the UN is authorized to undertake peacekeeping missions, initially when belligerents had agreed on a cease-fire and both requested the presence of UN peacekeepers to maintain the truce. Over time peacekeeping evolved into "peacemaking" missions as the UN was drawn, when the Security Council saw fit, into situations involving hot conflicts such as within "failed states" or "ethnic cleansing." Although the UN found it difficult to respond appropriately and successfully in the former Yugoslavia and failed even to try to stop genocide in Rwanda in 1994, "peacekeeping" was far more successful in the former Belgian Congo (Zaire), Cyprus, Namibia, El Salvador, Cambodia, and Mozambique.

f. Tribunals

The war crimes judgments at Nuremberg and Tokyo established the principle of "universal jurisdiction" intended to end the impunity of those who commit crimes against humanity or crimes of war. According to the principle of "universal jurisdiction," UN members have the authority individually or collectively to conduct a trial against persons accused of such crimes. The UN also has the power to establish international tribunals for this purpose, as with the 1993 War Crimes Tribunal for the former Yugoslavia. The effort to establish a genuine and permanent world court is envisioned in the Statute of Rome of 1998 that would establish the International Criminal Court (ICC) at The Hague. The Statute of Rome gives detailed attention to definitions of crimes falling within the Court's jurisdiction as well as the rights of defendants. It recognizes, for the first time, the seriousness of sexual violence, and it would establish command responsibility (of officers) as a basis of liability as well as deprive soldiers of the defense of "respondent superior" (following orders) in the commission of a crime. Presently awaiting ratification by states parties, the ICC is opposed by the United States government first on the grounds that the Court would not be subject to Security Council oversight, and second, because the Rome Statute did not guarantee demands for "100 percent protection" of American military personnel.

4. INSTRUMENTS AND ORGANIZATIONS REGIONAL IN SCOPE

In Africa, the Americas, and Europe, regional instruments and organizations have been developed for the protection and implementation of human rights. The efforts of African members of the UN were instrumental in the adoption in 1965 of the International Convention on the Elimination of All Forms of Racial Discrimination. Subsequently, African states created the regional Organization for African Unity (OAU) and in 1981 promulgated their own Charter of Human and People's Rights. The Charter was innovative in including so-called "third-generation" rights (e.g., the right to development) and in counterbalancing rights with duties. A Commission was set up in Banjul, Gambia, to monitor implementation of the Charter and to receive complaints. To date the record of the Commission is undistinguished (at best), because of newly independent states' jealousy of their sovereignty and their unwillingness to fund the Commission.

The OAU and its Charter were predated by an inter-American system with a Convention (1969), a Commission (in Washington, DC), and a Court (in Costa Rica) that covers many Latin American and Caribbean members of the Organization of American States, or OAS. (Although the United States is a signatory of the treaty, through self-serving illogic it refuses to recognize the jurisdiction of the Court). Despite the intransigence of military dictatorships, the Commission has had some significant successes, as for instance, in conducting a number of on-site investigations into disappearances and atrocities perpetrated by dictatorial regimes. The Inter-American Court has treaty powers to require states parties to change laws in conformity with rulings upholding the Convention. Although individuals have no direct right of access to the Court, the Commission can appear as a party on their behalf. And despite limitations on its activities resulting from inter-American politics, the Court has scored some major advances in human rights law, including a decision protecting freedom of expression and a decision that could be a precedent requiring governments to pay reparations to families of young men or women who have been "disappeared" by the military.

There is no international, regional human rights regime for Middle Eastern countries or for Asia or the newly independent Pacific states. However, jurists, rights theorists, and advocates in many Muslim states have convened to review the compatibility of human rights norms with the Qur'an and the teachings of the Prophet. The Cairo Declaration of Human Rights in Islam was created in 1990. In addition, the 48 states continuing membership in the British Commonwealth may advance human rights initiatives, although only 16 Commonwealth members recognize the authority of the Privy Council, which comprises the supreme court of the United Kingdom.

The most successful regional regime for human rights has occurred in Europe. In 1950, the Council of Europe promulgated the European Convention on Human Rights that was unique in combining provisions of the Universal Declaration with trial procedures of the common law. Furthermore, it established a Commission that could refer cases for final decision to a European Court sitting in Strasbourg. State signatories had a duty, in the event of adverse judgments, to bring their laws into conformity with the Convention. Most significantly, Article 25 enabled "any person, non-governmental organization, or group" to petition the Commission alleging a violation of their rights. Consequently, in ratifying the European Convention in 1953, states parties agreed to allow their citizens to bring them, or their laws and court decisions, before the bar of international justice. The European Court is recognized for the quality of its well-reasoned decisions, and it now adjudicates the interpretation of human rights standards for 41 countries, thereby building a body of specific and positive human rights law. It has become a constitutional court for almost the entire continent, and a model for a future world court.

5. International Citizens' Advocacy Groups

Globally, the strongest and most consistent champions of human rights have been grassroots and international citizens' research and advocacy groups. Known collectively as Non-Governmental Organizations, or NGOs for short, the majority of these groups are grassroots in that they are open to anyone sharing their mission, their funding comes from individual contributions and grants, and they are able to mobilize large numbers of ordinary persons to protest, to demonstrate, and to lobby and pressure governments and intergovernmental organizations (IGOs) on behalf of human rights and the victims of abuses. Although usually having low budgets in comparison with government operations, NGOs can disseminate information and influence public opinion with great rapidity through electronic and print media. See Appendix B for a short, selected group of NGOs.

NGOs make a critical contribution to human rights issues in several ways, although most do not limit themselves to one kind of influence. First, some (e.g., Amnesty International, Human Rights Watch, The Red Cross) identify particular persons whose rights have been violated, such as "prisoners of conscience," monitor the treatment of these persons, and advocate for their release or custody in conformity with their rights. Second, many (e.g., Bread for the World, Human Rights USA Resource Center, Oxfam) conduct research on conditions—political, economic, environmental, and the like—threatening human rights; publicize these findings; and raise funds to address problems (e.g., famine) and to advocate for changes in policies. Third, a number of NGOs (e.g., the Red Cross and the Red Crescent and Heifer International) dedicate themselves primarily to humanitarian relief.

Fourth, through the sheer scale of their activities and persistence, NGOs are able to keep world attention focused on human rights issues and the need for action. For example, the World Conference on Human Rights in Vienna held during 1993 included heads of states, over 2,000 delegates from 171 nations, and nearly 4,000 representatives of over 800 NGOs. Together the deliberations of this assembly resulted in The Vienna Declaration and Program of Action reaffirming the indivisible and interrelated nature of human rights. The 1995 UN Fourth World Conference on Women, which was held in Beijing, enabled NGOs representing women's rights to draw attention to the continued and serious violation of women's rights. When China, joined by Indonesia, Malaysia, and Singapore, endorsed the "Bangkok Declaration," asserting the cultural relativity of human rights norms, more than 100 Asian-Pacific NGOs publicly issued their parallel declaration, strongly affirming the universality of human rights norms.

A fifth way in which NGOs (e.g., Fellowship of Reconciliation, Peace Brigades International) exert influence is by recruiting and training private individuals for special roles in conflict areas. These persons are trained to be observers, fact-finders, and on some occasions, agents who offer safe conduct or sanctuary, or who serve as negotiators in strife-ridden areas. Sixth, most NGOs engage in one or more types of political advocacy to change laws or policies. Often expert members work with special agencies of the UN or other IGOs to assist in the drafting of reports and new treaties, and they send delegates to international conferences. Local chapters will expose or hold hearings on the activities of a government, as well as lobby and exert other forms of pressure. Through what has been called the "boomerang effect," local chapters of NGOs have succeeded, through influence and pressure on their own government (e.g., France or Great Britain), in leading their governments to change their attitudes and policies toward flagrant human rights violators. The boomerang effect was very effective in leading to the pariah status of the former racist government of South Africa, and it has had considerable effect against China.

CONCLUDING COMMENT

My intention has been to provide readers of this book with some helpful background on the extent and complexities of the international human rights regime, as it is commonly known. Such an account cannot avoid touching on some of the more notable advances or successes of the UN and this regime, as well as some of its more dismal limitations or failures. The literature on the human rights regime and the UN is immense. Those interested in a positive account with an optimistic prognosis for the future might begin with Paul Gordon Lauren's detailed but engaging *The Evolution of International Human Rights: Visions Seen* (Philadelphia: University of Pennsylvania Press, 1998). An equally engrossing narrative of the advance of human rights, but one less sanguine in tone and much more critical of both the UN and the United States, is Geoffrey Robertson, *Crimes Against Humanity: The Struggle for Justice* (New York: The Free Press, 2000).

appendix b

Selected Research and/or Activist Nongovernmental Organizations (NGOs), Selected Intergovernmental Organizations (IGOs), with Other Selected Resources

Selected NGOs and Web Sites

African Centre for Democracy and Human Rights Studies *http://www1.umn.edu/ humanrts/africa/ACOHRS.htm*

African Commission on Human and People's Rights *http://www.achr.org*

Albert Einstein Institute *http://www.aeinstein.org*

Alliance for Democracy *http://www.thealliancefordemocracy.org*

American Friends Service Committee *http://www.afsc.org*

Amnesty International *http://www.amnesty.org*

Arab Organization for Human Rights *http://aohr.org*

Ariga: Human Rights and Peace Groups *http://www.ariga.com/humanrights.org*

Asian Forum for Human Rights and Development *http://www.forumasia.org*

Asian Human Rights Commission *http://www.ahrchk.net*

Bread for the World *http://www.bread.org*

Carnegie Council on Ethics and International Affairs *http://www.ccia.org*

Carter Center *http://www.cartercenter.org*

Center for Human Rights Education *http://www.hrusa.org*

Centro por la Justicia y el Derecho Internacional *http://www.cejil.org*

Children's Defense Fund *http://www.childrensdefense.org*

Comitè des Nations Unie Contra la Torture *http://www.vpb.admin.ch/franz/cont/au/aut_0.1.2.1.html*

Derechos: Human Rights in Latin America *http://www.derechos.org*

Franklin and Eleanor Roosevelt Institute *http://www.feri.org*

Hague Appeal for Peace *http://www.haguepeace.org*

Human Rights USA Resource Center *http://hrusa.org*

Human Rights Watch *http://www.hrw.org*

Heartland Alliance *http://www.heartland_alliance.org*

Heifer International: Fighting Hunger, Caring for the Earth *http://www.heifer.org*

Indigenous People's Human Rights Project *http://www.hrusa.org*

Institute for International Law and Justice *http://www.nyuiilj.org*

International Alliance for Women *http://www.womenalliance.org*

International Commission of Jurists *http://www.icj*

International Committee of the Red Cross *http://www.icrc.org*

International Federation of the Red Cross and Red Crescent Societies *http://www.ifcr.org*

International Forum on Globalization *http://www.ifg.org*

International Gay and Lesbian Human Rights Commission *http://www.iglhrc.org*

International Labour Organization *http://www.ilo.org*

International League for Human Rights *http://www.ilhr.org*

Israel-Palestine Center for Research and Information *http://www.ipcri.org*

Jobs with Justice *http://www.jwj.org*

The Justice Project *http://www.thejusticeproject.org*

Karamah: Muslim Women Lawyers for Human Rights *http://www.karamah.org*

La Majer Obrera *http://www.majorobrera.org*

National Law Center on Homelessness and Poverty *http://www.nlchp.org*

National Network for Immigrant and Refugee Rights *http://www.nnirr.org*

Nuclear Age Peace Foundation *http://www.wagingpeace.org*

Oxfam International *http://www.oxfam.org*

Peace Brigades International *http://www.peacebrigades.org*

People's Movement for Human Rights Education *http://www.pdhre.org*

Physicians for Social Responsibility *http://www.psr.org*

Project South: Institute for the Elimination of Poverty and Genocide *http://www.projectsouth.org*

South Asia Human Rights Documentation Center *http://www.hri.ca*

Southern Poverty Law Center *http://www.splcenter.org*

"We the Peoples" Initiative *http://www.wethepeoples.org*

Women in Black *http://www.geocities.com/EndTheOccupation*

Women's International League for Peace and Freedom *http://www.wilpf.org*

World Council of Churches *http://www.wcc-coe.org/wcc/english.html*

Selected IGOs and Web Sites

Council of Europe, European Commission against Racism and Intolerance *http://www.coe.int*

European Court of Human Rights *http://www.echr.coe.int*

International Court of Justice *http://www.icj.org*

International Criminal Court *http://www.icc-cpj.int*

Organization of American States *http://www.oas.org*

Organization of African Unity *http://www.itcilo.it/actrav/actrav-english.htm*

United Nations, Centre for Human Rights *http://www.un.org*

United Nations, UNESCO *http://portal.unesco.org*

United Nations, Office of the High Commissioner for Human Rights *http://www .unhchr.hr.org*

World Health Organization *http://www.who.int/en*

Other Selected Resources

Amnesty International Report, Amnesty International

Human Rights Fax Hot Line: 41-22-917-0092, managed by the Special Procedures Branch of the Centre for Human Rights in Geneva

Human Rights Bulletin, International League for Human Rights

Human Rights Law Journal, a major journal

Human Rights Quarterly, a major journal

Human Rights Newsletter, UN Centre for Human Rights

Human Rights Review, a major journal

Human Rights World Watch Report, Human Rights Watch

Notes of the High Commissioner for Human Rights, No. 1: Making Human Rights a Reality, UN Office of the High Commissioner for Human Rights

UN CD-ROM, *Human Rights: Bibliographical Data and International Instruments,* 1997

United Nations Chronicle, UN Office of the Secretariat

The United Nations and Human Rights, 1945–1995, UN Office of the High Commissioner and Centre for Human Rights

Universal Human Rights, a major journal

Index

A

Absolutism, 49, 54, 56
Abuse, 94
  of children by teachers in Africa,
    75
  guarantees against, 94
  of human rights, 97
Accommodation, strategy of,
    97–108
Additive goods, 32
Ad hominem, 67
Advance of human rights/decline
    of traditional cultures, 70–71
Ad verecundiam, 75
Afghanistan, 26
Africa, 8, 72, 104

adoption of the Universal Decla-
    ration of Human Rights
    (UDHR) in, 58
availability of small firearms in,
    73
beating of children by teachers
    in, 75
famine in, 28
female circumcision in, 33
group roles in, 76
human rights concepts in, 60
strategy of accommodation in,
    104
Ahl al-kitab, 111
Alien, 56
Amnesty International, 80, 91
Anarchical Fallacies (Bentham), 19

Anikwata, Virginia (case study), 33–41
  justifications, 38–41
  right to asylum, 34–38
An-Na'im, Abdullahi Ahmed, 90, 108
Apostasy, law of, 89, 111
Appeals, 14
Application, 2
Arguments, trade-off, 83–87
Asia, 57, 104
  adoption of the Universal Declaration of Human Rights (UDHR) in, 58
  family values in, 76
  human rights concepts in, 60
  protection from arbitrary government in, 76
  strategy of accommodation in, 104
Asylum, right to, 34–38
Authority of law, 109
Autonomy regimes, 54
Aziz, Nikhil, 66

B

Basic goods, 9, 32
Bentham, Jeremy, 19
Bill of Rights, 20
bin Mohamad, Mahathir, 44
Boylan, Michael, 39, 90, 118–25
Buddhism, 61
Buddhist Tamils in Sri Lanka, 62

C

Capital punishment of minors, 67
Carter, Jimmy, 80
Caste system in India, 70
Categorical Imperative, 31
Causal claim, 68–69

Causal complaint, 66
Child betrothal, 104
Children
  exploitation of, 72
  protection from discrimination, 45
  right to opt out of traditional practices, 104–5
China
  international human rights norms in, 81
  national sovereignty in, 81
  slave labor in, 72
  trade-off arguments in, 83–84
  transformational strategy in, 96
Circumcision, female, 33, 104
Civil liberties, 85
Civil rights, 57
Claiming rights, 11
Coincidence, 71
Compelling reasons, 13
Concept of human rights, 1, 2–13
  correlative duties, 6–8
  entitlements, 4–6
  individual discretion, 10
  moral rights, 12–13
  objects of rights, 8–9
  social context, 3–4
  universalizability, 10–12
Conceptual analysis, 1
Content of law, 109
Contingent features of human life, 64
Convention against Torture and Other Cruel, Inhuman, or Degrading Treatment or Punishment, 41
Convention on the Elimination of All Forms of Discrimination Against Women (CEDAW), 45, 78
Convention on the Rights of the Child (CRC), 45, 78, 80
Coomaraswami, Radhika, 79

Core of human rights, 52
Correlation, 70–71
  between rights and duties, 6–8
Correlative
  duties, 6–8
  obligations, 36
CRC. *see* Convention on the Rights
  of the Child (CRC)
Cross-cultural negotiations, 87–88,
  89–127
  defining, 90
  internal validation, strategy of,
  108–18
  strategy of accommodation for,
  97–108
  transformational strategy, 92–97
  worldview integration, strategy
  of, 118–25
Cultural determinism, 64
Cultural diversity, 65, 99
Cultural relativism, 36, 48

D

Death penalty, 91
Debating the universality of
  human rights, 42–88
  causal claim, 68–69
  diversity, human rights, and
  cross-cultural negotiation,
  87–88
  ethical relativism, 48–66
  imperialism charge, 66–68
  irrelevancy of human rights
  claim, 77–82
  universalism *versus* exceptionalism, 43–48
Declaration of Independence, 14
Defeasible rights, 40, 49, 50
Democracy, 2
  participatory, 96
Democracy's Discontent (Sandel),
  44

Deng, Francis, 93
Derogable rights, 50
Dhimma, 111
Dialectical
  interaction, 122, 125–26
  justifications for human rights,
  28–32
  negotiations, 90–91
Dialogic process, 94–95, 125
Discrimination against women, 76
Diversity, human rights, and cross-
  cultural negotiation, 87–88
Diya, 112
Doctrine of natural rights, 15–16
Donnelly, Jack, 22, 24, 52, 71, 97
Drydyk, Jay, 63, 92
Dworkin, Ronald, 22, 23

E

Education, equal opportunity of,
  101
Egypt, 45
Employment, fair practices in, 101
English Reform Acts, 20
Enlightenment, 15
Entitlements, 4–6, 7, 35, 94
Epistemological objections, 17–19
Equality, 2
  in education, 101
  gender, 110–18
Equal rights, 10
Esoteric knowledge, 16
Ethical relativism, 46–66
  challenge, 46–47
Europe
  death penalty in, 91
  human rights concepts in, 60
  social democracies in, 60
Exceptionalism, 43–48
Exceptionalists, 71
Existence of human rights, 1
External judgment, 105, 107

F

Female circumcision, 33, 104
Feminism, 116
Flathman, Richard, 22
Forms of human rights, 52
Franck, Thomas, 59, 74
Fraser, Malcolm, 44
Freedom of conscience, 12, 103
Fundamental moral rights, 20–21

G

Gandhi, Mohandas (Mahatma), 63,
    97
Gender equality in Islam, 110–18
General Assembly, 58
Genetic fallacy, 57
Genocide, 61, 73
    prevention of, 97
Germany
    economic development in, 85
    social and economic rights in, 85
Gewirth, Alan, 28–32
Glendon, Mary, 58
Global problems facing humanity,
    74
Global trade in small firearms, 73
Golden Rule, 31
Golding, Martin, 3, 22
Good reasons approach, 22–25
    problems with the, 25–28
Goods, categories of, 9
Gratuities, 4

H

Habermas, Jürgen, 96
Hadith, 55
Hampshire, Stuart, 43
Haq, Farhart, 114
Hard relationships, 61

Heuristics, 34
Higgins, Rosalyn, 43
Hindu discrimination against
    Chandals, 106
Holidays with pay, 101
Homeomorphic equivalents, 63
Howard, Rhoda, 22, 24, 71, 104
Humanity
    crimes against, 97
    global problems facing, 74
Human rights
    abuse of, 97
    the Anikwata case, 33–41
    concept of, 1, 2–13
    and cross-cultural negotiations,
        87–88, 89–127
    debating the universality of,
        42–88
    existence of, 1
    incomplete conception of, 92
    irrelevancy of, 77–82
    justification of, 1, 13–32
    protection of, 87
    reasoning about, 1–41
    and trade-off arguments, 83–87
Human Rights Watch, 91

I

ICCPR. *see* International Conven-
    tion on Civil and Political
    Rights (ICCPR)
Ijitihad, 110, 116
Immigration and Naturalization
    Service (INS), 33
Imperialism charge, 66–68
Imperialism criticism, 53
Inada, Kenneth, 61
Inalienable rights, 9, 10, 16
Incommensurability claim, 56, 77
India
    caste system in, 70
    exploitation of women in, 72

Hindu discrimination against
Chandals in, 106
Individual discretion, 10
Infringement of rights, 103
Internal judgment, 105
Internal validation, strategy of, 90,
108–18
criticism of, 117–18
International Bill of Human Rights,
3, 14, 91, 95, 102
International Convention Against
Torture, 33
International Convention on Civil
and Political Rights (ICCPR),
44, 59, 89, 100
International Monetary Fund
(IMF), 68, 86
Interpretations of human rights, 52
Iran, 116
transformational strategy and, 96
Irrelevancy criticism of human
rights, 56, 66, 77–82
Islam and Human Rights (Mayer),
117
Islam/Islamic cultures, 62, 89, 110;
see also Muslims
conflicts with international
human rights, 111
gender equality in, 115
strategy of internal validation
and, 108–18

J

Jefferson, Thomas, 3, 16
Jim Crow laws, 103
Jizya, 111
Justice, 2
Justification of human rights, 1,
13–32
dialectical justifications, 28–32
difficulties with natural rights,
17–20

good reasons approach,
22–25
natural law and natural rights,
15–16
from natural rights to human
rights, 20–22
problems with the good reasons
approach, 25–28
Justifications, 2
Juvenile criminals, 100

K

Kant, Immanuel, 31
Khomeini, Imam, 111
King, Martin Luther, 97
Kumarantunga, Chandrika, 79
Kwasi, Wireda, 8
Kyoto Accord, 82

L

Latin America, human rights con-
cepts in, 60
Law of nature, 15
Life, critical concerns of, 90
Locke, John, 3, 14, 15, 17
Logical inconsistency, 46
Logical objections to natural rights,
17, 18
Lovelave, Sandra, 75–76

M

Mahbubani, Kishore, 85
Maliseet Indians, 75–76
Marcel, Gabriel, 58
Mayer, Ann Elizabeth, 78, 1174
Melden, A.I., 22, 23, 25
Mernissi, Fatima, 70
Meyers, Diana, 9

Middle East, human rights
problems afflicting the,
78–79
Moral errors, 48
Morally justified rights claim, 13
Moral rights, 12–13
Muslims, 55, 70
gender equality among, 110
group classifications of, 111
irrelevancy of human rights,
78
rights of women, 111–13
role of *shari'a*
strategy of internal validation
and, 108–18
Muzaffar, Chandra, 66

N

Najmabadi, Afasaneh, 116
National interest, 77
National sovereignty, 81
Natural law, 15–16
Natural rights, 14, 15–16
difficulties with, 17–20
objections to, 17–20
Natural rights theory, 2
Neglect, 94
Nicaragua, 67
Nondefeasible rights, 50
Nonderogable rights, 50
Nonsubtractive goods, 32
North America/United States
death penalty in, 91
economic development in, 85
human rights concepts in, 60
importance of fundamental
rights in, 20
international human rights
norms in, 81
political liberalism in, 57
protection of social and economic rights, 79–80

O

Objections, 17–20
to natural rights, 17–20
Objects of rights, 8–9, 36
Official culture, 78
concept of, 75
Orientalism, 57
Orwell, George, 11
Othman, Norani, 79, 108

P

Paid holidays, 101
Paine, Thomas, 3
Pannikar, Raimundo, 62
Parochial tradition, 16
Participatory democracy, 96
Periodic holidays with pay, 51
Personal Worldview Imperative
(PWI), 39, 120
Political liberalism, 57
Political liberties, 85
Pollis, Adamantia, 63
Poll tax, 111
Practical objections to natural
rights, 17, 19
Practice of rights, 13
Privileges, 4
Prostitution in Thailand, 71–72
Psychopaths, moral rights of, 25
*Purdah and the Status of Women in
Islam* (Haq), 115

Q

Qawamu, 111
Qur'an, 110

R

Reagan, Ronald, 67, 80
Relativism, 55

Religious law. *see Shari'a*
Right(s)
  to asylum, 34–38
  basic, 10
  defeasible, 49, 50
  derogable, 50
  and duties, correlation between, 6–8
  equal, 11
  to food and water, 10
  fundamental, 20–21
  inalienable, 9, 10, 16
  infringement of, 103
  to life, 10
  moral, 12–13
  natural, 15–16
  nondefeasible, 50
  objects of, 8–9
  self-administrative aspect of, 36
  to trial by jury, 7
  to work, 100
Rights and Persons (Melden), 23
Rushdie, Salman, 111

S

Said, Edward, 57
Sandanistas, 68
Sandel, Michael, 44
Satanic Verses (Rushdie), 111
Satha-Anand, Suwanna, 72
Schwab, Peter, 63
Search and seizure, 7
Second Treatise of Government (Locke), 14
Self-administrative aspect of rights, 36
Sen, Amartya, 85
Shari'a, 89, 109–12
Shue, Henry, 50
Singapore
  economic development in, 86
  effects of modernization/global-ization in, 74
Sisters of Islam, 79
Slave trading, 93
Social behavior, 22
Social context, 3–4, 36
Social contract theory, 16
Social determinism, 64
Socially constructed, 24
Social protection, 63
Social responsibility, 74
Sociopaths, moral rights of, 25
Soft relationships, 61
Somalia, humanitarian intervention into, 72
South Korea, economic development in, 86
Sri Lanka, 62, 79, 96
  Buddhist Tamils in, 62
State of nature, 16
Strategy
  of accommodation, 97–108
  of internal validation, 90, 108–18
  of worldview integration, 118–25
Subjectivism, 55
Substance of rights, 8–9
Sunna, 55
Sweden, death penalty in, 91

T

Taiwan
  economic development in, 86
  effects of modernization/globalization in, 74
Taking Rights Seriously (Dworkin), 23
Taliban, 26
Taylor, Charles, 62
Thailand, prostitution in, 71–72
Theory of rights, 2
Trade-off arguments, 63, 66, 83–87
Traditional culture, 78
Transformational strategy, 92–97

critics of, 96
prospects of, 96–97
Tribal law, 76

U

United Nations, 14, 53, 97
  Commission on Human Rights,
    53
Universal Declaration of Human
    Rights (UDHR), 42, 44, 89
*Universal Human Rights in Theory
    and Practice* (Donnelly), 98,
    105
Universal Islamic Declaration of
    Human Rights, 58–59, 78
Universalism *versus* exceptional-
    ism, 43–48
Universality of human rights,
    42–88
  debating, 42–88
  ethical relativism and, 46–66
  versus exceptionalism, 43–48
  six charges against, 44–46
Universalizability of rights, 10–12,
    21
U.S. Constitution, 7, 67, 80
  right to trial by jury, 7
U.S. Supreme Court, 80

V

Value pluralism, 49, 52, 54
Vienna Declaration and Pro-
    gramme of Action, 42

W

Waive a right, 10
Western Europe
  importance of fundamental
    rights, 20
  political liberalism in, 57
Widow inheritance, 104
Wiredu, Kwasi, 93
Women
  discrimination against, 76
  equal rights for, 93
  in India, exploitation of, 72
  physical abuse of, 75
  rights of, 26, 111–13
    in Afghanistan, 26
    in Muslim states, 111–13
  right to opt out of traditional
    practices, 104–5
World Bank (WB), 68
World Conference on Human
    Rights, 42
World Organization Against Tor-
    ture USA, 33
Worldview integration, strategy of,
    118–25

Y

Yanomamo, 64, 65